AF473768

I want to dedicate this book to my ancestors;
my parents, Younghye and Jongchol Han;
my mother-in-law, Loretta Genelin; and especially
the two brilliant people who inspire me
every day, Roberto and Nara Han Sifuentes.

— **Aram Han Sifuentes**

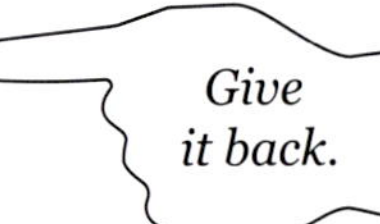
Give
it back.

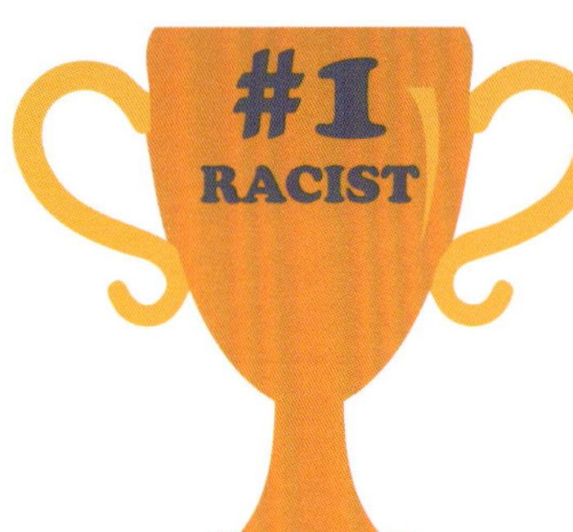
#1
RACIST

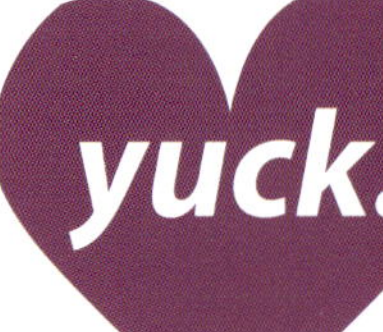
yuck.

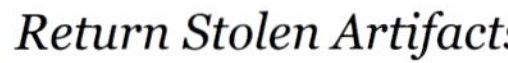
Return Stolen Artifacts

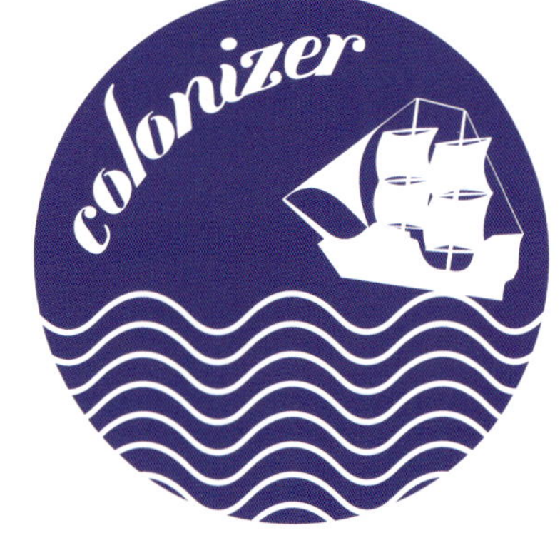
colonizer

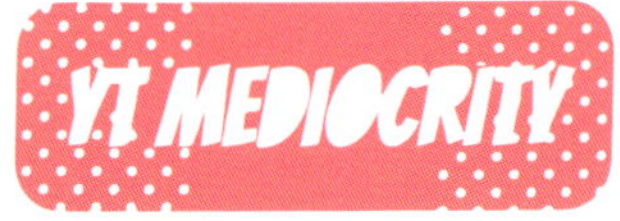
YT MEDIOCRITY

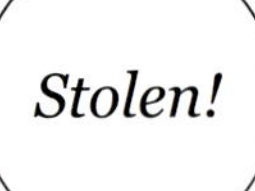
Stolen!

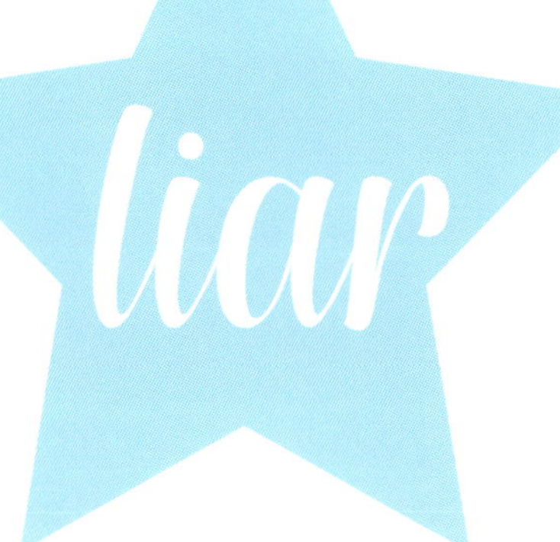
liar

Your ancestors
took this from
my ancestors.

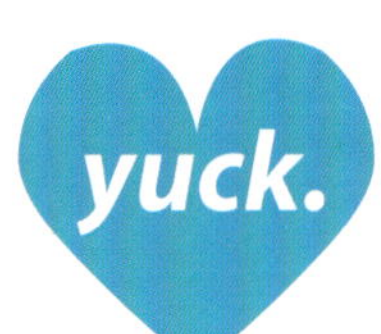
yuck.

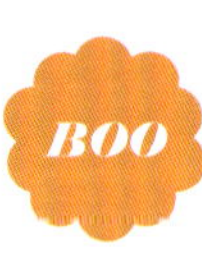
BOO

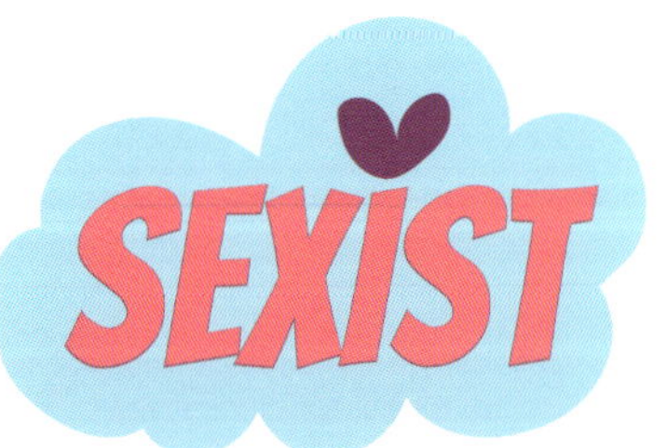
SEXIST

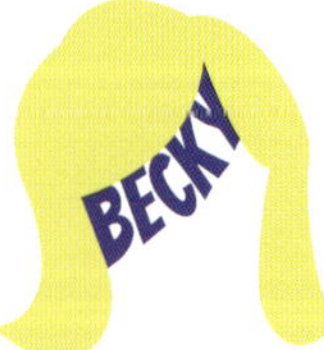
BECKY

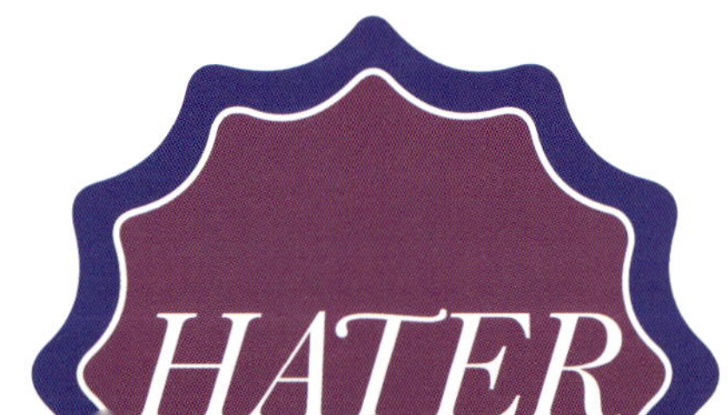
HATER

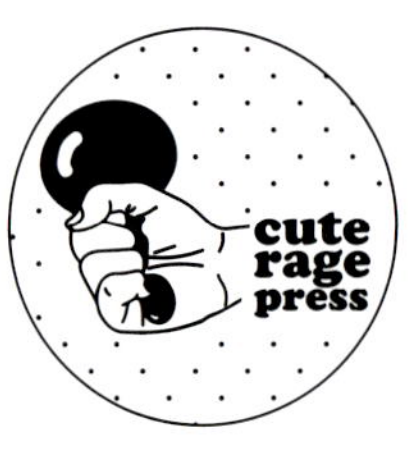
cute
rage
press

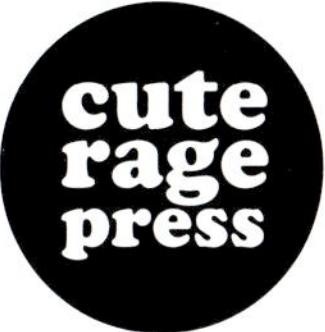

culture vulture

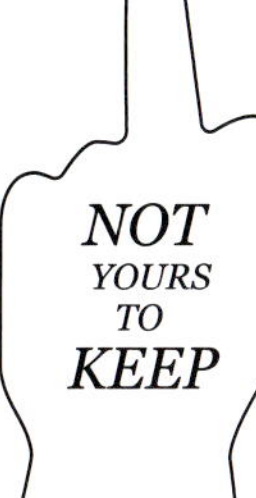

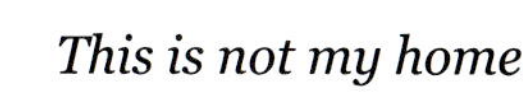

Colonized!

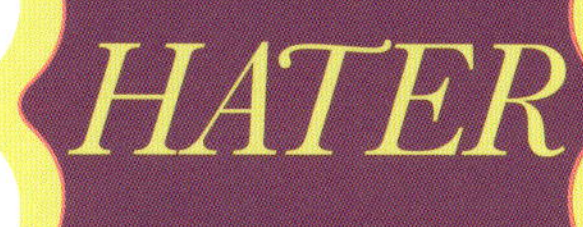

FAKE

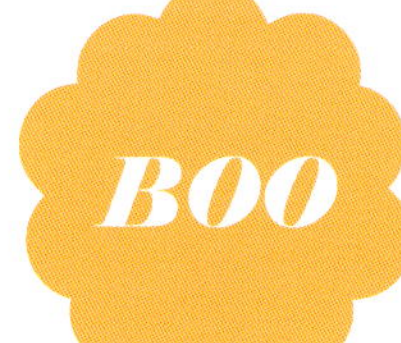

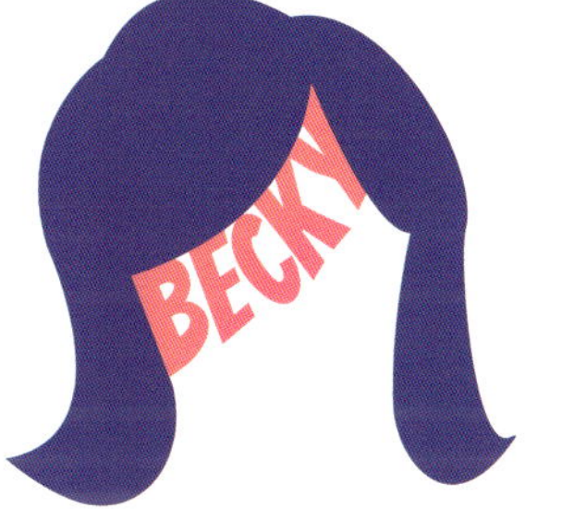

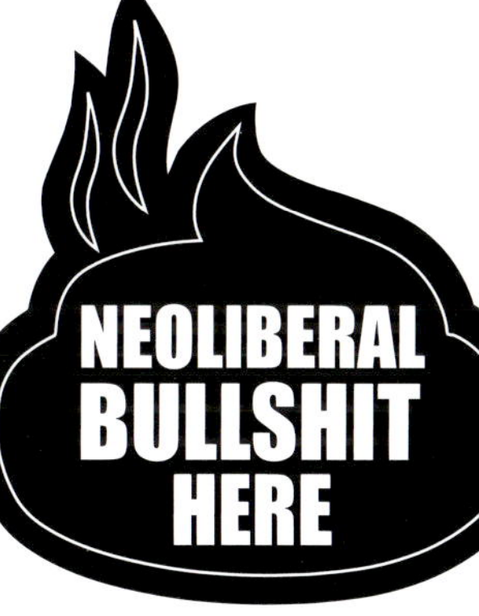

This was never yours.

Repatriate!

liar

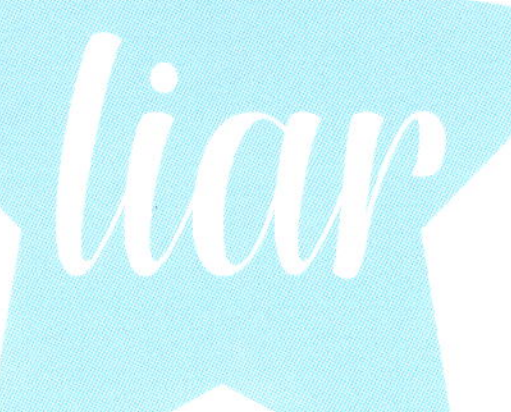

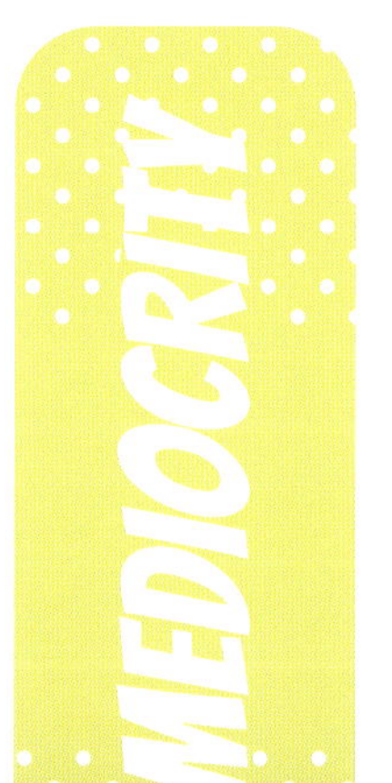

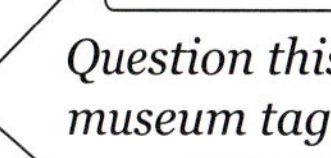

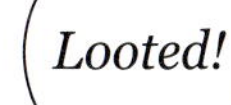

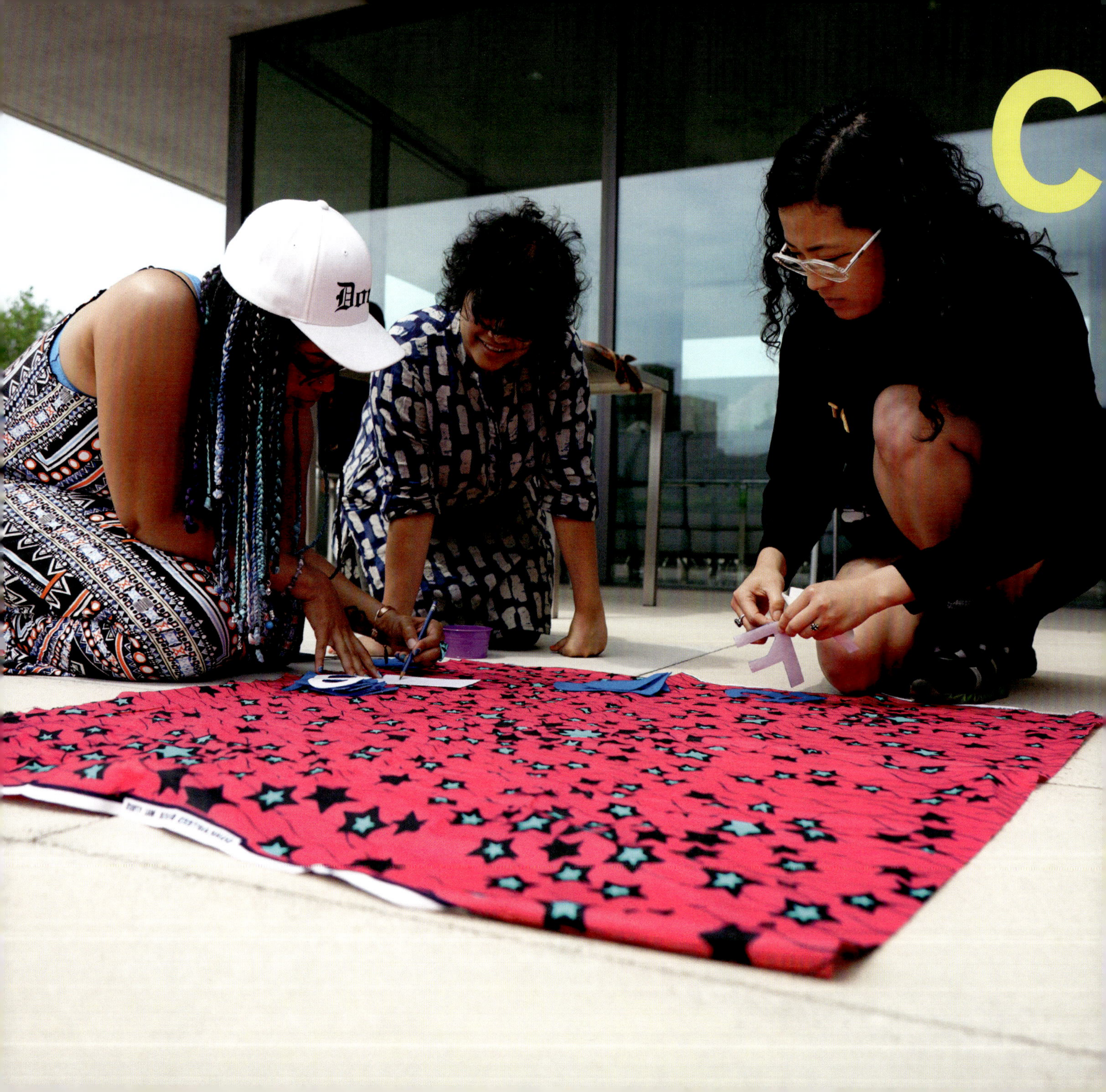

ONTENTS

WE ARE NEVER NEVER OTHER

ARAM HAN SIFUENTES

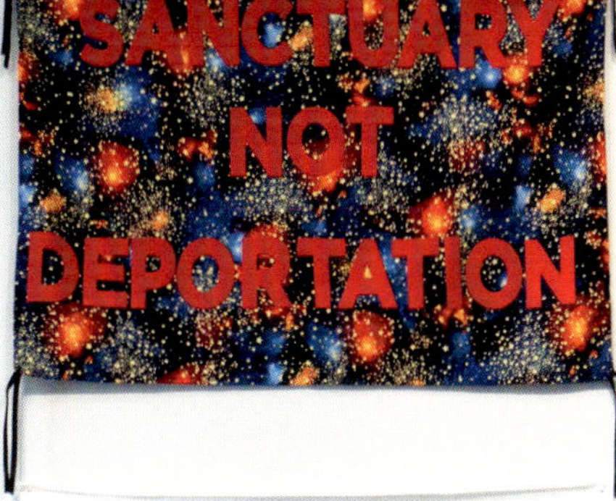
SANCTUARY
NOT
DEPORTATION

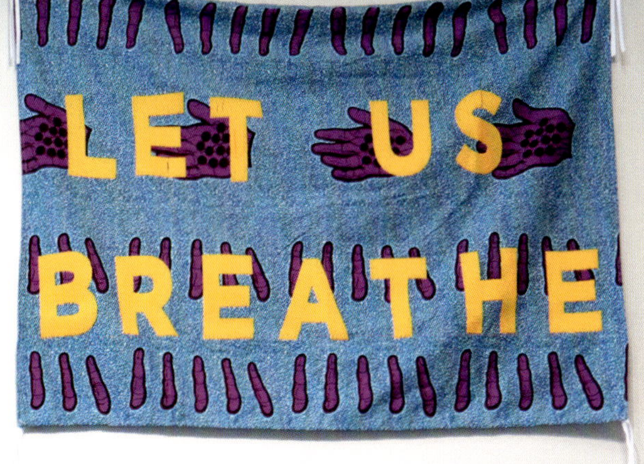
LET US
BREATHE

PROTEST
BANNER
LENDING
LIBRARY

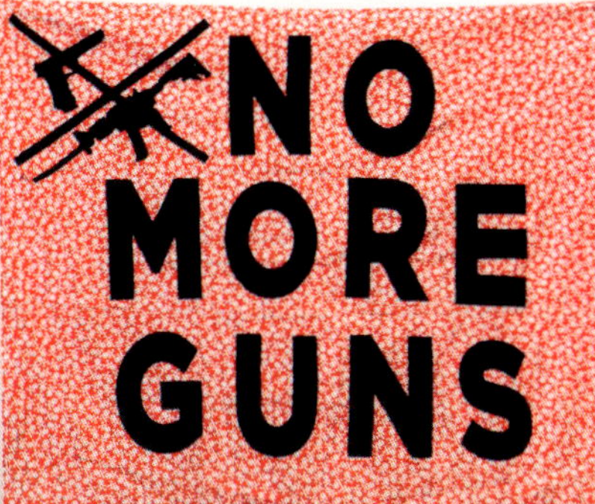
NO
MORE
GUNS

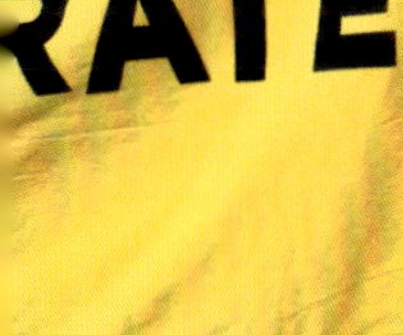

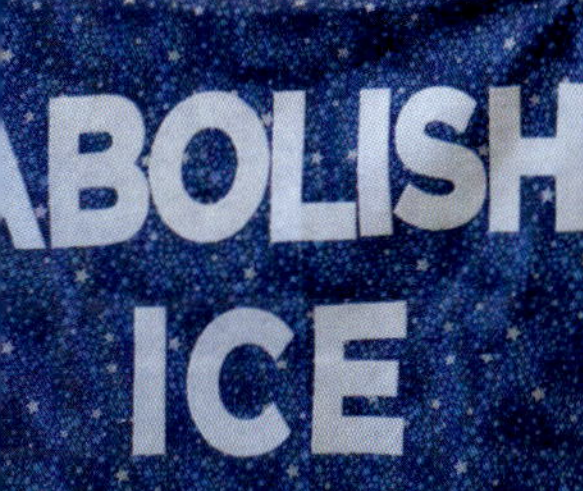
ABOLISH
ICE

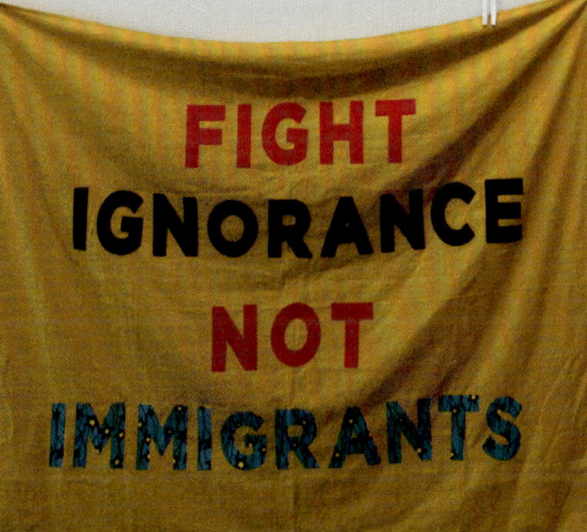
FIGHT
IGNORANCE
NOT
IMMIGRANTS

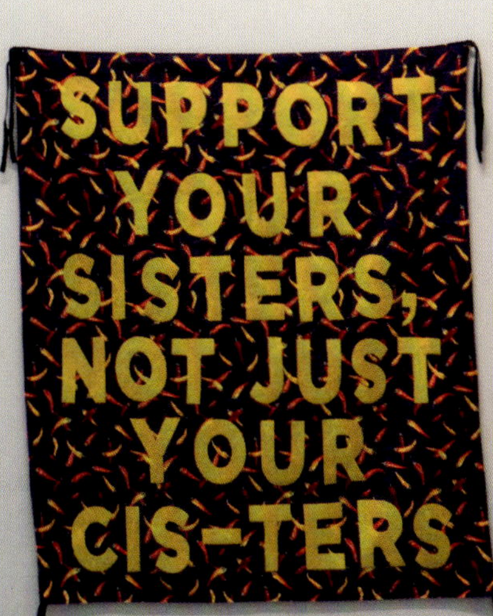
SUPPORT
YOUR
SISTERS,
NOT JUST
YOUR
CIS-TERS

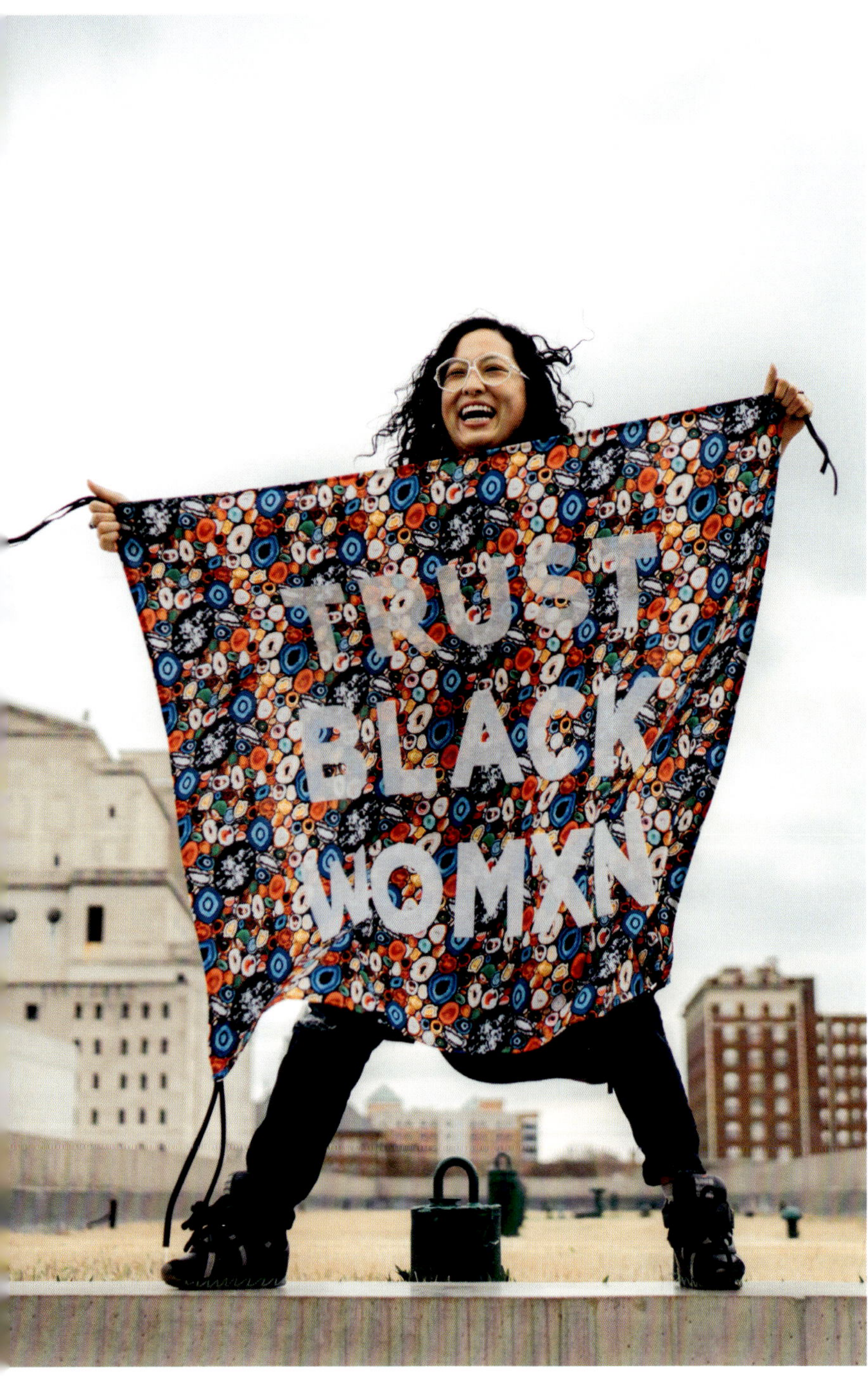

Who sits comfortably at the center? Who is pushed to the peripheries and has to fight to be seen, acknowledged, and considered? *In Ghostly Matters: Haunting and the Sociological Imagination*, **social theorist Avery Gordon writes, "Complex personhood means that even those called 'Other' are never never that."[1] My goal as an artist is to disrupt, unsettle, and rupture dominant narratives to assert, demand, and claim space for those who are commonly othered, particularly immigrants of color. We are never never other, and especially in this moment of widespread national and international xenophobia and hate, we have to push beyond the margins and occupy the center.**

As an artist and arts educator, I am constantly asked if art can create social change? Over the years, I have been writing notes in an attempt to answer this question. The following points are particularly intended to respond to the concerns of BIPOC artists. In this ongoing and constantly evolving text, many of the listed points are layered and overlap with one another. Rather than a comprehensive list, this is a constellation of thoughts and realizations.

Telling Our Stories

Through art, music, and writing, we have the power to tell our own stories. These stories are often not told, actively forgotten, and/or suppressed, perverted, distorted, and oversimplified by dominant culture. Through art, we tell our own stories and truths on our own terms.

Centering: Shifting the Frame

By telling our own stories, we shift the frame and put ourselves in the center. We live in a society where most things are defined by whiteness. When we tell stories and truths from our own perspective, we rupture white narratives and define ourselves and our experiences to ourselves and our communities.

Art allows us to imagine and present alternate pasts, presents, and futures. Through art, we can see our imaginations come to fruition.

Representation

By telling our own stories, we claim space. We become visible. Representation is: "I see you. I am you. You are not alone. You are important. We are proud." There is something profoundly powerful about seeing the many nuances and complexities of your story and your experiences reflected back to you. It's a sigh of momentary relief. Then we fight for more.

Pushing Back: Talking Back to Power

This is one of my favorite ways to use art: to talk back to power. Vulnerable communities, such as non-citizen immigrants, do not have freedom and space to talk back to power without fear of reprisal. Art can create this space under the guise of creativity.

A Pathway to Healing

In our society, so many pathways to healing are cut off, corporatized, or just made inaccessible (including art).[2] It is undeniable that art is a pathway to healing, and even if this society makes it hard for us to make art in our everyday lives, we must do so for our well-being.

Sharing Collective and Community Knowledge

I feel immense joy and power when I make art with my communities. In many non-Euro-Western cultures, "art" is made collectively, not by an individual. Making art together creates spaces for our knowledge —connected through lived experiences — to be shared and uplifted. These spaces of collective making become radical spaces to speak, listen, validate each other, talk through our political differences, share stories and resources, learn about the self and others, and playfully come up with strategies to live and fight.

Imagination and Action

Art is the language of imagination. Art allows us to imagine and present alternate pasts, presents, and futures. Through art, we can see our imaginations come to fruition. I use art in this way to create socially engaged projects — such as voting stations for those who cannot legally vote — that reimagine what civic engagement could look like if it were truly made accessible to all. At its best, art can push against structures of capitalism, white supremacy, and power to imagine and create new worlds. Once we see these worlds, it is up to us to make them a part of our everyday. Imagination and dreams are the inspiration for action. We demand change because we can see different and better worlds. Imagination is what gives us hope. The seeds for action are indignation with the way things are and imagination for the way things can be.

In these ways, art is integral to an ecosystem fighting for change.[3] Making art is radical. In our collective making, sharing, expressing joy, and creating culture, we declare that we are never never other. We are here. We are resilient. And we will continue to fight for our human rights to create better worlds.

1. Avery F. Gordon, Ghostly Matters: Haunting and the Sociological Imagination (Minneapolis, MN: New University of Minnesota Press, 2008), 4.

2. One of my best friends, somatic therapist Willi Farrales, said this to me in a phone conversation.

3. William Estrada made this point while lecturing in one of my fall 2019 classes at the School of the Art Institute of Chicago (SAIC).

IMAGE CAPTIONS

1 PAGE 7 *Installation view of* Protest Banner Lending Library *at University Galleries of Illinois State University, 2019. Photo: Jessica Bingham.*

2 *Aram Han Sifuentes, Pulitzer Arts Foundation, St. Louis. Courtesy of Pulitzer Arts Foundation. Photo: Virginia Harold.*

3 *Aram Han Sifuentes,* We Are Never Never Other, *2018. PVC-coated vinyl. 137 1/3 x 264 inches. Courtesy of Pulitzer Arts Foundation. Photo: Alise O'Brien.*

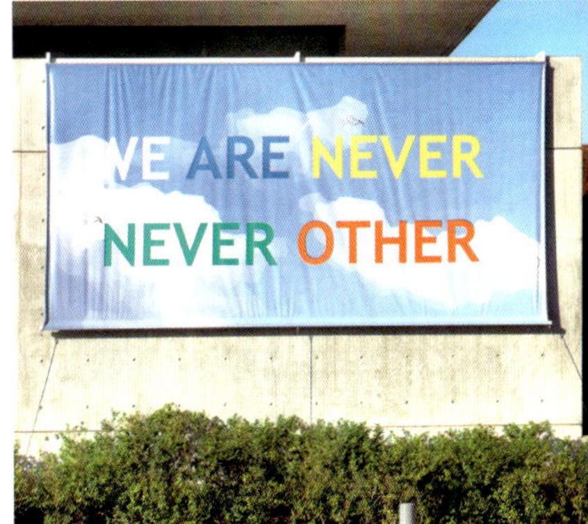

ARAM HAN SIFUENTES

The Genius of the Collective

Grace Kyungwon Hong
Director of the Center for the Study of Women, and Professor of Asian American Studies and Gender Studies, University of California, Los Angeles

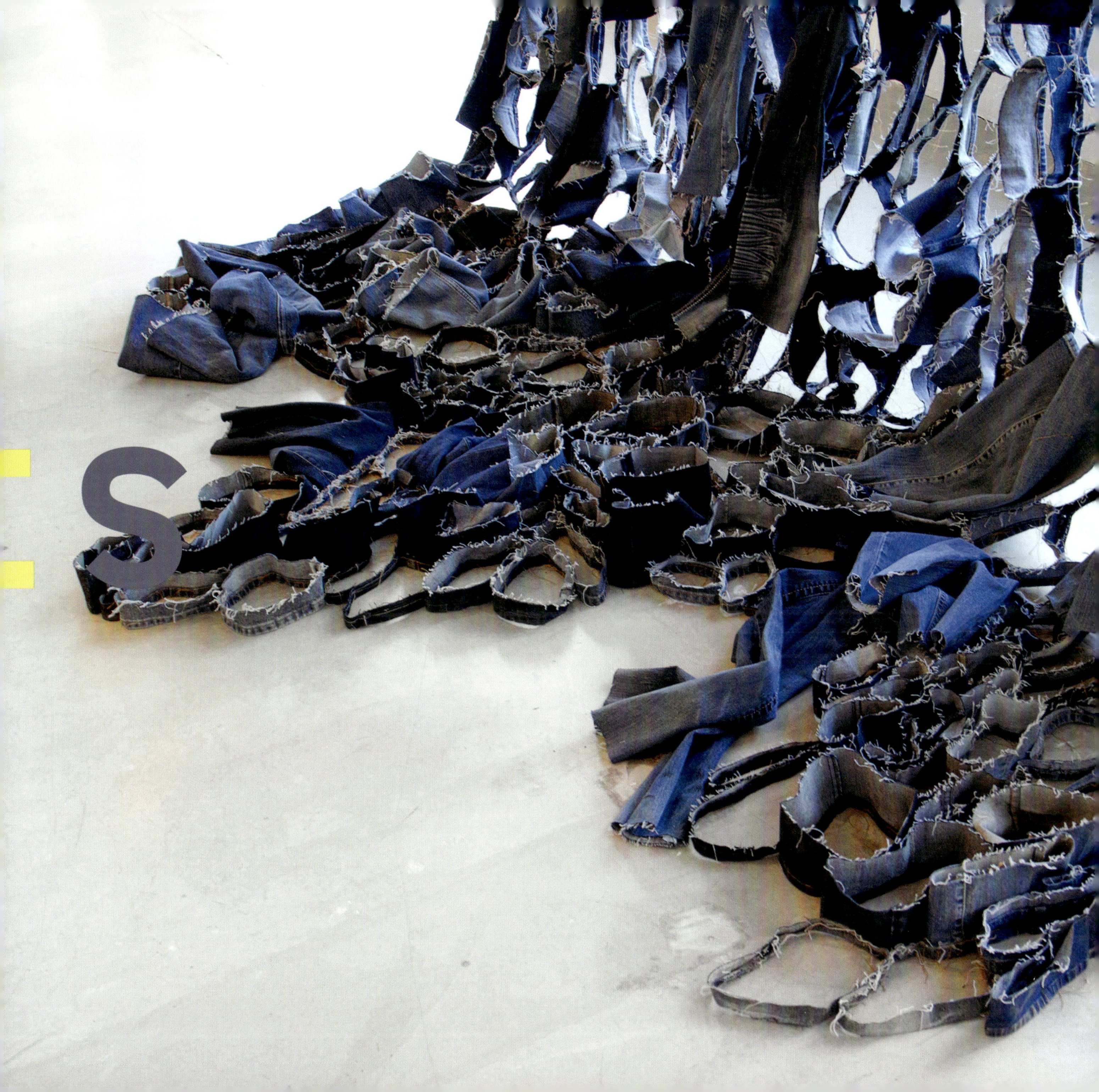
S

To properly situate Aram Han Sifuentes' work, it is necessary to know not only the trajectory of fiber arts as an arts practice, but also to be versed in the histories of labor migration to the United States, the genealogy of citizenship as a technology of racialized and gendered violence, and the cultures and aesthetics of social movement organizing as a means of crafting alternative visions of community and belonging.

Han Sifuentes' interest in fiber arts emerges from having been taught to sew by her Korean immigrant parents who run a dry cleaning and alterations business. Her parents' experience is common amongst South Korean immigrants of their generation who are overresented in small business entrepreneurship.[1] Regardless their education and training in their country of origin, immigrants often face barriers to entry to many professions once in the United States and thus find starting their own small business a more viable path to economic survival.[2] Han Sifuentes' family history is particularly poignant in this regard: her mother is an artist who had no access to an arts career upon migrating to the United States and made her living as a seamstress.

The context of immigrant entrepreneurship and gendered racialized labor exploitation means that Han Sifuentes' framing of her work departs from the dominant narrative of fiber arts, which tends to follow a specific Euro-American feminist historiography. This narrative situates the craft of sewing, weaving, and embroidery as labor that became feminized and devalued as work and leisure became separated into public and private spheres during the Industrial Revolution, which introduced the mass production of fabric and clothing.[3] Later, this narrative goes, the advent of second-wave feminism of the 1960s and 1970s enabled the reclamation of this feminized craft as art, which contemporary feminist artists have both taken up and re-envisioned.[4]

Han Sifuentes' approach to her work highlights what that narrative elides, that is, that the contemporary division of labor is not only gendered but racialized, in that Asian and Latina workers in the global assembly line, and immigrant women in the U.S. from Asia and Latin America, perform the majority of the sweated, low-waged clothing construction labor for the garment industry.[5] These immigrant women did not experience the 1960s and 1970s as the era of second-wave feminism. Instead, the 1965 Immigration and Nationality Act paved the way for their migration to the United States, as they were unmoored from their countries of origin by U.S. war and militarism and by capitalist development. Lisa Lowe writes, "Asian immigrant women's work must be understood within the history of U.S. immigration policies and the attempts to incorporate immigrants into the developing economy, on the one hand, and within the global expansion of U.S. capitalism through colonialism and global restructuring, on the other."[6]

Han Sifuentes' piece *A Mend: A Collection of Scraps from Local Seamstresses and Tailors (Chicago)* perhaps most explicitly situates her art practice in this latter genealogy. Han Sifuentes collected remnants of jeans altered by two dozen seamstresses and tailors in the Chicago area, in the process interviewing them about their migration histories, work experiences, and family. Since these tailors and seamstresses are mainly called upon to shorten jeans, most of the scraps collected and donated are the last few

1. As Bogan and Darity note, "By 1990, Korean Americans ranked the highest in self-employment rates" (p. 2008). Bogan, Vicki, and William Darity Jr. "Culture and entrepreneurship? African American and immigrant self-employment in the United States." The Journal of Socio-Economics 37, no. 5 (2008): 1999–2019.

2. Min, Pyong Gap. "Korean immigrant entrepreneurship: a multivariate analysis." Journal of Urban Affairs 10, no. 2 (1988): 197–212.

3. Halter, Daryl. "Introduction: A theoretical framework for women's work in forming the industrial revolution." In Daryl Halter, ed. European Women and Pre-Industrial Craft. Bloomington: Indiana University Press, 1995.

4. For an analysis of second-wave feminism and the fiber arts movement, see Fowler, Cynthia. "A sign of the times: Sheila Hicks, the fiber arts movement, and the language of liberation." The Journal of Modern Craft 7, no. 1 (2014): 33–51. For a discussion of fiber arts, craft, and contemporary feminism, see Myzelev, Alla. "Creating digital materiality: third-wave feminism, public art, and yarn bombing." Material Culture 47, no. 1 (Spring 2015): 58–78. See also Montgarrett, Julie. "Textile art and feminist social activism: the Daily Diminish project." Textile 15, no. 4 (2017): 396–411. See also Agosin, Marjorie, ed. Stitching Resistance: Women, Creativity, and the Fiber Arts. Kent: Solis Press, 2014.

inches of hem, which Han Sifuentes has sewn together to create a large net-like tapestry that hangs from ceiling to floor. This visual resemblance to netting, along with the faded blue color of denim and the fraying pieces of

The context of immigrant entrepreneurship and gendered racialized labor exploitation means that Han Sifuentes' framing of her work departs from the dominant narrative of fiber arts, which tends to follow a specific Euro-American feminist historiography.

cut-off hems, call to mind a fishing net turned ragged by long exposure to the sea. Larger pieces of denim adorn this piece, like entangled flotsam and jetsam. Referencing the migrant histories of these seamstresses and tailors as they themselves traveled overseas as well as the labor of their mending and alterations, *A Mend* also serves as a visual metaphor for the network of immigrant workers that Han Sifuentes created in the process of making this piece. She writes, "I continue to visit many seamstresses and tailors in the area. Many of them have also been collecting jeans remnants for my project. From this collection of oral histories, I'm interested in seeing the similarities among the immigrant workers' stories in order to understand a collective identity, and hear about their hand labor."[7] In turning scraps which would otherwise be deemed worthless and end up as waste into a work of art, *A Mend* does not so much make visible the invisible labor that allows for the transformation of mass-produced clothing to fit a diversity of embodiments, but instead creates something new from that which is discarded in that process.

Han Sifuentes' more recent work builds on her ongoing interest in labor and migration to focus on the contradictions of citizenship and nationalism for racialized and disenfranchised people. Two recent projects, *U.S. Citizenship Test Sampler* and the *Official Unofficial Voting Station*, underscore the ways in which the violence of exclusion from the rights and responsibilities of citizenship are not solved by eventual inclusion, but are instead exacerbated and rendered more complex. Instead of refortifying the nation-state and its bad-faith promises of universal citizenship, these projects advance a radically different vision of governance as created by and through uneven, heterogeneous, localized communities and characterized by intimate, if ephemeral, connection and collaborative work. Indeed, Han Sifuentes not only envisions such communities, but through her process of making art, which relies heavily on workshops and other collaborative practices, creates the conditions to realize them.

U.S. Citizenship Test Sampler is a case in point. The central piece in this collaborative project is a scroll of fabric that Han Sifuentes originally planned to embroider with all 100 questions in the U.S. Citizenship Test booklet, from which immigrants applying for citizenship are quizzed as a part of the naturalization process. This scroll is as yet unfinished, perhaps gesturing to the endless nature of the demands made of immigrants to prove their worthiness for citizenship. While Han Sifuentes' creation is one element, this project is collaborative, in that it not only comments on the citizenship test, but materially intervenes in the process. Seeking other immigrants to contribute samplers, Han Sifuentes conducted workshops that

5. Fernandez-Kelly, Patricia. "The global assembly line in the new millennium: a review essay." Signs 32, no. 2 (Winter 2007): 509–521. Chin, Margaret. Sewing Women: Immigrants and the New York City Garment Industry. New York: Columbia University Press, 2005. Bonacich, Edna and Richard P. Appelbaum, Behind the Label: Inequality in the Los Angeles Apparel Industry. Berkeley: UC Press, 2000.

6. Lowe, Lisa. Immigrant Acts: On Asian American Cultural Politics. Durham: Duke University Press, 1997, 158.

7. Han Sifuentes, Aram. "A Mend: A Collection of Scraps from Local Seamstresses and Tailors (Chicago)." https://www.aramhansifuentes.com/a-mend.

IMAGE CAPTIONS

1 PAGE 11

Aram Han Sifuentes, A Mend: A Collection of Scraps from Local Seamstresses and Tailors (Chicago) *(detail), 2011–13. Jeans scraps and gold denim thread. 14 x 10 x 4 feet. Courtesy of the artist. Photo: Hyounsang Yoo.*

doubled as citizenship test classes in collaboration with immigrant rights organizations in the Chicago area. In these workshops, participants studied for the test by embroidering one of the questions onto a sampler, accompanied by an illustration if they chose. Han Sifuentes then displays and sells these samplers, each priced at the cost of applying for naturalization, and passes funds along to the immigrant creator of that particular sampler. While at face value, these workshops seem to prioritize U.S. citizenship, since the ostensible goal that brings everyone together is naturalization, it becomes clear that the workshops themselves create spaces and relations of belonging and community in which the nation-state is extraneous and irrelevant. Han Sifuentes writes, "By facilitating these workshops, I quickly realized that bringing people together through the act of sewing was as important as the final finished work. The workshops spoke to a long history of creating a sense of community through participating in sewing circles — sewing becoming just a medium for conversation. In these intergenerational sewing circles, we teach one another to sew while talking about our relationships with the needle and thread, which often speaks to personal immigrant labor histories."[8]

These samplers, which Han Sifuentes calls "a living archive," provide unexpected glimpses of poignant nostalgia, sly humor, and ironic critique.[9] In one sampler, the artist, Isara Suntichotinun, has answered the question, "What is one promise you make when you become a U.S. citizen?" with "give up loyalty to other countries" stitched underneath. Placed in blank squares framed by long threads in the middle of the sampler, the question and its answer overlays, but does not entirely obscure, a circular background image, lushly embroidered in vibrant shades of blue, red, pink, and green, of a room in the artist's childhood home in Thailand. A ceiling fan is visible in the upper part of the image, a door to the left, and at the center bottom, a beautifully intricate depiction of a triangular wedge-shaped lounging pillow common to Thai households. In contrast to the plain, unadorned squares in which the words of the question and its answer are enclosed, the idyllic background image of comfort and leisure conveys a powerful sense of nostalgia that poignantly illustrates the affective ties — indeed, the *loyalty* — to the country of origin that can never be fully relinquished, despite the U.S.'s demand to do so as a requirement of naturalization. The poignancy of the piece is further underscored by the fact that it took so long to make that the artist had to change his age and the date of the piece, which he did by stitching a 1 over the 0 in his age (changing it from 20 to 21) and a 7 over the 6 in the date (changing it from 2016 to 2017). Suntichotinun's refusal to pick out the original stitching, preferring instead to sew a new number on top, creates a palimpsestic record of duration that gestures to the depth of emotional attachment to the childhood home that inspired this sampler's painstaking sewing.

Another sampler by Kyong Choe, age 50 in 2014, features the question "What does the President's Cabinet do?" along with the answer "advises the president." This sampler is adorned with an embroidered line drawing of a 2-drawer file cabinet, the bottom cabinet slightly open, cheekily bringing to mind a scene in which the so-called leader of the free world seeks advice from a piece of office furniture. A third sampler by Gaby, age 49 in 2018, features the question "Name one American Indian tribe in the United States." The answer, "Navajo," is accompanied by a sewn-on printed patch featuring the adage

8. U.S. Citizenship Sampler Project's Facebook page, accessed April 25, 2020, https://www.facebook.com/USCitizenshipTestSampler/timeline.

9. Ibid.

10. For a Black feminist analysis of the masculinist tendencies of charismatic leadership in the post-Civil Rights era, see Erica Edwards, Charisma and the Fictions of Black Leadership. Minneapolis: University of Minnesota Press, 2012.

"Water is Sacred/No Pipeline," referencing the months-long fight against the Dakota Access Pipeline led by the Standing Rock Sioux tribe. Embroidered water droplets traverse the patch and onto the sampler linen, connecting the two spaces. Gaby's sampler gestures to the importance of solidarity with Native nations even, or perhaps especially, at the moment of naturalization, that is, at the moment of incorporation into a settler colonial state built on constant and ongoing attempts to undermine Native sovereignty.

While not a part of the exhibition that inspires this volume, another of Han Sifuentes' projects, the *Official Unofficial Voting Station: Voting for All Who Legally Can't*, amplifies and extends the themes of citizenship and its contradictions that we see in *U.S. Citizenship Test Sampler*. First initiated to coincide with the 2016 presidential election, the *Official Unofficial Voting Station* was launched at the Jane Addams Hull-House Museum in Chicago, and allowed non-citizens, minors, undocumented people, and others with no avenue for political representation in the electoral system to stage a performance of agency. The second iteration was scheduled for fall of 2020 and was planned to be larger and more ambitious. For the 2020 election, Han Sifuentes created *Voting Kits for the Disenfranchised*, which she distributed to artists, activists, and organizations across the country so they could establish their own stations and stage guerrilla voting station take-overs, including virtually.

Another thematic of her work is the power of collective social protest, as exemplified by her ongoing project *Protest Banner Lending Library*. For this project, Han Sifuentes stages workshops during which she teaches people from all walks of life the basic sewing skills necessary to create protest banners for marches, rallies, and actions. She has conducted these workshops all over the U.S. and internationally, and makes sure to organize workshops with local grassroots community organizations wherever she is invited to travel. Inspired by the limitations of her own non-citizen status (she has since naturalized) and her new status as a mother, Han Sifuentes has shifted more of her practice to workshops, teaching others to contribute to social movements in a variety of ways. If workshop attendees cannot themselves attend a protest because of exigencies such as childcare or vulnerability to arrest due to non-citizen status, they have the opportunity to learn the skills to create the material infrastructures of protest. In this way, *Protest Banner Lending Library* also makes visible the largely unheralded and uncredited labor, mainly of women of color, that underwrites the charismatic, largely male leadership made most visible by public and spectacularized events such as rallies and protests.[10]

Han Sifuentes' art practice thus makes crucial interventions in many of the deeply held values that have long animated more traditional definitions of art. Her emphasis on workshops, art education, and the ability of everyday people — immigrants and people of color in particular — to make art challenges the notion of individual genius. Inspired by collectivity rather than solipsism, solidarity rather than self-interest, Han Sifuentes' art practice brings into being a radically different vision of art as community.

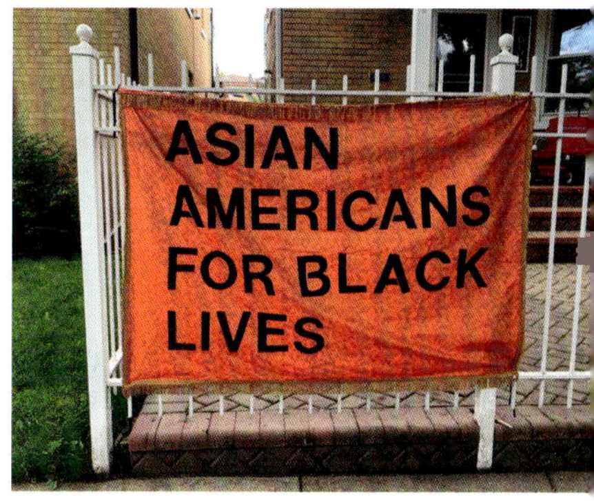

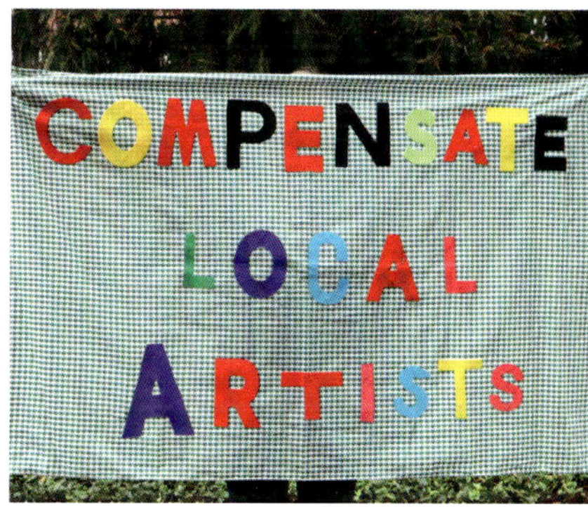

2 *Protest banner made by Sabba Elahi and donated to the* Protest Banner Lending Library. *Photo: Aram Han Sifuentes.*

3 *Protest banner by Joseph Wilcox, Chad Kouri, and Liana Faletto and donated to the* Protest Banner Lending Library. *Photo: Ishita Dharap.*

FORGET
GREATNE
WORK FO
PEACE

Kendra Paitz
Director and Chief Curator,
University Galleries of
Illinois State University

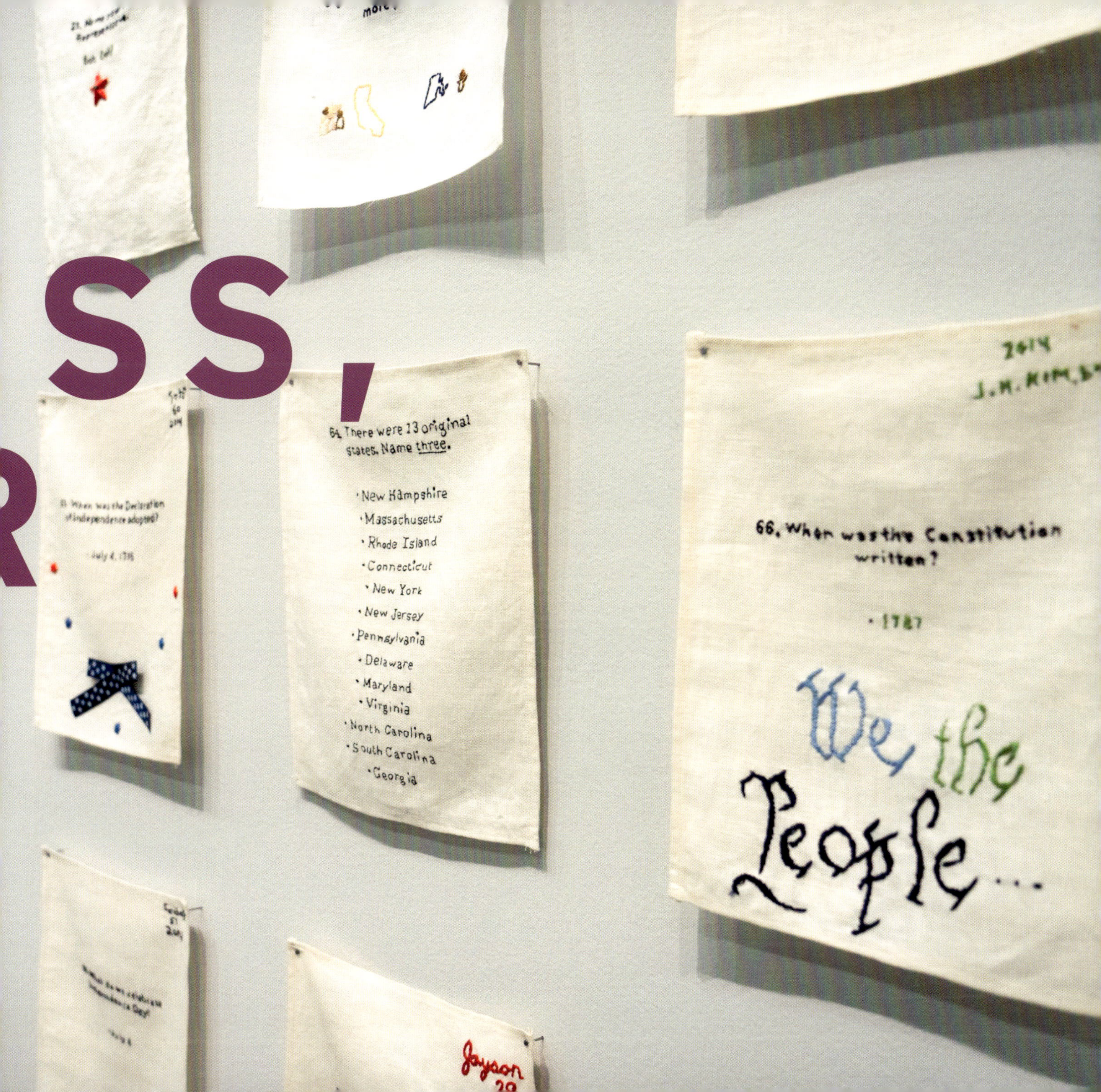
SS,
R
64. There were 13 original states. Name three.
• New Hampshire
• Massachusetts
• Rhode Island
• Connecticut
• New York
• New Jersey
• Pennsylvania
• Delaware
• Maryland
• Virginia
• North Carolina
• South Carolina
• Georgia
66. When was the Constitution written?
• 1787
We the People...
2014
Jayson

You cannot buy the Revolution. You cannot make the Revolution. You can only be the Revolution. It is in your spirit, or it is nowhere.[1]

— URSULA K. LE GUIN

Aram Han Sifuentes is at the forefront of decolonizing institutional spaces. She is an immigrant woman of color who is making textiles that protest injustice, demand accountability, facilitate empowerment, and generate community. This impressive list of attributes barely accounts for the multiplicity of her works' impacts. While many artists have been leaders in social activism, Han Sifuentes' practice bridges the histories of resistance, feminism, and citizenship, and the disciplines of graphic design, textiles, and participatory art in surprising ways. In the artist's words, her work stems from "growing up in an immigrant working-class family in which the arts were inaccessible," so she wants to "ruptur[e] and re-imagin[e] what art can do."[2]

A Mend

In the first sentence of her artist statement, Han Sifuentes points out that she has been sewing since the age of six because her mother is a seamstress. She writes, "Sewing is my medium to investigate identity politics, immigration and immigrant labor, possession and dispossession, citizenship and belonging, dissent and protest, and race politics in the United States."[3] (American artist Faith Ringgold [b. 1931], who was partially inspired by her own mother's work as a seamstress and fashion designer, and her political story quilts come to mind.) For *A Mend: A Collection of Scraps from Local Seamstresses and Tailors (Chicago)* (2011–13), Han Sifuentes visited shops like her mother's to ask questions about seamstresses' and tailors' backgrounds and collect scraps from seemingly endless piles of jeans. She did not simply drop in and expect people to contribute to her project. Instead, she utilized their services and compensated them, an equitable and demonstrable valuation of her collaborators' time and labor.

Through stitching, Han Sifuentes transformed the denim remnants, each with its own history, into a semi-monumental draping honeycomb sculpture that forms a composite of those histories. Suspended from overhead, organic forms and negative spaces that both reference the body and speak to its absence, gently cascade downward and pool across the floor. The rounded cuffs and wrinkled tubes in washes of iciest azure to inkiest indigo evidence varying degrees of disintegration. The frayed edges address both the materiality and durability of this ubiquitous blue fabric. The phrase *blue collar* came into widespread use after WWII to describe positions of manual labor for which people often wore jeans that could get dirty;[4] here, the reconstructed denim bridges jobs classified as *blue collar* and those as *sweated labor*. To demonstrate the limited employment options many immigrants face, Han Sifuentes narrativized in chart form the basic oral histories she collected from the individuals [see page 29]. At a glance, we can see that she encountered 23 people from South Korea, Iraq, Palestine, and Mexico, and that most did not work in the garment industry before coming to the United States. They were teachers, artists, stay-at-home parents, a nurse, a banker, a graphic designer,

1. Ursula K. Le Guin, The Dispossessed: An Ambiguous Utopia, 1974, quoted in The Verso Book of Dissent: Revolutionary Words from Three Millennia of Rebellion and Resistance, ed. Andrew Hsiao and Audrea Lim (London and Brooklyn, New York: Verso Books, 2016), 268.

2. Aram Han Sifuentes, author's studio visit with the artist, Chicago, April 24, 2018.

3. Aram Han Sifuentes, "Artist Statement," accessed October 15, 2020, https://www.aramhansifuentes.com/artist-s-statement.

4. Forrest Wickman, "Working Man's Blues: Why do we call manual laborers blue collar?," Slate, May 1, 2012. https://slate.com/business/2012/05/blue-collar-white-collar-why-do-we-use-these-terms.html.

IMAGE CAPTIONS

1 PAGE 17 *Installation view of Aram Han Sifuentes'* U.S. Citizenship Test Sampler: A Community of Non-Citizens Proving Worth of Citizenship Through Stitching Samplers *at University Galleries of Illinois State University, 2019. Photo: Jessica Bingham.*

and a corporate businesswoman. Only two identified as being in a related field: a clothing retailer and a children's clothing manufacturer.

Six years later, Han Sifuentes returned to this project, centering the humanity of the individuals and their situations. These newer wall-mounted works are similarly titled but with one word's difference — *A Mend: A Collection of Stories from Local Seamstresses and Tailors (Chicago)* (2019). In golden thread on quilted rectangular denim scraps, she embroidered contour drawings of hands holding fabric and text-based fragments of the stories collected from the seamstresses and tailors. One passage reads, "In 1997 my husband's father passed away. My husband was going to Korea for the funeral and he told me he wasn't coming back. He left and I even drove him to the airport to be supportive. He left me and our children. They were in 3rd and 4th grade. Even though I was stricken with grief, I had to work hard for my children." Another states, "Because of the economic crisis of the IMF, we essentially came empty handed." Han Sifuentes cites Lebanese-Dutch artist Mounira Al Solh (b. 1978) as an inspiration. For her series *I Strongly Believe in our Right to Be Frivolous* (2012–2017), Al Solh created portraits of Middle Eastern and North African migrants she met in Kassel, Germany, and Athens, Greece.[5] Drawn on yellow legal pads in ink, graphite, marker, and paint, the works include embroidered elements of each person's story as they "have made — or are making — the transition from the status of refugees into citizens."[6] Like Al Solh, Han Sifuentes poetically addresses both the inequity faced by, and resilience of, many seeking to find their way in a new country.

U.S. Citizenship Test Sampler

What does it mean to be a citizen of the United States? Questioned about the title of her 2014 book, *Citizen: An American Lyric*, poet and scholar Claudia Rankine (b. 1963, Jamaica) responds, "There are two worlds out there; two Americas out there. If you're a white person, there's one way of being a citizen in our country; and if you're a brown or a black body, there's another way of being a citizen and that way is very close to death. It's very close to the loss of your life. It's very close to the loss of your liberties at any random moment. And so I wanted that to be considered."[7] Even with that knowledge, or perhaps without it, hundreds of thousands of people are naturalized each year.[8] With *U.S. Citizenship Test Sampler* (2012–present), Han Sifuentes aims to dismantle the structural and systemic injustice identified by Rankine through building community support systems for non-citizens.

To apply for citizenship through naturalization in the United States, one must have had a Green Card for three to five years, meet eligibility requirements, and go through a ten-step process that includes taking the U.S. Naturalization Test and having a personal interview.[9] In 2012, overlapping with the period of working on *A Mend*, Han Sifuentes began *U.S. Citizenship Test Sampler: 100 Questions and Answers*. On a towering scroll of linen, she started hand-sewing in black thread the 100 questions and their answers. The 25-foot work-in-progress was sold in 2016 for $680, then the cost of taking the test. The artist had already worked for 300 hours to stitch 53 of the entries, meaning she was paid a rate of $2.27 per hour — drastically below the federal minimum wage during the years of this project: $7.25 per hour — a pointed

5. Hendrik Folkerts, "Mounira Al Solh," documenta 14, accessed August 2020, https://www.documenta14.de/en/artists/13500/mounira-al-solh.

6. Folkerts, "Mounira Al Solh."

7. Claudia Rankine, "In 'Citizen,' Poet Strips Bare the Realities of Everyday Racism," interview by Eric Westervelt, NPR, January 3, 2015, https://www.npr.org/2015/01/03/374574142/in-citizen-poet-strips-bare-the-realities-of-everyday-racism.

8. "The number of U.S. naturalizations rose to 843,593 persons in 2019, up 11% from 761,901 in 2018." See U.S. Citizenship and Immigration Services, "Naturalization Fact Sheet," last updated November 18, 2020, https://www.uscis.gov/news/news-releases/naturalization-fact-sheet#:~:text=The%20number%20of%20U.S.%20naturalizations,from%20837%2C168%20applications%20in%202018.

9. "How to Become a US Citizen," USA.gov, last updated November 6, 2020, https://www.usa.gov/become-us-citizen.

commentary on the devaluing of immigrant- and hand-labor.

One year after starting *100 Questions and Answers*, Han Sifuentes began *U.S. Citizenship Test Sampler: A Community of Non-Citizens Proving Worth Through Stitching Samplers* (2013–present), a series of workshops centered around studying for the naturalization test. She explains,

> There's a lot of frustration being an immigrant here. We're in a constant place of working to prove ourselves. There's frustration about the narrative about fiber and whitewashed histories. Textile history says an immigrant or person of color who is sewing or weaving becomes an invisible laborer instead of an artist. This is a chance to reappropriate and reclaim that history by creating a sewing circle of immigrants.[10]

Each participant selects a question from the exam and stitches both the question and answer on a piece of linen scaled to reference a sheet of paper. If desired, they can embellish with additional stitches, patches, beads, imagery, and designs. The completed samplers range from simple letters, to Maita's cheerfully blazing yellow sun that embraces a list of our First Amendment rights in red and blue star-shaped beads, and Karina's elaborate and emotional full-bleed turquoise and pink faceless young girl with the response "give up loyalty to other countries."

Each of the 120 samplers is available to purchase for the current cost of taking the naturalization exam: $725. (If the cost of taking the test increases, so does the price of each sampler.) When one sells, Han Sifuentes gives the full proceeds to the maker. This reciprocity recalls artist Nari Ward's (b. 1963, Jamaica) *Naturalization Drawing Table* (2004), inspired by his own process of naturalization to the U.S. Participants completed the artist's versions of naturalization applications and went through a series of bureaucratic procedures that simulated the process, and in return, received prints from the artist. Han Sifuentes also opens possibilities of support that otherwise may have been inaccessible, both through self-described "intergenerational sewing circles" and monetizing their craft. The archive of samplers serves as an empathetic reminder that immigration statistics are abstractions; these works embody the individuals who dream of becoming citizens of the United States. Han Sifuentes, who specialized in Latin American Studies with a focus on immigration policy at UC Berkeley, describes this as one of her "forever projects."[11]

Official Unofficial Voting Station: Voting for All Who Legally Can't

After consistently hearing the phrase "the disenfranchised" on CNN, Han Sifuentes learned that 28% of the U.S. population cannot legally vote.[12] As listed on her website, this includes "youth under 18, non-citizens, incarcerated and formerly incarcerated people (depending on state laws), residents of U.S. territories, and those without government-issued IDs (depending on state laws). This monumental number does not even factor in voter suppression."[13] "Frustrated by bureaucracy,"[14] she envisioned *Official Unofficial Voting Station: Voting for All Who Legally Can't* (2016–present). She has worked with more than a dozen collaborators, including artists, institutions, and activists to realize the Stations, allowing much freedom on the part of the organizers and participants in terms of ballots, activities, decorations, and environments. The *Official Unofficial Voting Stations* have taken

10. Han Sifuentes studio visit, 2018.

11. Han Sifuentes studio visit, 2018.

12. Han Sifuentes studio visit, 2018.

13. Aram Han Sifuentes, "The Official Unofficial Voting Station," accessed November 2020, https://www.aramhansifuentes.com/the-official-unofficial-voting-stat.

14. Han Sifuentes studio visit, 2018.

the forms of a DJ'ed party at the Museum of Contemporary Art in Chicago; candidate-piñata smashing at Handwerker Gallery in Ithaca, New York; "bloody" fingerprinting in Mexico City; and a mobile station in the trunk of a car in Washington, D.C., among many others.

Artist Jenny Holzer's (b. 1950, United States) *Sign on a Truck* (1984) comes to mind. Organized by the artist during the U.S. presidential election, a huge electronic screen on a semi-truck trailer featured artists' visual and audio works, as well as interviews with passersby. In Holzer's words, they "were discussing not just the candidates but the issues that come up at election time — a time when Americans are willing to talk about politics, and what they really want to happen or not happen in the world."[15] While Holzer cited giving people an opportunity to express themselves in a similar format to the candidates, Han Sifuentes has offered a means of making visible the politically disenfranchised. The Stations have embraced polyvocality, sharing the raucous, hilarious, assertive, brilliant, sensitive perspectives of people who are excluded from the democratic process.

Protest Banner Lending Library

Han Sifuentes started another "forever project" the same year: *Protest Banner Lending Library* (2016–present). She began this project immediately after the 2016 U.S. presidential election as a way to channel her anger when "the risks of going to protests were too high."[16] Her first banner declared DUMP TRUMP in black block letters adhered to a cheerful fabric rectangle (an aqua background filled with small pug dogs) surrounded with gold fringe. Soon, many more followed. Han Sifuentes continued making banners herself, and generated ways for others to do so. She has led in-person banner-making workshops, educated institutions on how to lead them in lieu of her presence, provided online and written tutorials, and developed virtual workshops during the coronavirus (COVID-19) pandemic. Han Sifuentes has basically created an open-source model; she does not have to be banner maker, workshop leader, or protester but she has served in all of those roles and has clearly outlined for others how to do so. In four years, the Library has expanded to include hundreds of banners made by the artist and workshop participants, with the materials often provided by hosting institutions. Unlike historical decorative tapestries commissioned to demonstrate power, these contemporary textile placards are created to demonstrate *against* power.

The generosity of *Protest Banner Lending Library* extends beyond the provision of materials and instruction; it functions as an actual library for donating or checking out banners. When explaining the impetus for structuring the project in this way, Han Sifuentes discusses access and accessibility: "I'm working a lot with immigrant communities and undocumented people. I turned it into a library so people who don't feel safe going to a protest can contribute and feel safe. People who don't feel comfortable carrying a banner can make a slogan for others to use."[17] Han Sifuentes has devised a simple analog cataloging system to record the checkouts and returns: 4 x 6-inch notecards include handwritten entries for the slogan, maker's name, borrower's contact information, and where the banner was used. The history of each banner accumulates on its small accompanying card. To illustrate, a BLACK LIVES MATTER banner made by Han Sifuentes was borrowed five times from January 2017 through September 2018 for use at the Women's March in Washington, D.C.; an exhibition in Cuba; the Museum of Design in

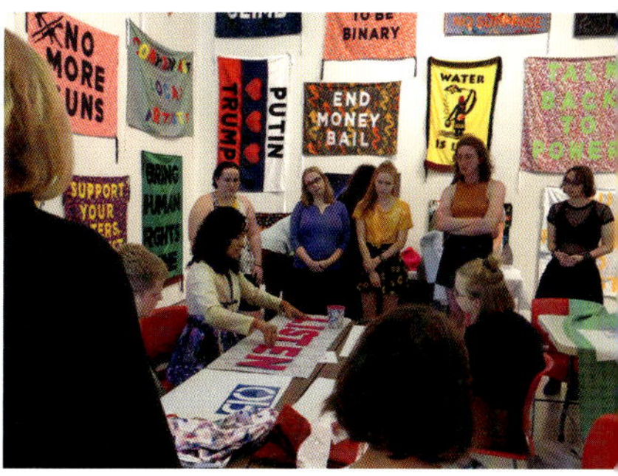

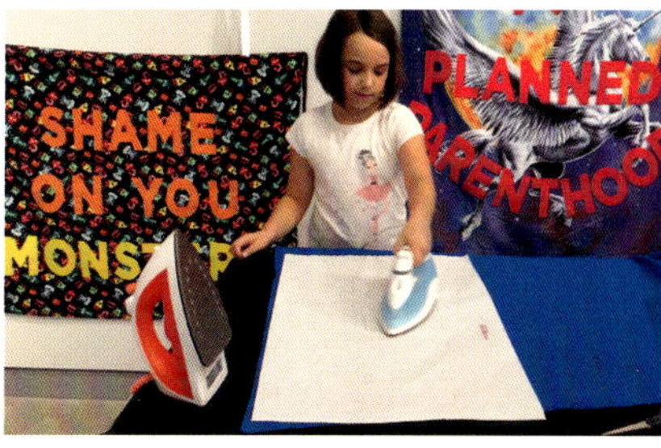

2 + 3 *Protest banner-making workshop, University Galleries of Illinois State University, Normal, 2019. Photos: Kendra Paitz.*

15. Jenny Holzer, "Jenny Holzer," in Inside the Studio: Two Decades of Talks with Artists in New York, ed. Judith Olch Richards (New York: Independent Curators International, 2004), 28.

16. Han Sifuentes studio visit, 2018.

17. Han Sifuentes studio visit, 2018.

Atlanta; and the Forward Union Fair in New York City. One reading CLIMATE CHANGE IS REAL made by Masum was checked out eight times between March 2017 and October 2019 for use in a class about environmental justice and climate change, and at events listed as Climate March, Refuse Fascism, MLK Jr. concert, PolicyLink Equity Summit, Change Fest, AMFM Feast, and Climate Strike.

Most of the banners follow the format of simply aligned capital sans serif block letters (traced from stencils) adhered to a horizontal rectangular fabric substrate. Eschewing the slick fabrication of mass production and sometimes including backward letters, awkward alignment, progressive spellings, and inside jokes, the banners are notably handmade and individualized. They are designed to make an immediate impact but the messages and visuality vary dramatically. Approaches include humorous slogans on whimsical fabrics, inspiring texts on solid backgrounds, angry declarations on preprinted imagery, and poignant pleas on geometric patterns. There are outliers to this structure too, from a triangular flag filled with a cascade of ampersands to reflect the myriad means of classifying one's individuality, to a hooded cape featuring a stack of letters spelling LIBERTY. Han Sifuentes discusses the "freeing" nature of the process, citing a Muslim student using her mother's hijabs to make a banner reading NOT MY SAFE SPACE.[18] As with banners created by American filmmaker and artist Cauleen Smith (b. 1967), with whom Han Sifuentes has collaborated, some are piercing in their combination of imagery and language.[19] For instance, one entry in the *Protest Banner Lending Library* features a haunting figurative drawing — made from cut black and red fabric — surrounded by text reading WATER IS LIFE, to emphasize the inextricable connection between humans and land and the need for active conservation of natural resources.

The banners' effectiveness lies, in part, in their portability; they can be folded, rolled, packed, mailed, and/or carried. Not only that, the "scale is reproducible," as artist and organizer Rick Lowe once pointed out while discussing other participatory works.[20] The banners are to be created, used, and re-used in public spaces. While selections are often temporarily housed within museums, galleries, and not-for-profit organizations, they are made to exit the institution. They are made to be hoisted overhead at a march for reproductive rights, waved at a rally about climate science, or carried at a demonstration against a detention center. Claiming both physical and psychological space, they are often photographed, thus extending their reach via news outlets and social media.[21] The banners themselves are resilient,[22] like many of their messages:

BLACK LIVES MATTER;
ABOLISH ICE;
NO GUNS;
NO WALL;
CLIMATE CHANGE IS EVERYONE'S PROBLEM;
WE ARE WATCHING YOU;
THEY TRIED TO BURY US. THEY DIDN'T KNOW WE WERE SEEDS;
LOVE RESISTS;
WE ARE IN THIS TOGETHER;
SUPPORT YOUR SISTERS, NOT JUST YOUR CIS-TERS;
FIGHT IGNORANCE NOT IMMIGRANTS;
MARS IS NOT AN OPTION;
THE FUTURE IS FEMALE AND BROWN;
OTRO MUNDO ES POSIBLE;
OUR HOPE IS MORE POWERFUL THAN THE SEA.

18. Han Sifuentes studio visit, 2018.

19. For more information on Cauleen Smith's banners, which are exhibited and sometimes activated via a processional, see "Waking Life: Siddhartha Mitter on the art of Cauleen Smith" at https://www.artforum.com/print/201905/siddhartha-mitter-on-the-art-of-cauleen-smith-79523. Other examples include ACT UP's (AIDS Coalition to Unleash Power) posters and banners demanding research, funding, public policies, and more to end the AIDS crisis; Decolonize This Place's collaborative actions to "resist, unsettle, and reclaim" New York City; and Renée Green's banners that together compose a poem.

20. Rick Lowe, "In Conversation: Rick Lowe and Lisa Lee," in Place and Revolution (Pittsburgh, Pennsylvania: Open Engagement in Print, 2015), 24.

21. For example, Han Sifuentes pointed out (during our April 24, 2018 studio visit) that the Asian Arts Initiative in Philadelphia started a library with 20 slogans collected by the program director from activists in town. People continued to check out the banners and use them in protests, then news organizations would cover the protests and publish images. It surprised her to see how far some of the banners had traveled.

22. Han Sifuentes estimates that only one out of 250 is no longer usable due to damage.

FORGET GREATNESS, WORK FOR PEACE

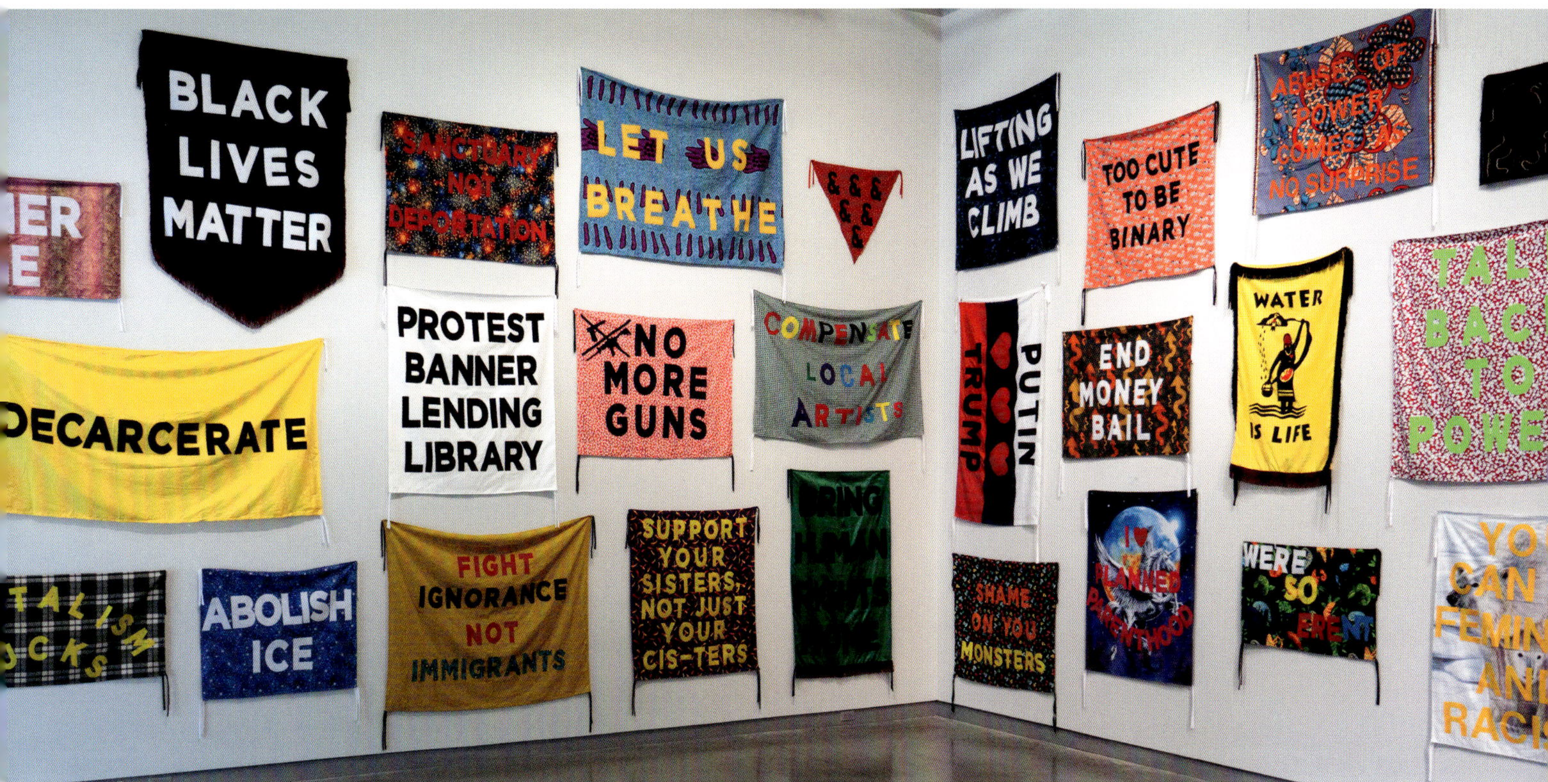

Given the ways Han Sifuentes offers opportunities and develops relationships, it is perhaps not surprising that each of the aforementioned projects is ongoing. As previously stated, she began *Protest Banner Lending Library* the day after the 2016 U.S. presidential election. This publication is going to print amid intense social, political, and ecological turmoil in the months surrounding the 2020 U.S. presidential election: with COVID-19 ravaging communities, the heartbreaking murder of George Floyd and resulting Black Lives Matter protests, and a devastating and record-breaking fire season, among countless examples. And at the moment of this writing, the current U.S. president continues to deny that president-elect Joe Biden won the election. It is even clearer how vital Han Sifuentes' work is and how urgently we need to use our voices and peacefully speak truth to power. Like Han Sifuentes, we must be the revolution.

The title of this essay is inspired by a banner donated to the Protest Banner Lending Library *by artist kg (Karolina Gnatowski).*

4 *Installation view of* Protest Banner Lending Library, *University Galleries of Illinois State University, 2019. Photo: Jessica Bingham.*

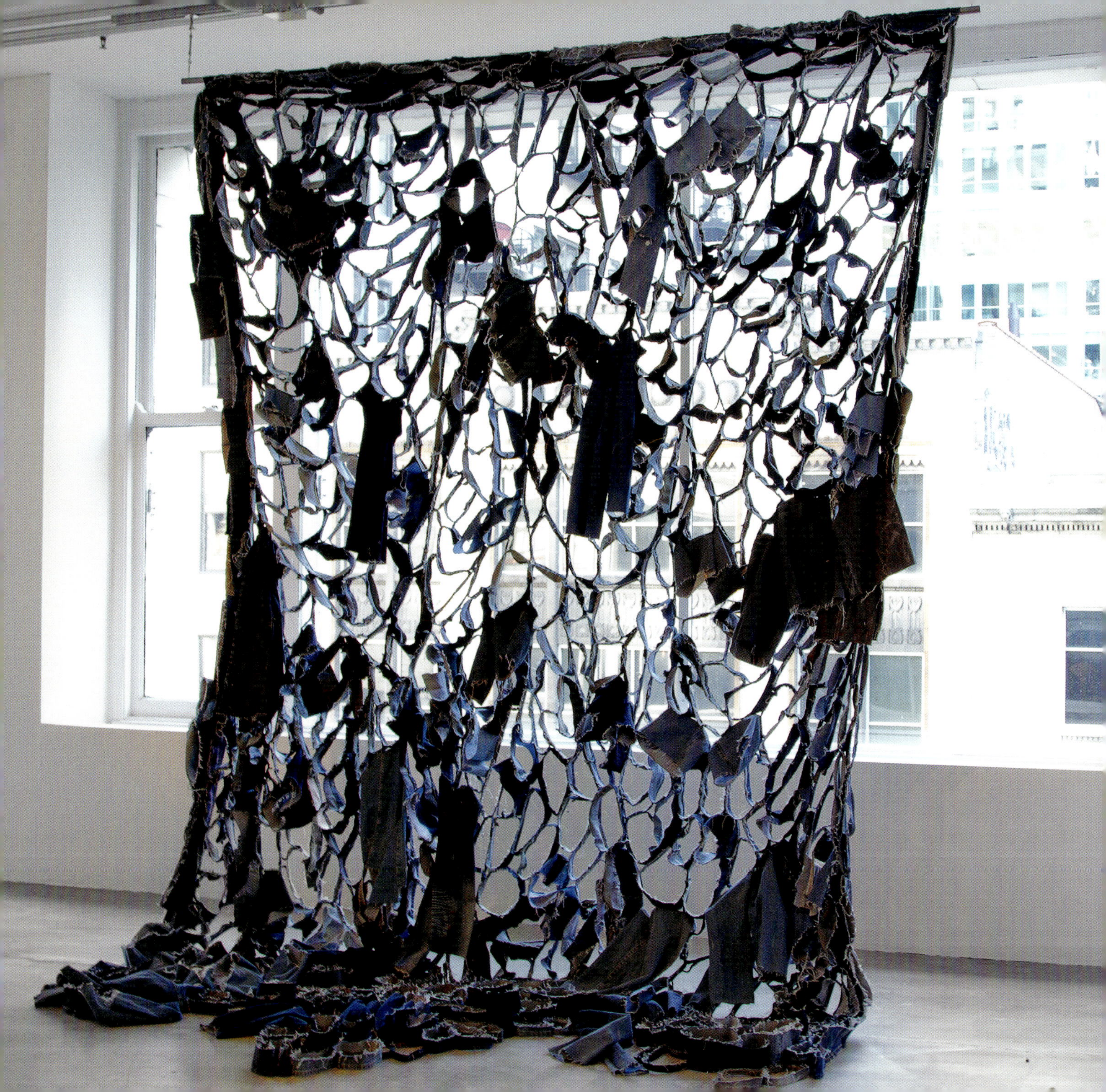

A MEND

A Collection of Scraps from Local Seamstresses and Tailors (Chicago)

2011-present

The politics of immigrant sweated labor in the United States inform my project, ***A Mend: A Collection of Scraps from Local Seamstresses and Tailors (Chicago)***. Because many immigrants do not speak English well and their credentials do not carry over to the United States, their employment options are usually limited. Many of them end up getting jobs that offer low wages, require repetitive manual labor, and are sometimes hazardous with no unions or collective bargaining protections. Inspired by my mother being a seamstress, I am interested in people who do sweated labor. Sweated laborers often work long and tedious hours for low wages, and often take extra work home or to places where work is unregulated.

I have been visiting tailors and seamstresses in the Chicago area. I have been using their services, talking to them about my project, asking them to donate their jeans remnants, and asking them:

From where did you immigrate?
How long have you been in the U.S.?
How long have you worked as a seamstress or tailor?
What type of work did you do before?
How much do you charge to hem a pair of jeans?
Do you enjoy this type of work?

While answering these questions, their stories slip out. I continue to visit many seamstresses and tailors in the area. Many of them have continued collecting jeans remnants for my project. From this collection of oral histories, I am interested in seeing the similarities among the immigrant workers' stories in order to understand a collective identity and hear about their hand labor.

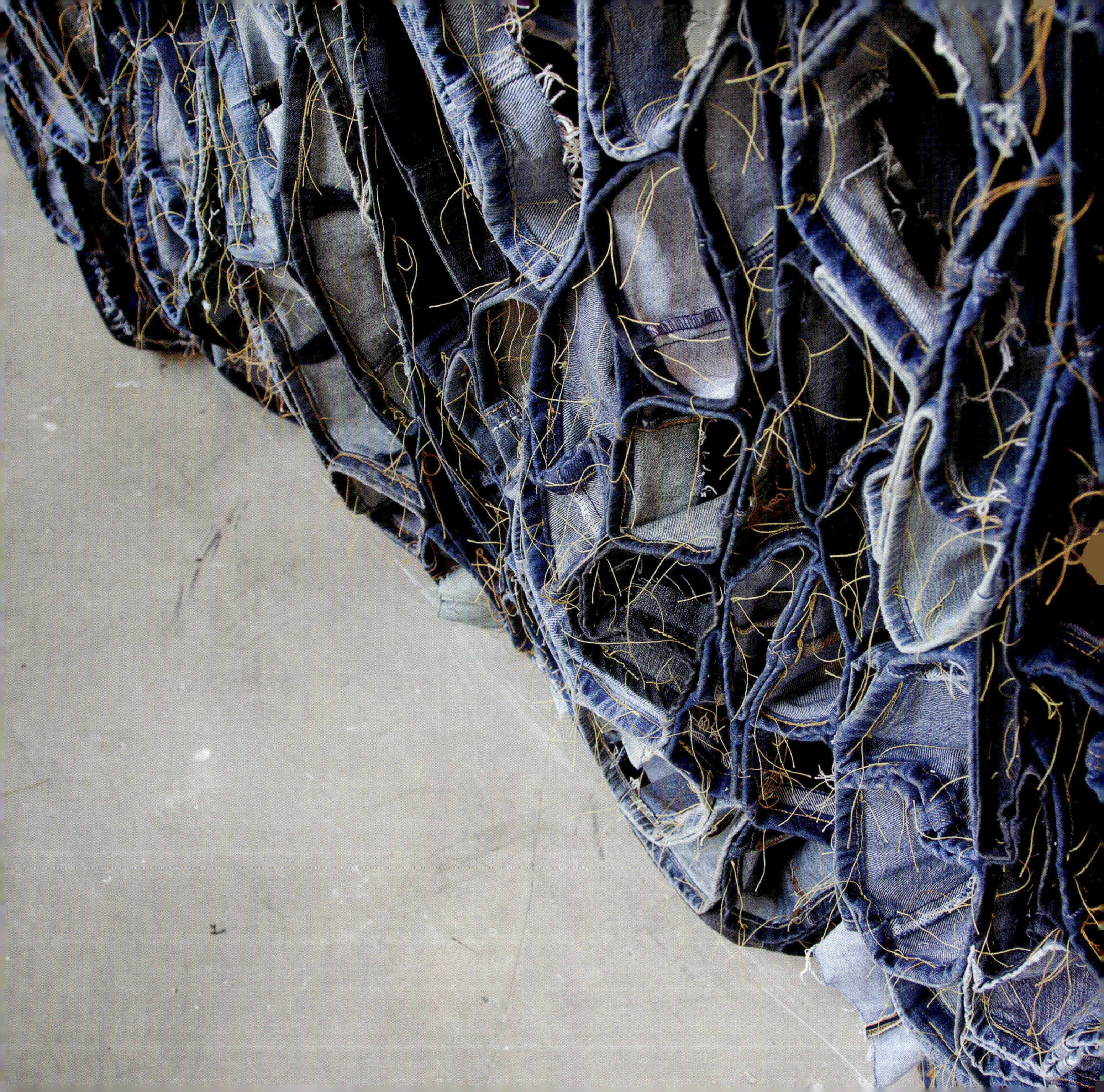

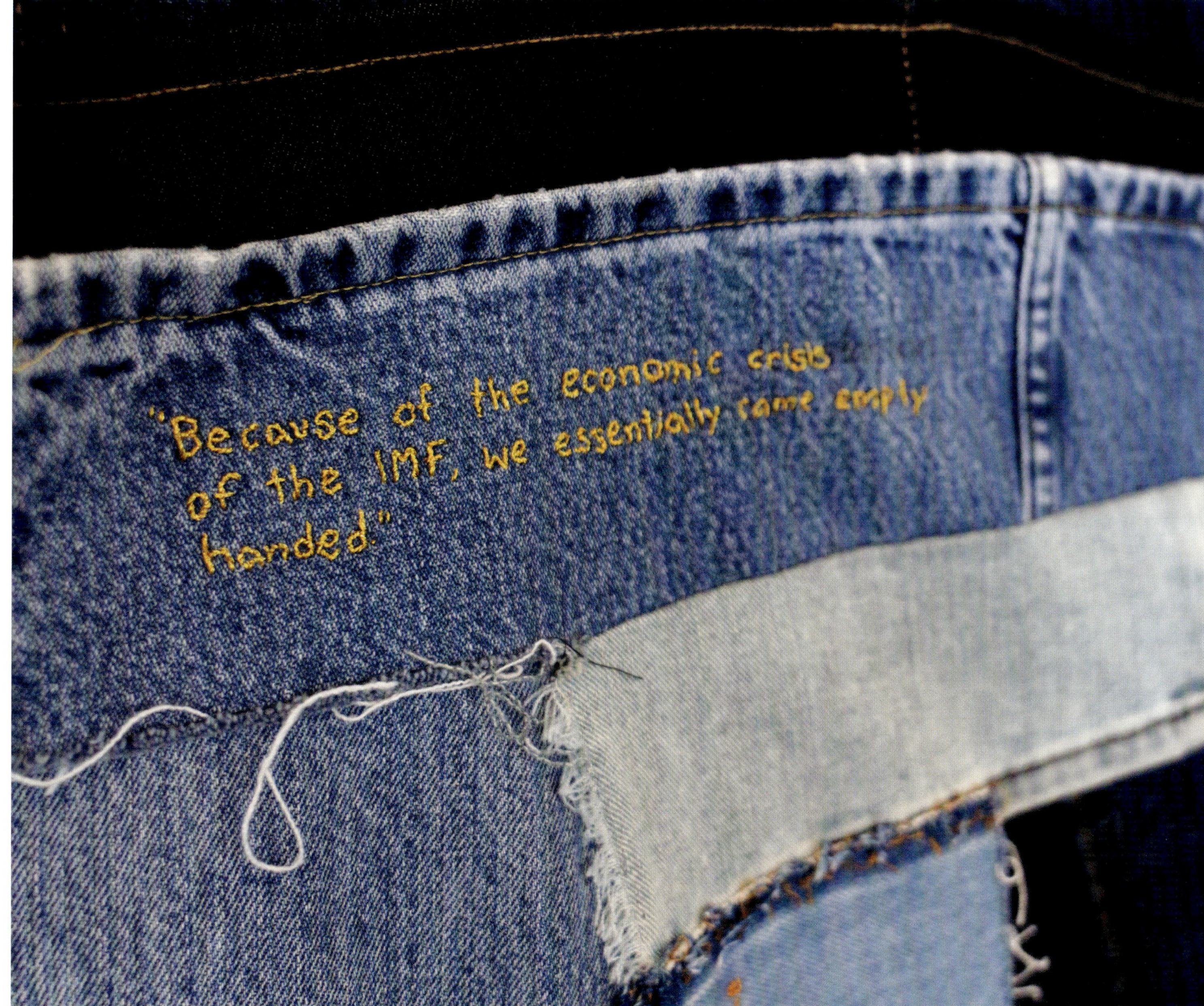

1 PAGE 24 *Aram Han Sifuentes,* A Mend: A Collection of Scraps from Local Seamstresses and Tailors (Chicago), *2011–13. Jeans scraps and gold denim thread, 14 x 10 x 4 feet. Photo: Hyounsang Yoo.*

2 A Mend: A Collection of Scraps from Local Seamstresses and Tailors (Chicago) *(detail). Photo: Hyounsang Yoo.*

3 *Aram Han Sifuentes,* A Mend: A Collection of Stories from Local Seamstresses and Tailors (Chicago) *(detail), 2019. Jeans scraps and gold thread, 33 x 46 inches. Photo: Aram Han Sifuentes.*

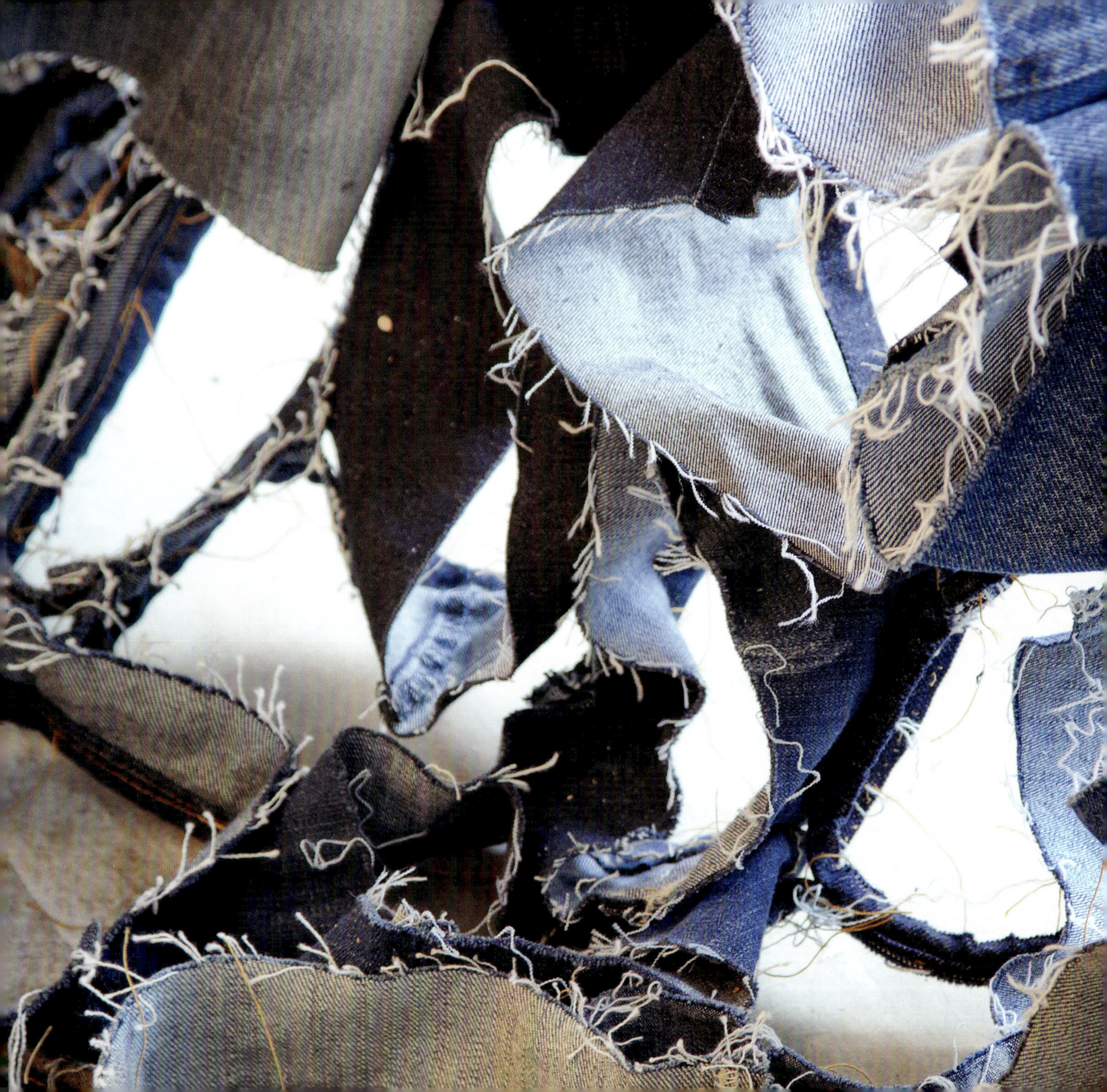

HEMMED JEANS SCRAPS CONTRIBUTED BY THE WORK OF 23 SEAMSTRESSES AND TAILORS.

FROM	HAS BEEN IN U.S. FOR (YEARS)	WORKING AS A SEAMSTRESS/ TAILOR (YEARS)	USED TO BE A	CHARGES TO HEM A PAIR OF JEANS (U.S. $)
S. Korea	30 years but went back for 8 years	12	Teacher	$12-18
S. Korea	30	10	Stay-at-home Mother	$10-20
S. Korea	30	24		$12-20
S. Korea	40	22	Nurse	$10-20
S. Korea	30	30	Stay-at-home Mother	$10-20
S. Korea	30	28	High School Teacher	$10-18.50
S. Korea	**"a long time now"**	**12**	**Stay-at-home Mother**	**$9.50-19.50**
S. Korea	25	25		$9.50-17.50
S. Korea	33	Over 20 years	Children's Clothing Manufacturer	$12-22
Iraq	20	16	Elementary School Teacher	$10-20
Palestine	40	20	Tailor	$11-15
S. Korea				**$16-24**
S. Korea	20	15	Graphic Designer	$20
S. Korea	30	22	Banker	$14-20
S. Korea	31	28	Artist (Painter and Ceramicist)	$11-20
Mexico	31	13		$13
S. Korea	32	15		$18
S. Korea	42	23	Teacher	
S. Korea			**Stay-at-home Mother "with maids"**	
S. Korea	**"a long time now"**	**23**	**Corporate Businesswoman**	
S. Korea	19	19	Clothing Retailer	$15-22
S. Korea	30	26	Stay-at-home Mother	$15-20
S. Korea	21	21	Artist (Painter)	$10-20

20 OF 23 ARE FROM SOUTH KOREA

...

AVERAGE YEARS IN U.S. = 29.26

...

CHARGING $9.50-$24 TO HEM A PAIR OF JEANS

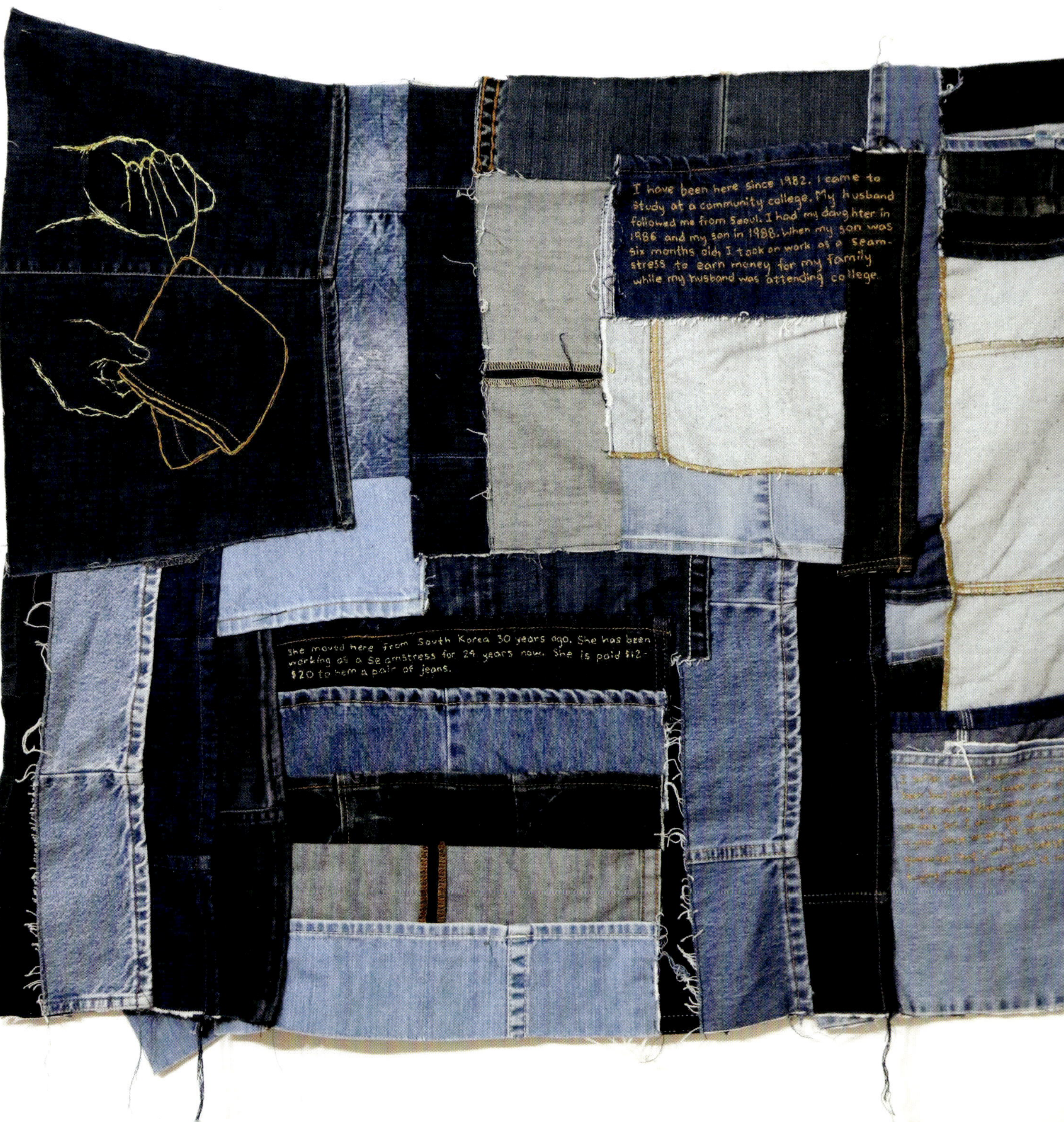

I have been here since 1982. I came to
study at a community college. My husband
followed me from Seoul. I had my daughter in
1986 and my son in 1988. When my son was
six months old, I took on work as a seamstress to earn money for my family
while my husband was attending college.
She moved here from South Korea 30 years ago. She has been
working as a seamstress for 24 years now. She is paid $12-
$20 to hem a pair of jeans.

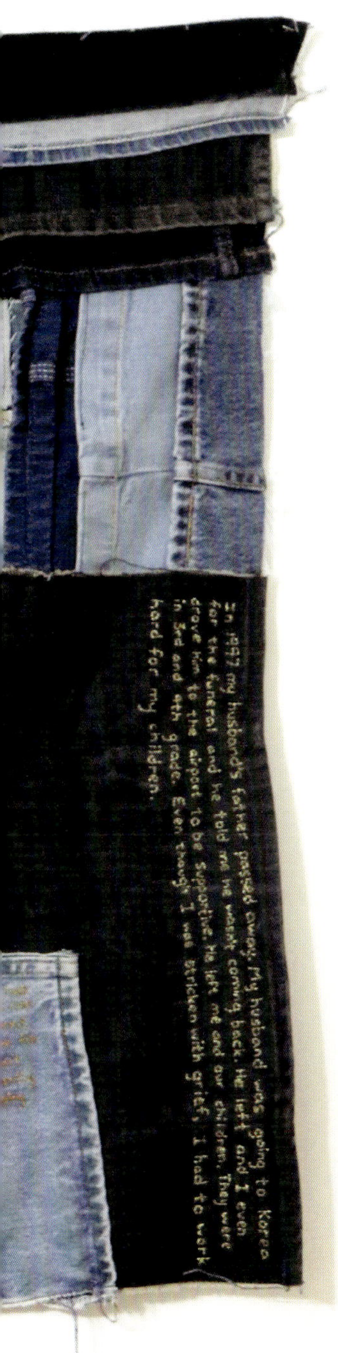

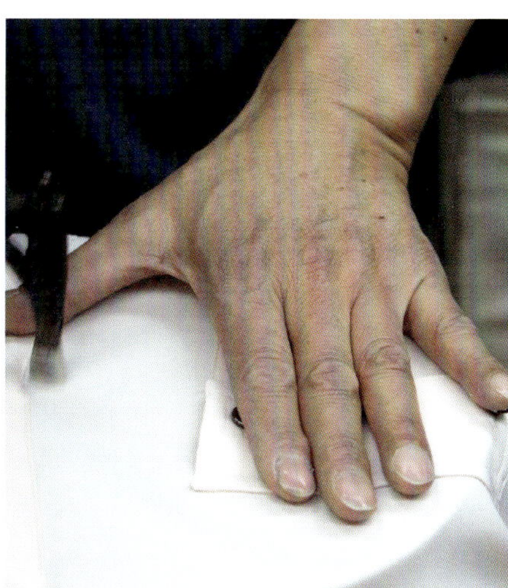

4 PAGE 28 A Mend: A Collection of Scraps from Local Seamstresses and Tailors (Chicago) (*detail*). *Photo: Hyounsang Yoo*

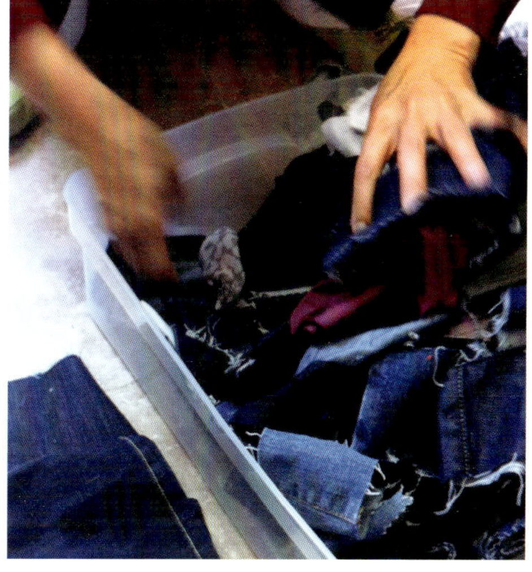

5 PAGE 30 *Aram Han Sifuentes,* A Mend: A Collection of Stories from Local Seamstresses and Tailors (Chicago) (*detail*), *2019. Jeans scraps and gold thread, 33 x 46 inches. Photo: Aram Han Sifuentes.*

6–8 A Mend: Photographs of the Hands of Local Seamstresses and Tailors (Chicago), *2011–13. Photos: Aram Han Sifuentes.*

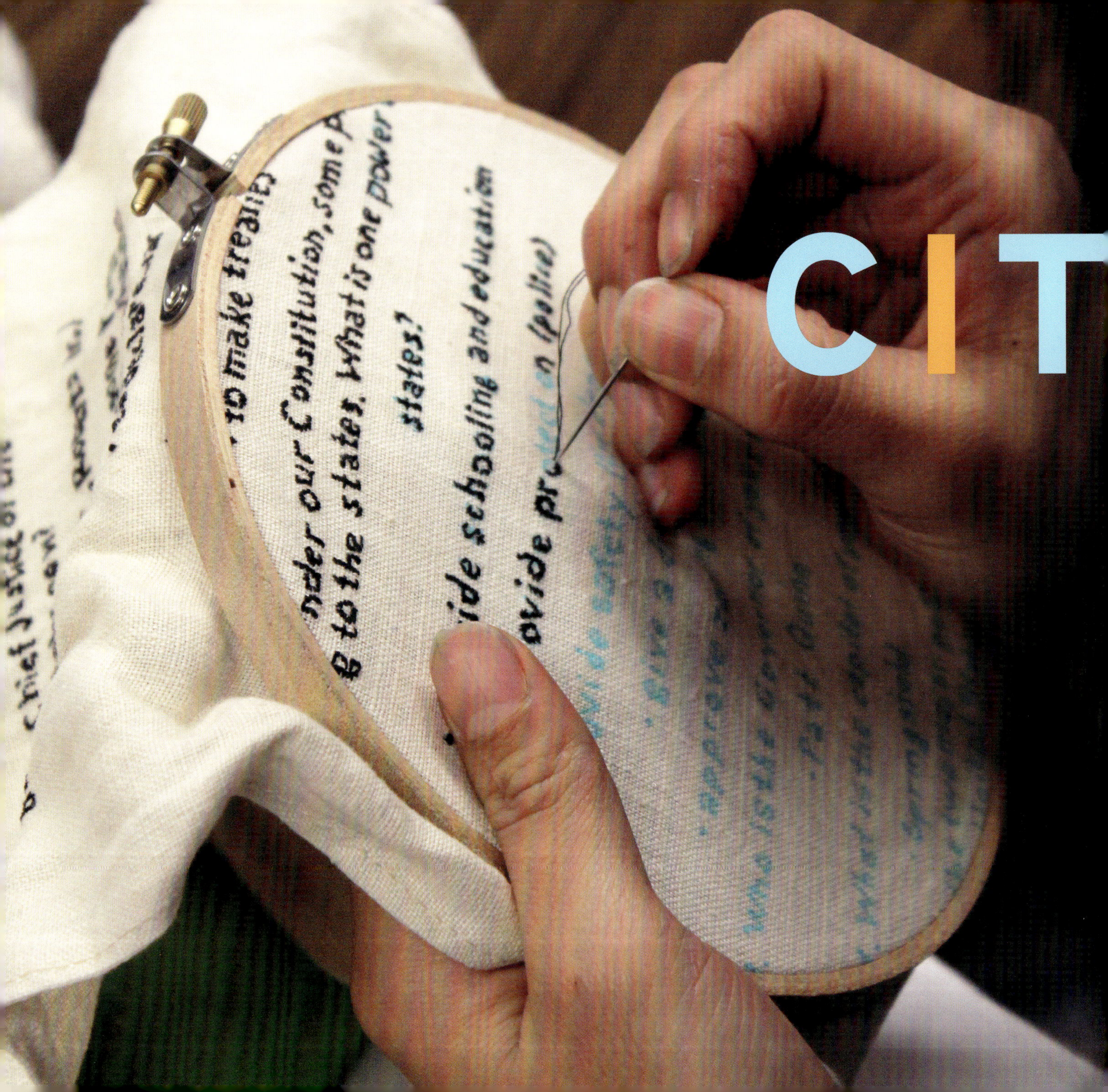

CIT

US
IZENSHIP
TEST
SAMPLER

A Community of Non-Citizens: Proving Worth of Citizenship Through Stitching Samplers

2012–present

U.S. Citizenship Test Sampler addresses the social and collective nature of needlework's history, the socio-historic role of women, and the value of non-citizen communities. Sewn samplers were used in Colonial America to teach needlework and the alphabet to young children, and in 2012, I began hand-sewing the 100 civic study questions and answers for the U.S. Naturalization Test. In December 2016, I sold the completed work for $680, then the cost of applying for naturalization. This action was motivated by the additional history of educated adolescent women embroidering decorative pictorial samplers that functioned as signifiers of worth to potential suitors. My citizenship was contingent on the sale of the work, and following that sale, I became a naturalized citizen in 2018. Through workshops, other non-U.S. citizens have contributed, and continue to contribute, to the pool of samplers, both augmenting the project and building a community. Each of their works can be purchased for $725, the current cost of applying for citizenship. If sold, the full amount goes to the maker of the sampler.

From start to finish, this project is about reclaiming the historical act of making samplers. The Colonial samplers were about assessing value – the value of the skills of the woman making them. In this industrial age, when embroidery and hand crafts are made by so-called invisible laborers, that assessment of hand work has been lost. This project reclaims this tradition, especially for the racialized immigrant working class.

PAGE 32 *Aram Han Sifuentes working on* U.S. Citizenship Test Sampler: 100 Questions and Answers, *2012.*

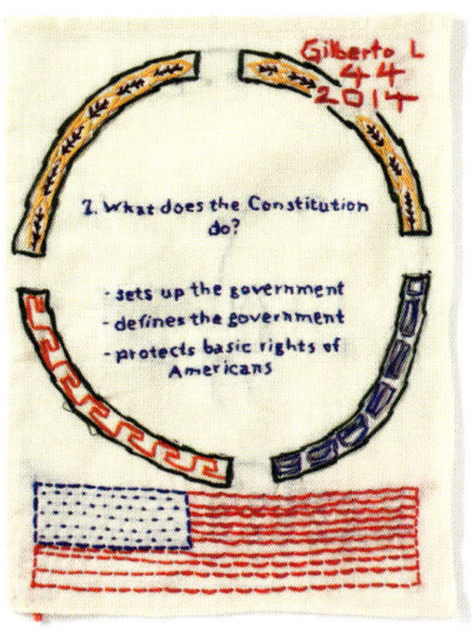

2

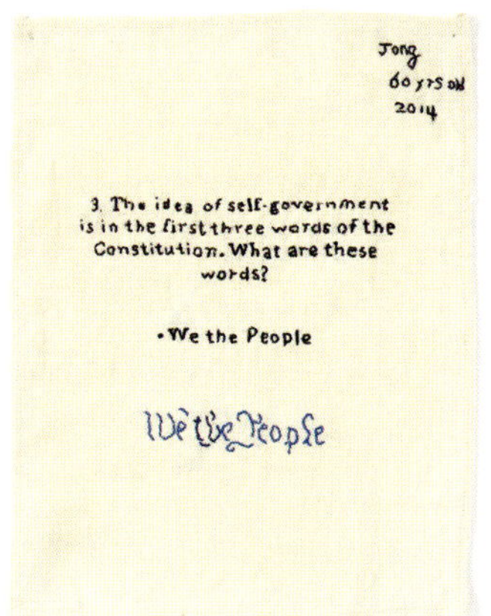

3

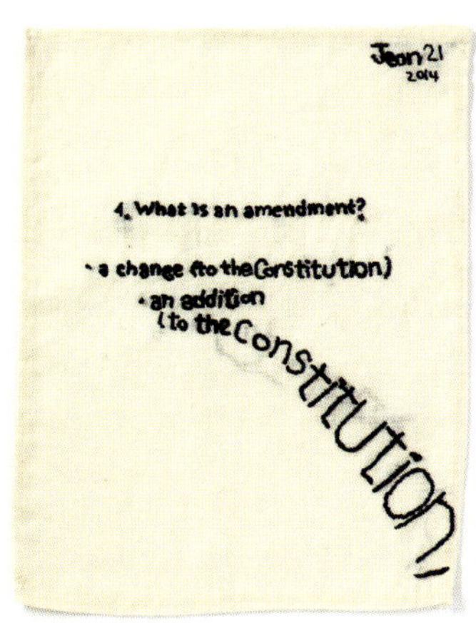

4

Young
59 yrs old
2014
8. What did the Declaration of Independence do?
• said that the United States is free (from Great Britain)

8

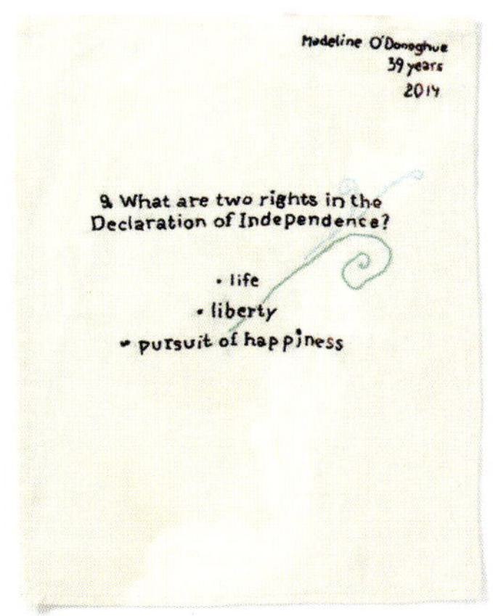

9

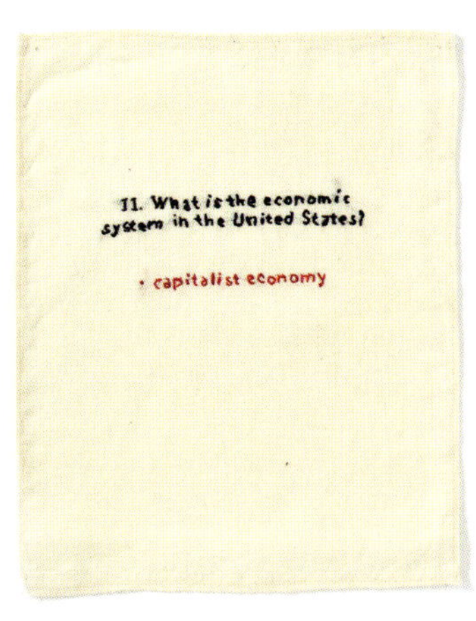

11

APARICIO
67
2014
16. Who makes federal laws?
Congress

16

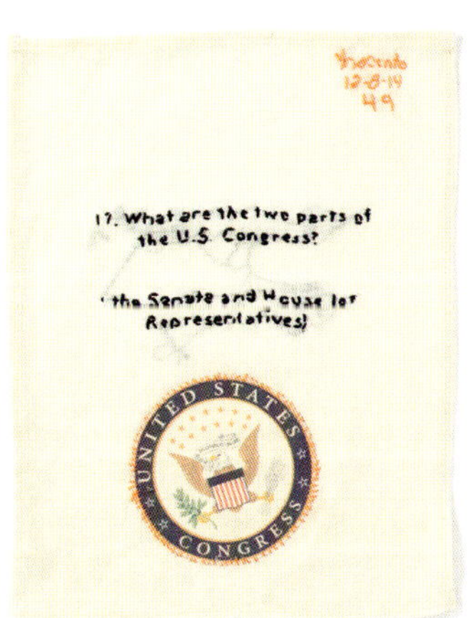

17

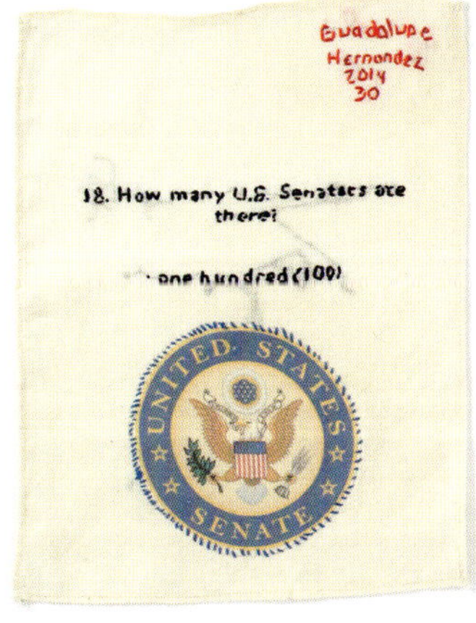

18

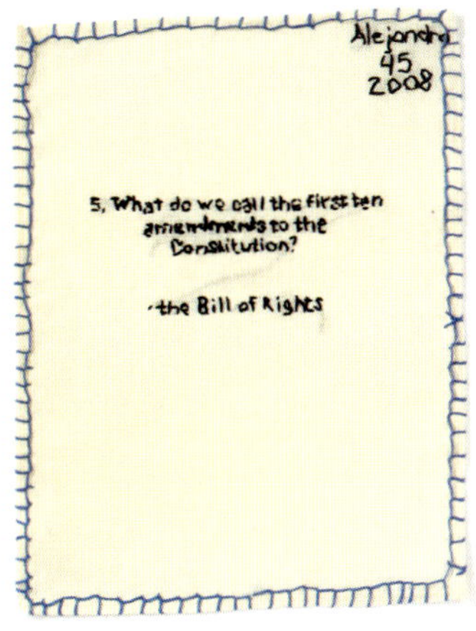

5

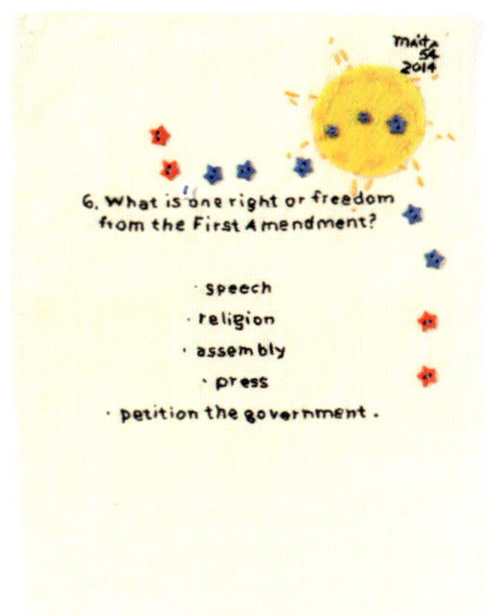

6

7

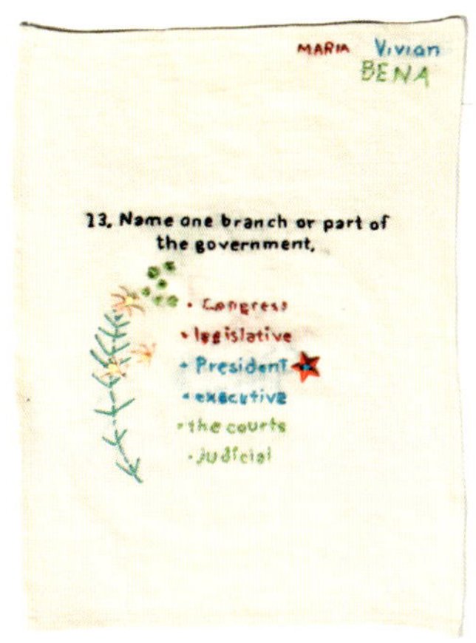

13

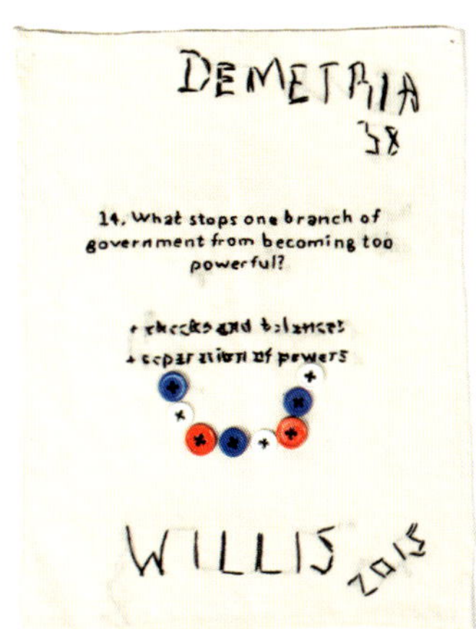

14

15. Who is in charge of the executive branch?

· the President

15

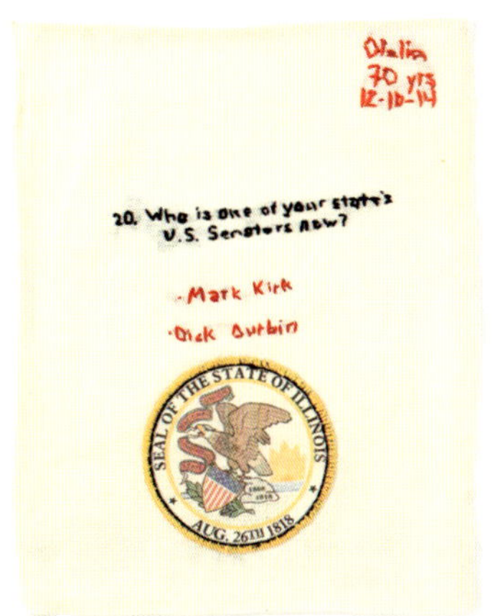

20

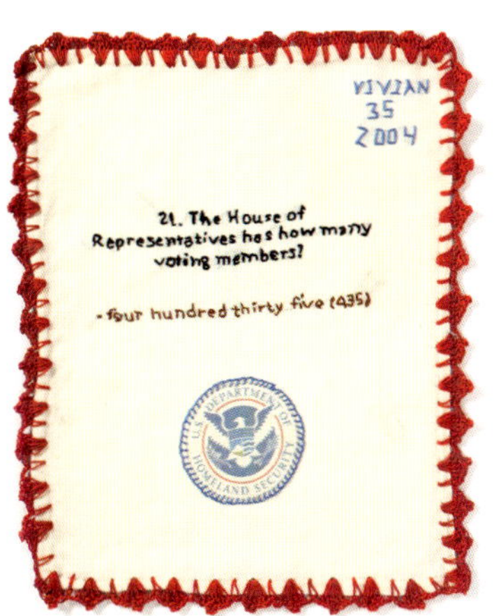

21

These numbers correspond to the question selected by each participant. Information provided by participants is listed — including names, year the sampler was completed, and country one moved from.

2 *Gilberto L., 2014, Mexico.*
3 *Jong, 2014, South Korea.*
4 *Jeon, 2014, South Korea.*
5 *Alejandra, Mexico.*
6 *Maita, Colombia.*
7 *Isidra, 2014, Mexico.*
8 *Young, 2014, South Korea.*
9 *Madeline O'Donoghue, 2014, Australia.*
11 *Havia, Mexico.*
13 *Maria, Vivian, and Bena.*
14 *Demetria, 2015.*
15 *Cristina, 2014, Mexico.*
16 *Aparicio, 2014, Mexico.*
17 *Ynocenta, 2014, Mexico.*
18 *Guadalupe Hernandez, 2014.*
20 *Ofelia, 2014, Mexico.*
21 *Vivian, Guatemala.*

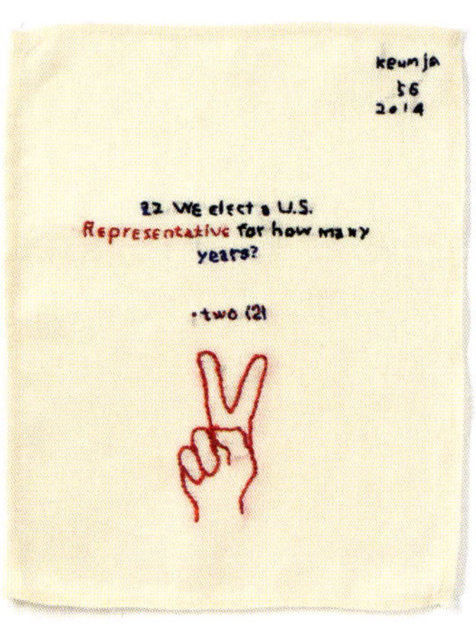

22

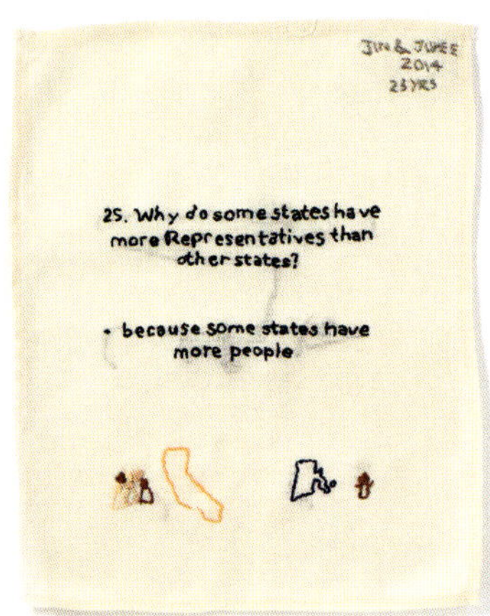

25

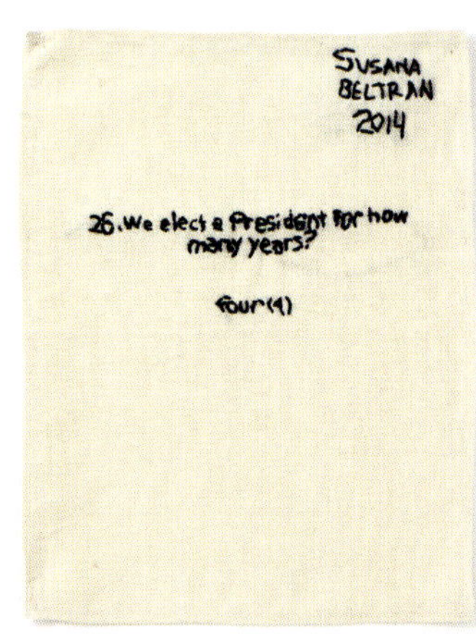

26

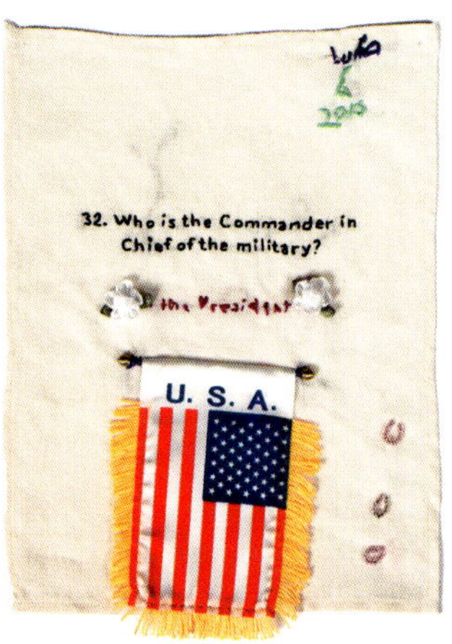

32

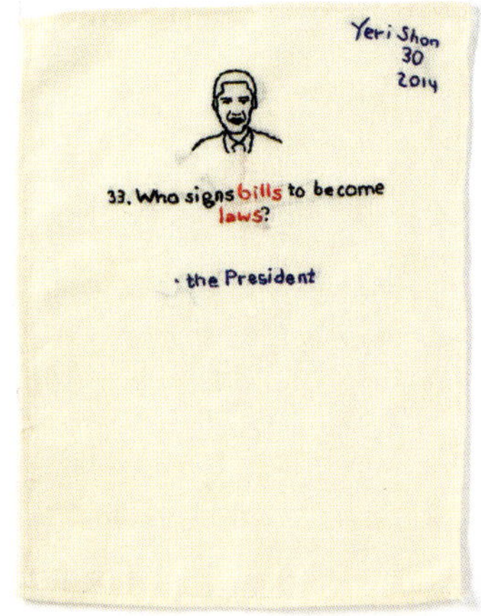

33

34

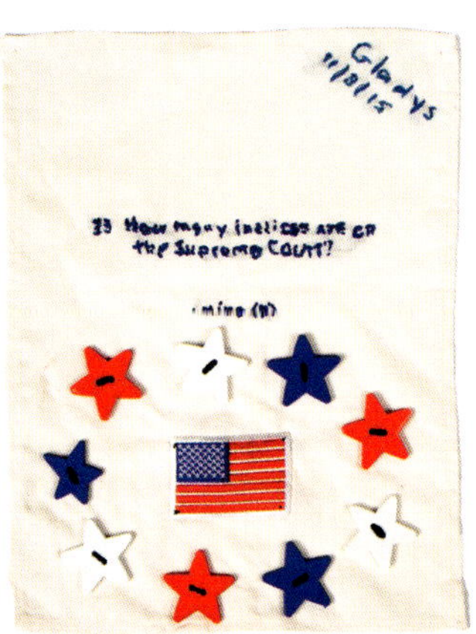

39

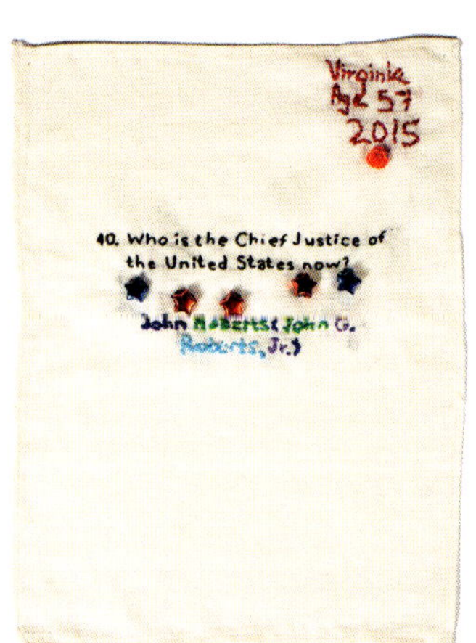

40

Carrie
23
2014
41. Under our Constitution, some powers belong to the federal government. What is one power of the federal government?
• to declare war

41

27

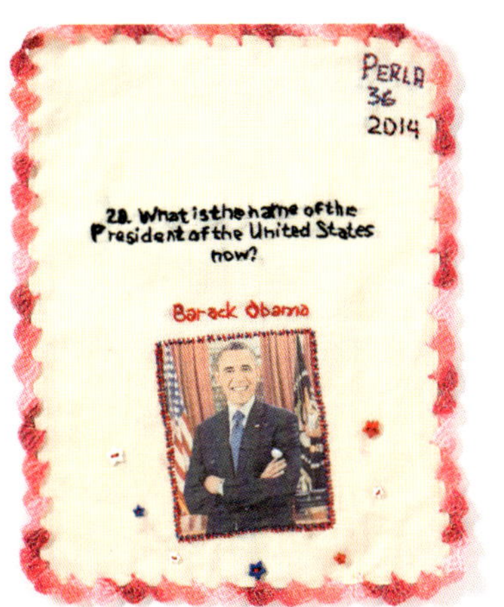

28

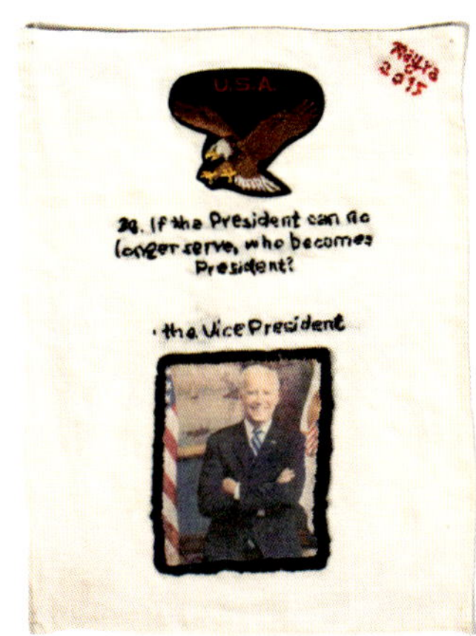

30

Kyong Choe
50 Years
2014

35. What does the President's Cabinet do?

• advises the President

35

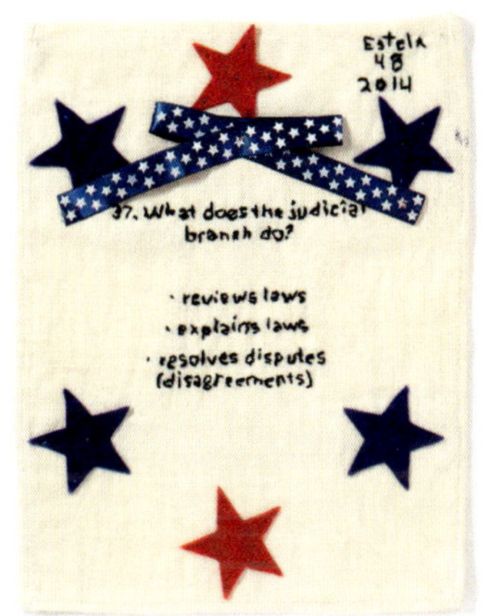

37

Hee Jeong
40
2014

38. What is the highest court in the United States?

• the Supreme Court

38

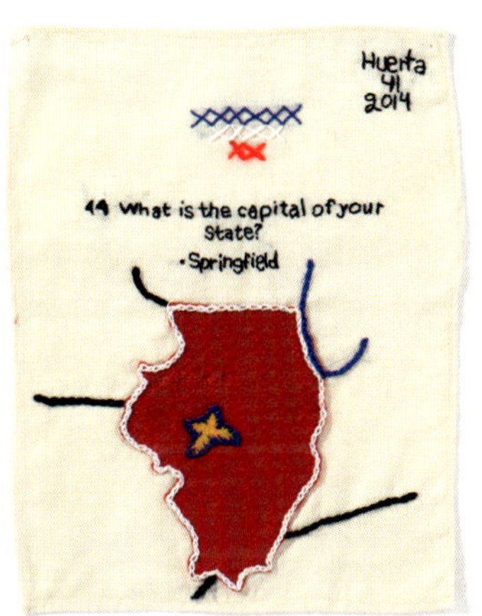

44

carmen
42
2014

45. What are the two major political parties in the United States?

• Democratic and Republican

45

22 *Keumja, 2014, South Korea.*

25 *Jin and Juhee, 2014, South Korea.*

26 *Susana, 2014.*

27 *Maria, 2014, Mexico.*

28 *Perla, 2014, Mexico.*

30 *Mayra, 2015, Mexico.*

32 *Lulia, 2016, Eretria.*

33 *Yeri, 2014, South Korea.*

34 *Joaquin, 2014, Mexico.*

35 *Kyong Choe, 2014, South Korea.*

37 *Estela, 2014, Mexico.*

38 *Hee Jeong, 2014, South Korea.*

39 *Gladys, 2015, Ecuador.*

40 *Virginia, 2015.*

41 *Carrie, 2014, South Korea.*

44 *Huerta, 2014, Mexico.*

45 *Carmen, 2014, Ecuador.*

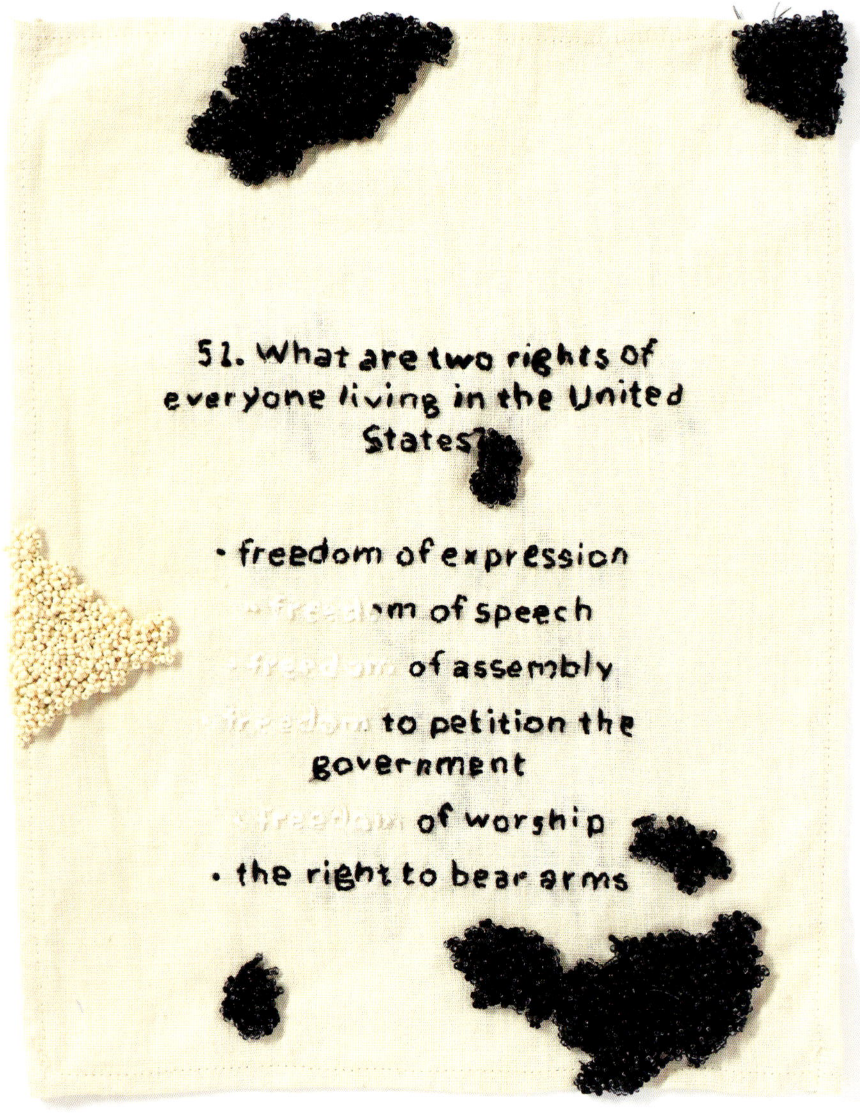

51. What are two rights of everyone living in the United States?

• freedom of expression

• freedom of speech

• freedom of assembly

• freedom to petition the government

• freedom of worship

• the right to bear arms

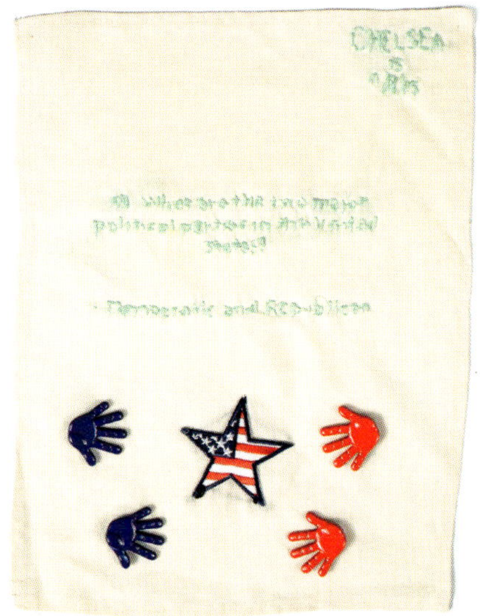

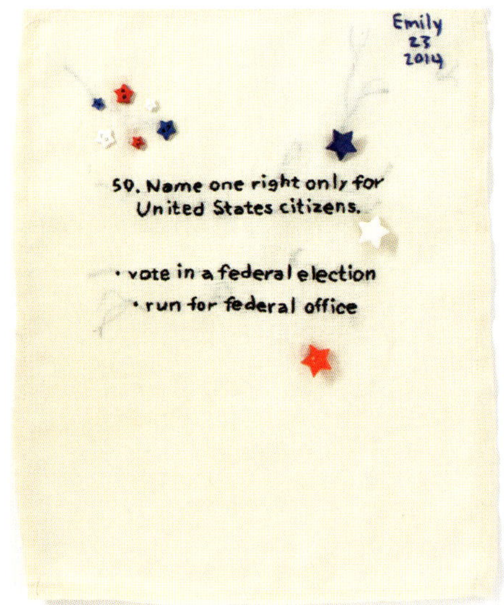

51 *Veronica, 2014, Spain.*

45.2 *Chelsea, 2015, Ecuador.*

50 *Emily, 2014, South Korea.*

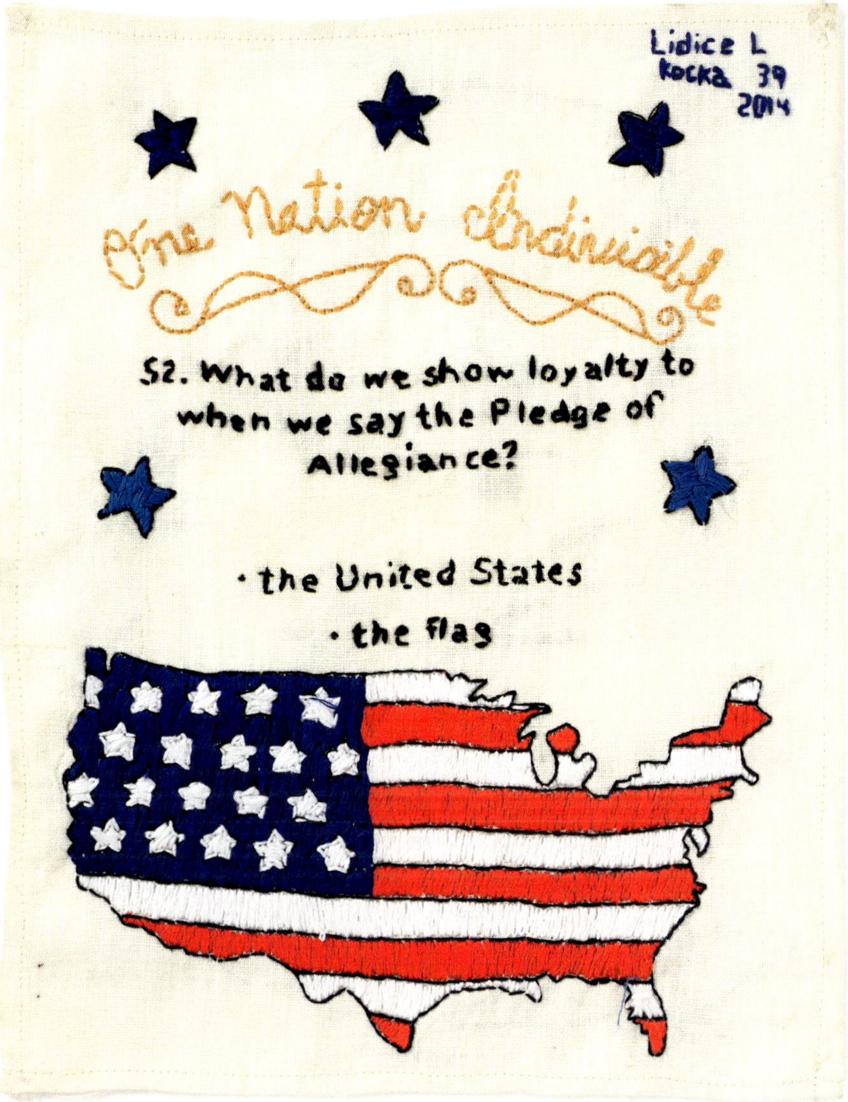

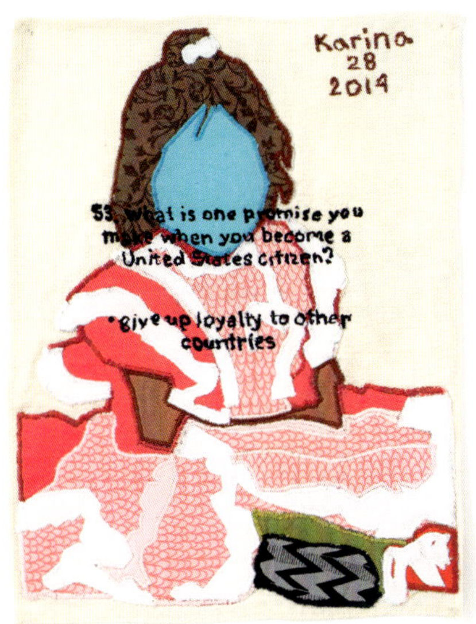

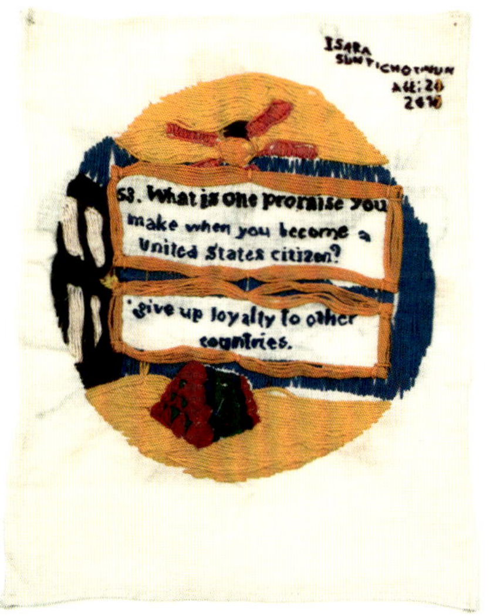

52 *Lidice, 2014, Mexico.*

53 *Karina, 2014, Mexico.*

53.2 *Isara Suntichotinun, 2017, Thailand.*

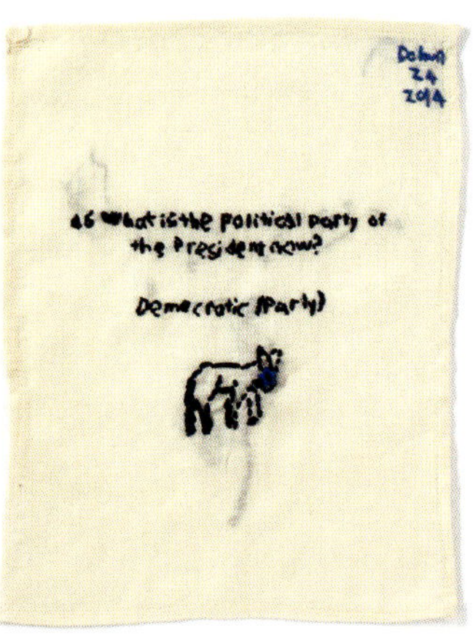

46

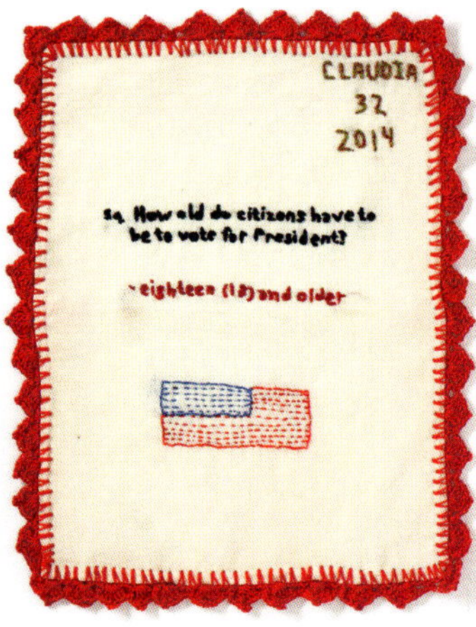

54

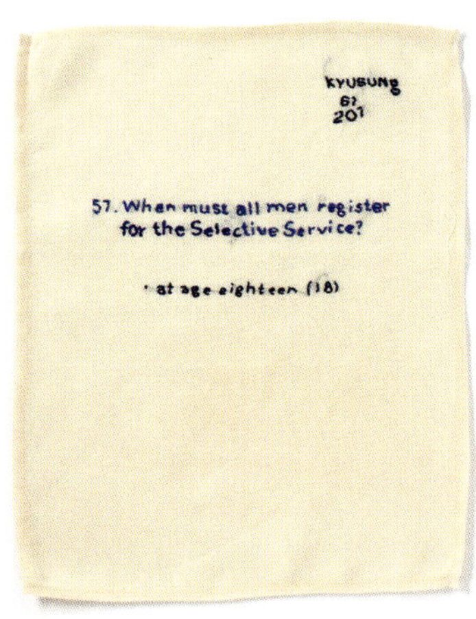

57

Soto
60
2014

63 When was the Declaration of Independence adopted?

• July 4, 1776

63

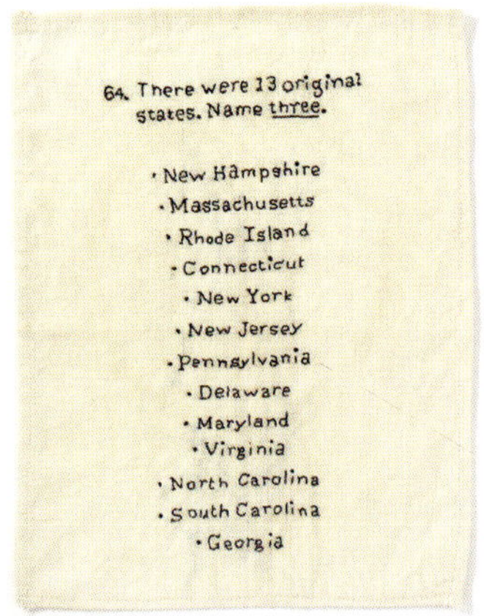

64

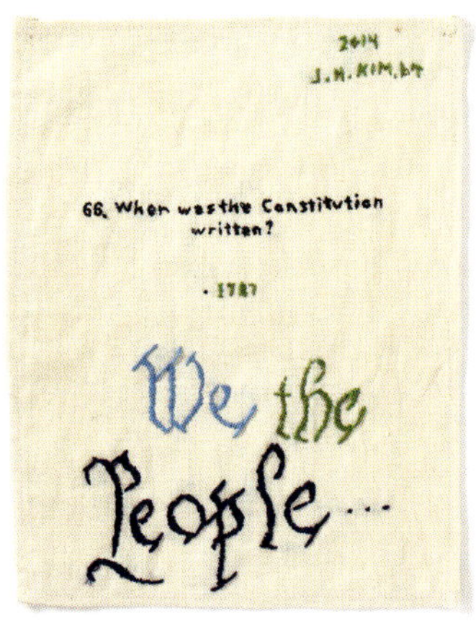

66

Cecy
2015

I ♡ USA

71. What territory did the United States buy from France in 1803?

the Louisiana Territory

71

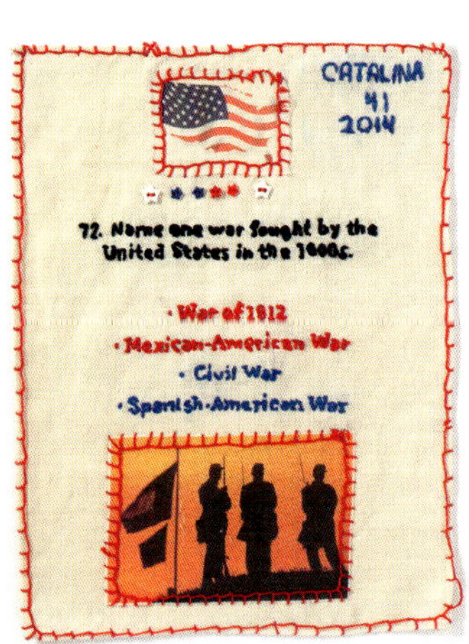

72

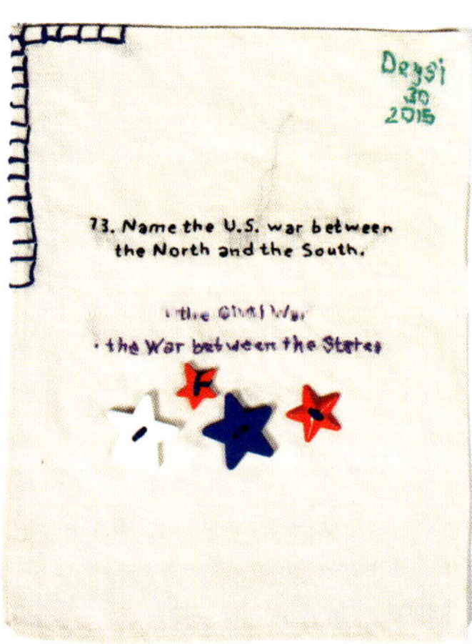

73

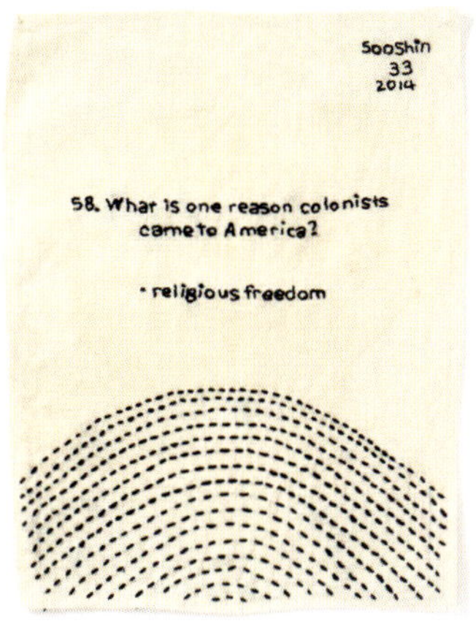

58

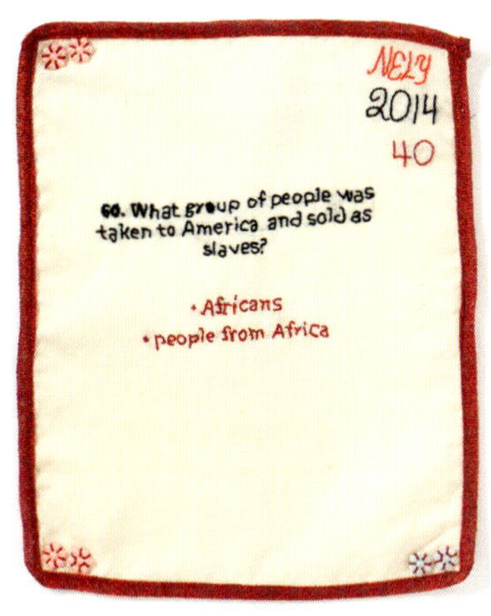

60

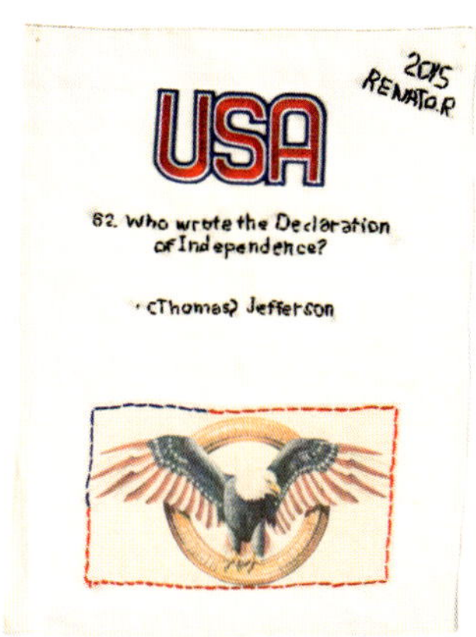

62

NATALIYA
KOTLOVA
2014
21 years old

68. What is one thing Benjamin Franklin is famous for?

• U.S. diplomat
• oldest member of the Constitutional Convention
• first Postmaster General of the United States
• writer of "Poor Richard's Almanac"
• started the first free libraries

68

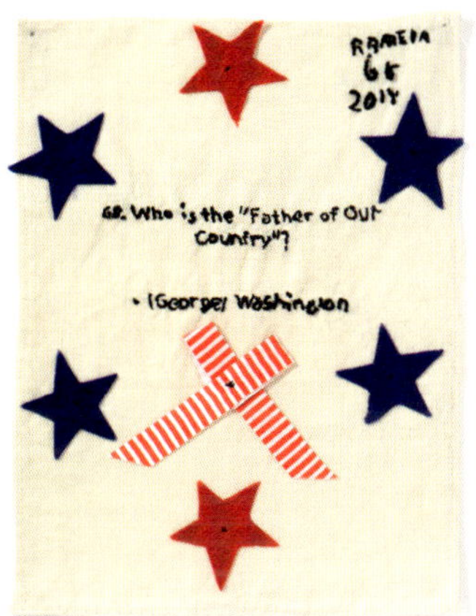

69

MARIA
60
2014

70. Who was the first President?

• (George) Washington

70

OFELIA
50
2014

75. What was one important thing that Abraham Lincoln did?

• freed the slaves

75

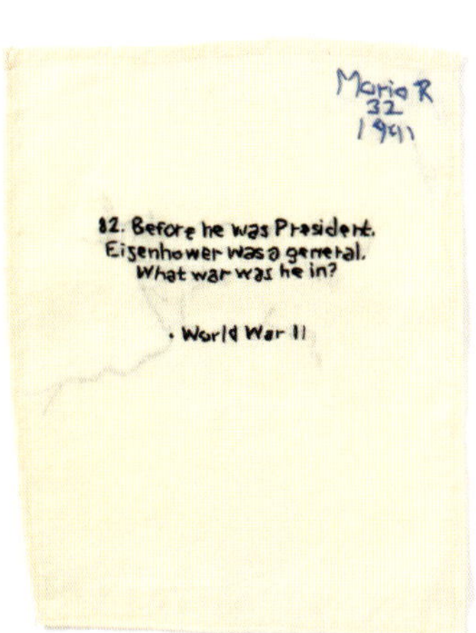

82

46 *Dohun, 2014, South Korea.*

54 *Claudia, 2014, Guatemala.*

57 *Kyusung, 2014, South Korea.*

58 *Soo Shin, 2014, South Korea.*

60 *Nely, 2014, Ecuador.*

62 *Renato, 2015.*

63 *Soto, 2014, Mexico.*

64 *Line, 2014, Denmark.*

66 *Joo Ho, 2014, South Korea.*

68 *Nataliya Kotlova, 2014, Russian Federation.*

69 *Rafaela, 2014, Mexico.*

70 *Maria, 2014, Mexico.*

71 *Cecy, 2015, Mexico.*

72 *Catalina, 2014, Mexico.*

73 *Deysi, 2015.*

75 *Ofelia, 2014, Mexico.*

82 *Maria R., Mexico.*

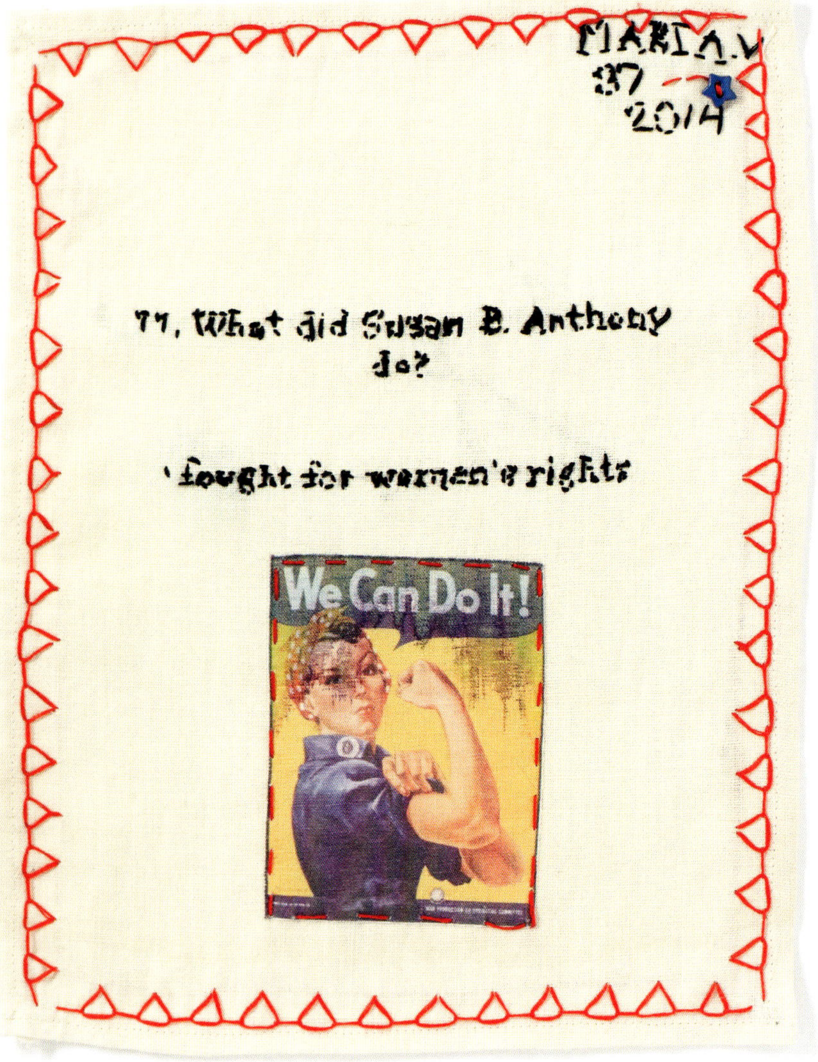

MARIA.V
37
2014

77. What did Susan B. Anthony do?

· fought for women's rights

We Can Do It!

77 *Maria, 2014.*

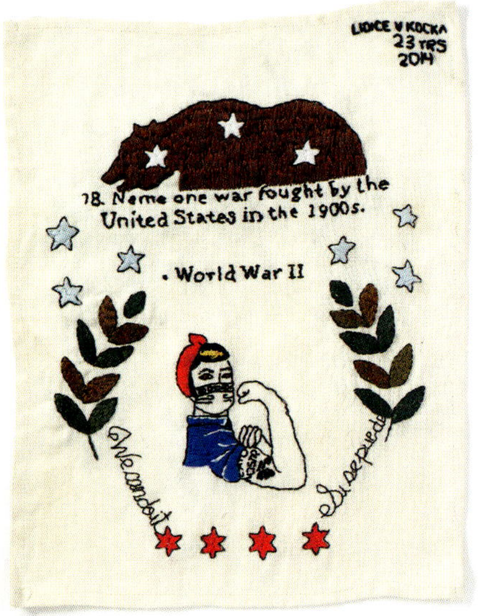

78 *Lidice, 2014, Mexico.*

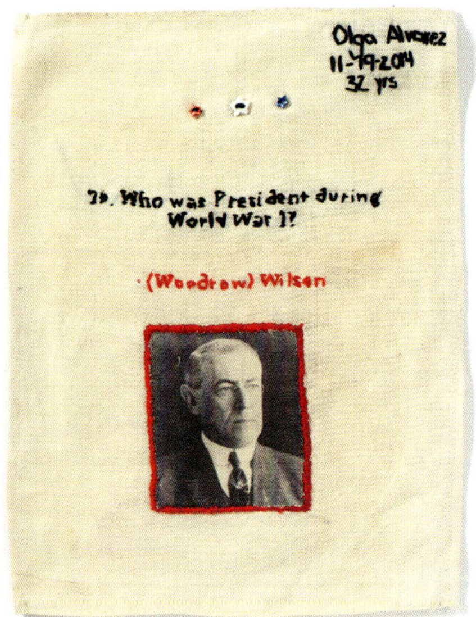

79 *Olga Alvarez, 2014, Mexico.*

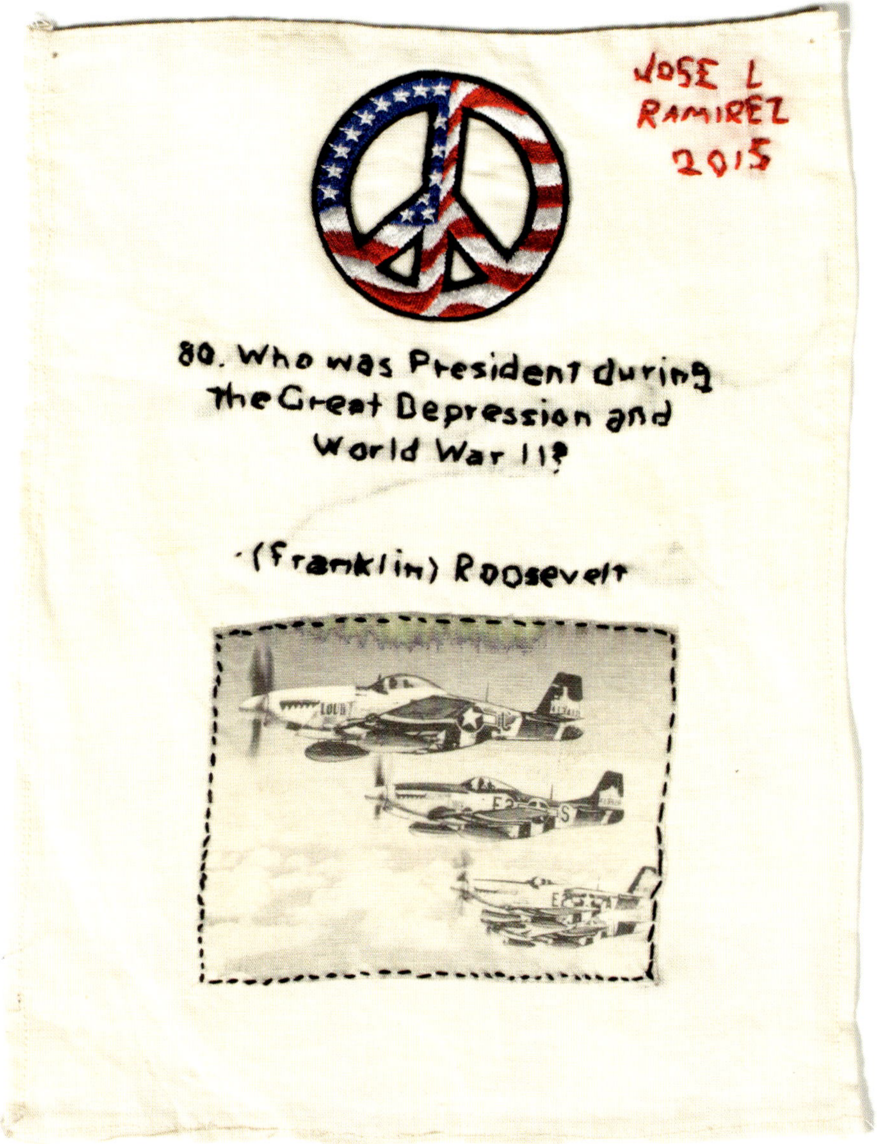

JOSE L
RAMIREZ
2015

80. Who was President during the Great Depression and World War II?

· (Franklin) Roosevelt

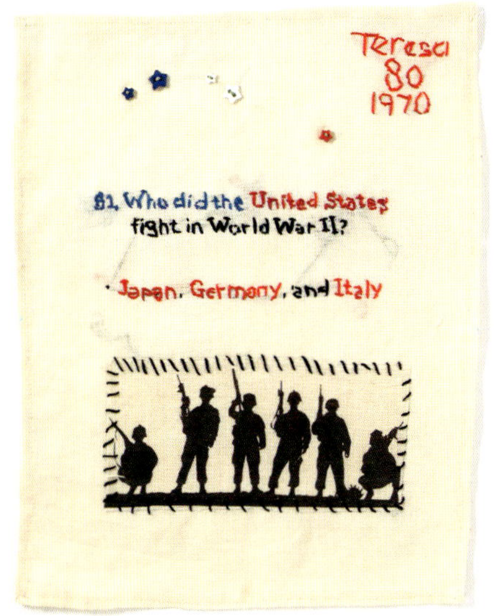

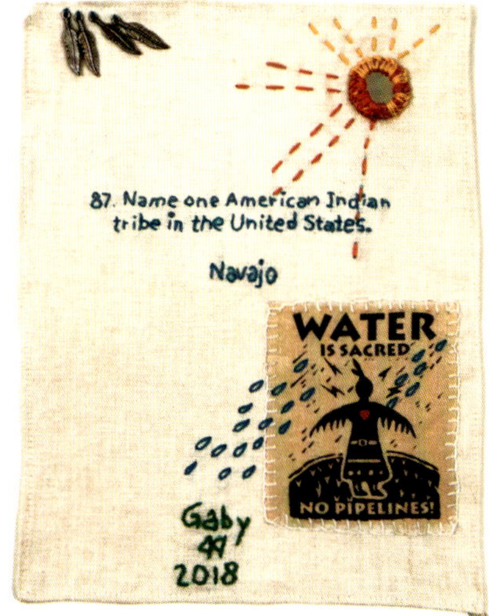

80 *Jose L. Ramirez, 2015, Mexico.*

81 *Teresa, Mexico.*

87 *Gaby, 2018, Netherlands.*

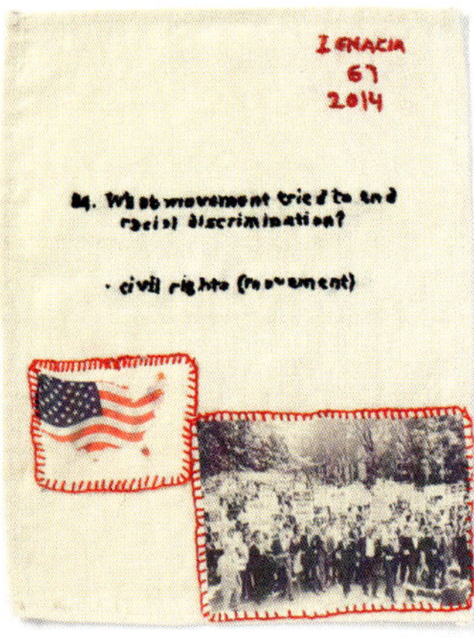

84

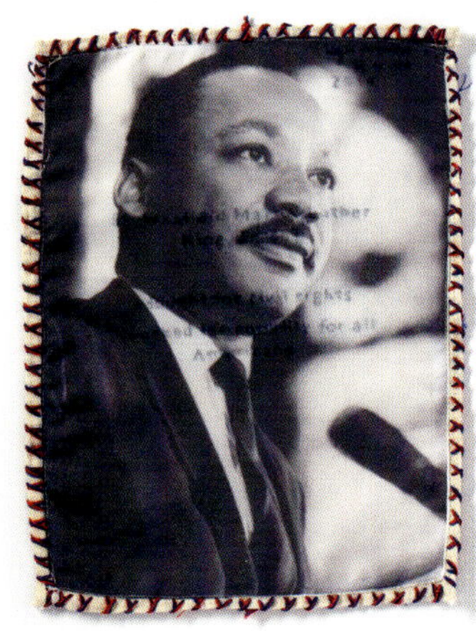

85

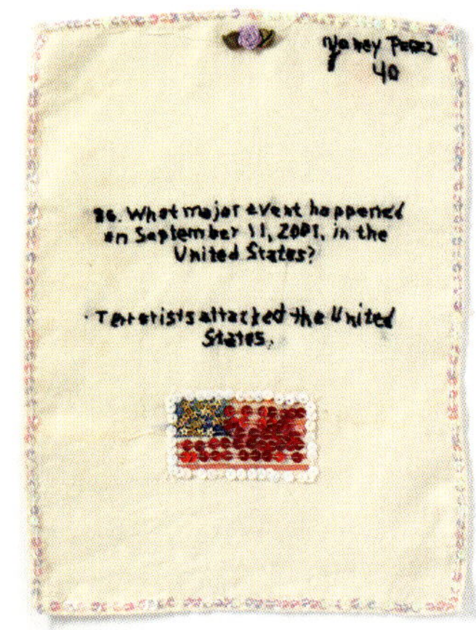

86

Alicia
12-3-14
27

90. What ocean is on the East Coast of the United States?

· Atlantic (Ocean)

90

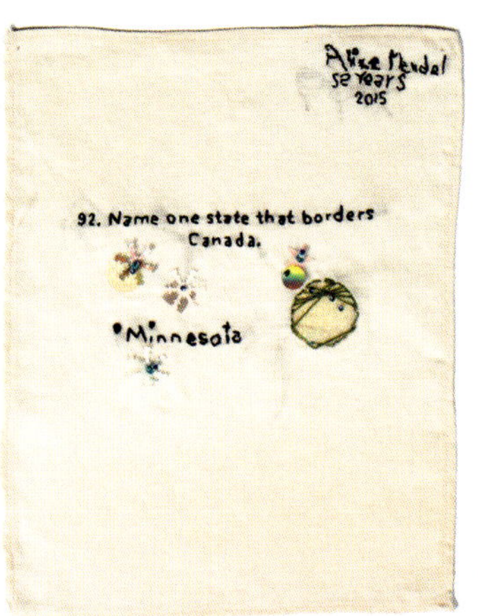

92

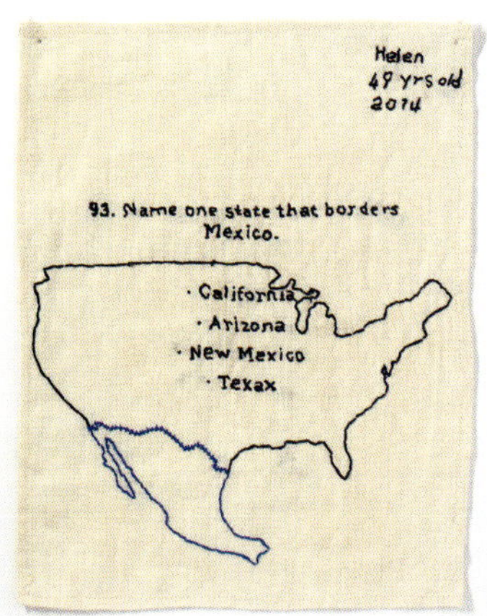

93

Krystal J.
13
2014

97. Why does the flag have 50 stars?*

· because there is one star for each state.

97

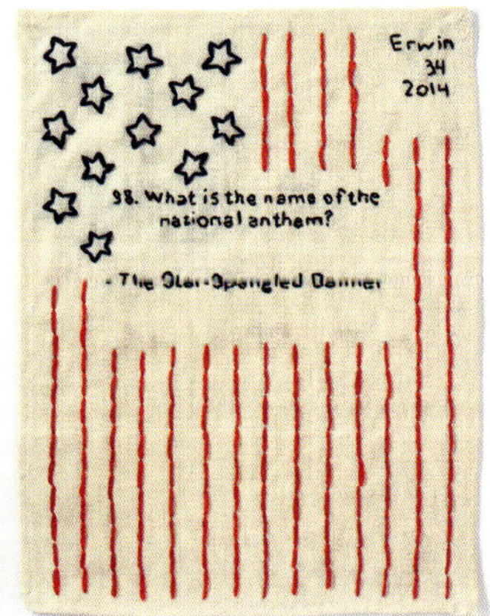

98

Garibay
51
2014

99. When do we celebrate Independence Day?

· July 4

99

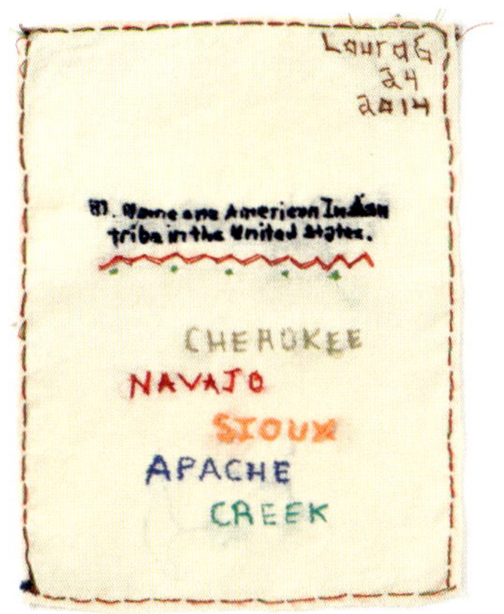

87

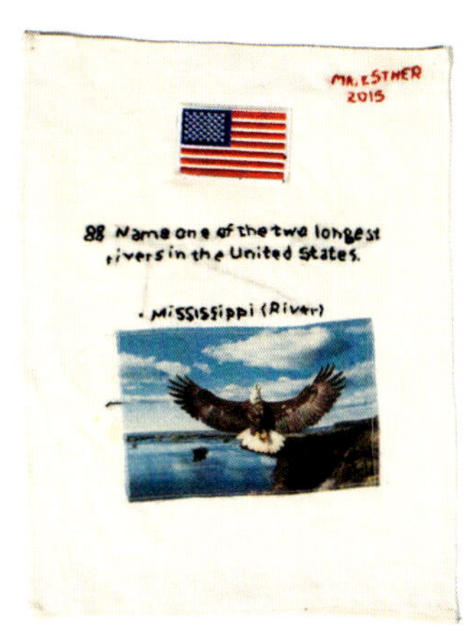

88

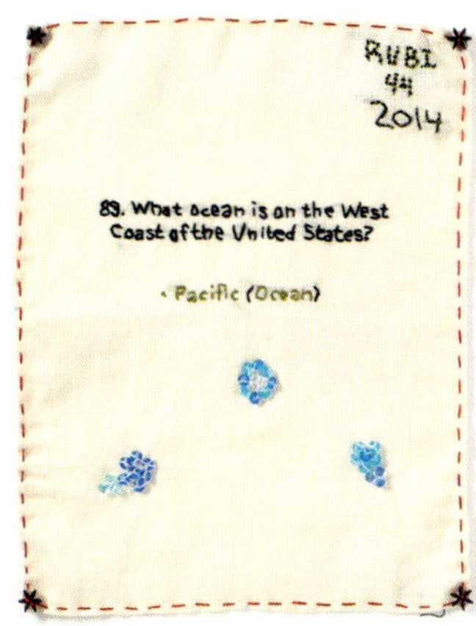

89

94

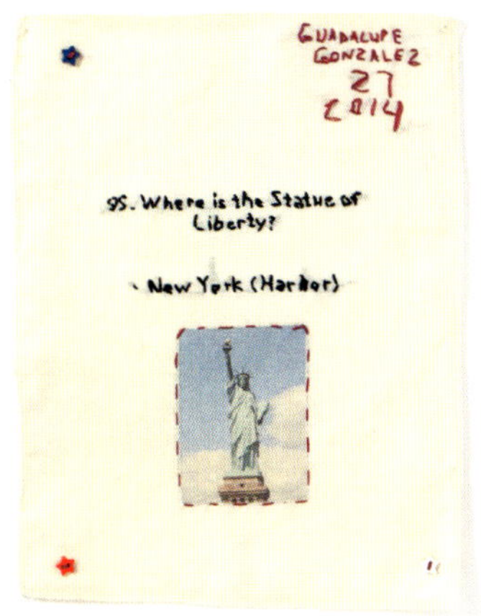

95

96

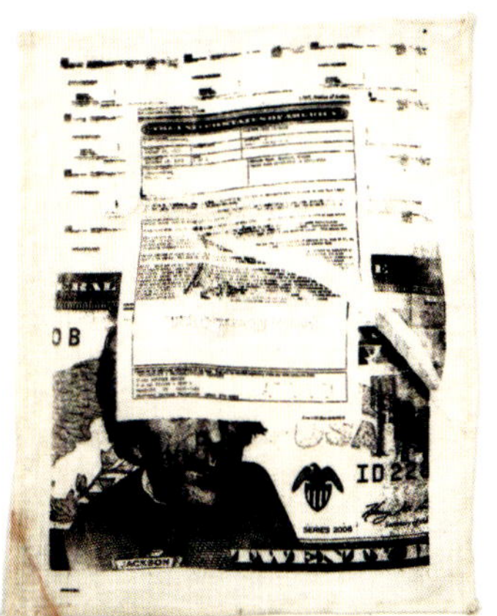

100.1

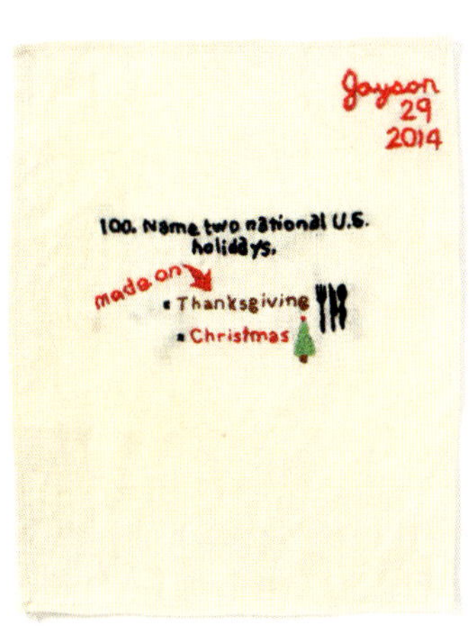

100.2

84 *Ignacia, 2014, Mexico.*

85 *Magali Almada, 2014, Brazil.*

86 *Yaney Perez, Mexico.*

87 *Laura G, 2014, Mexico.*

88 *Esther, 2015, Mexico.*

89 *Rubi, 2014, Mexico.*

90 *Alicia, 2014.*

92 *Alice Mendel, 2015.*

93 *Helen, 2014, South Korea.*

94 *Graciela, 2014, Mexico.*

95 *Guadalupe Gonzalez, 2014, Mexico.*

96 *Maria Theresa, 2014.*

97 *Krystal, 2014, South Korea.*

98 *Erwin, 2014, Netherlands.*

99 *Garibay, 2014, Mexico.*

100.1 *Joseph Mora, 2018, Mexico.*

100.2 *Jayson, 2014, Hong Kong.*

PR

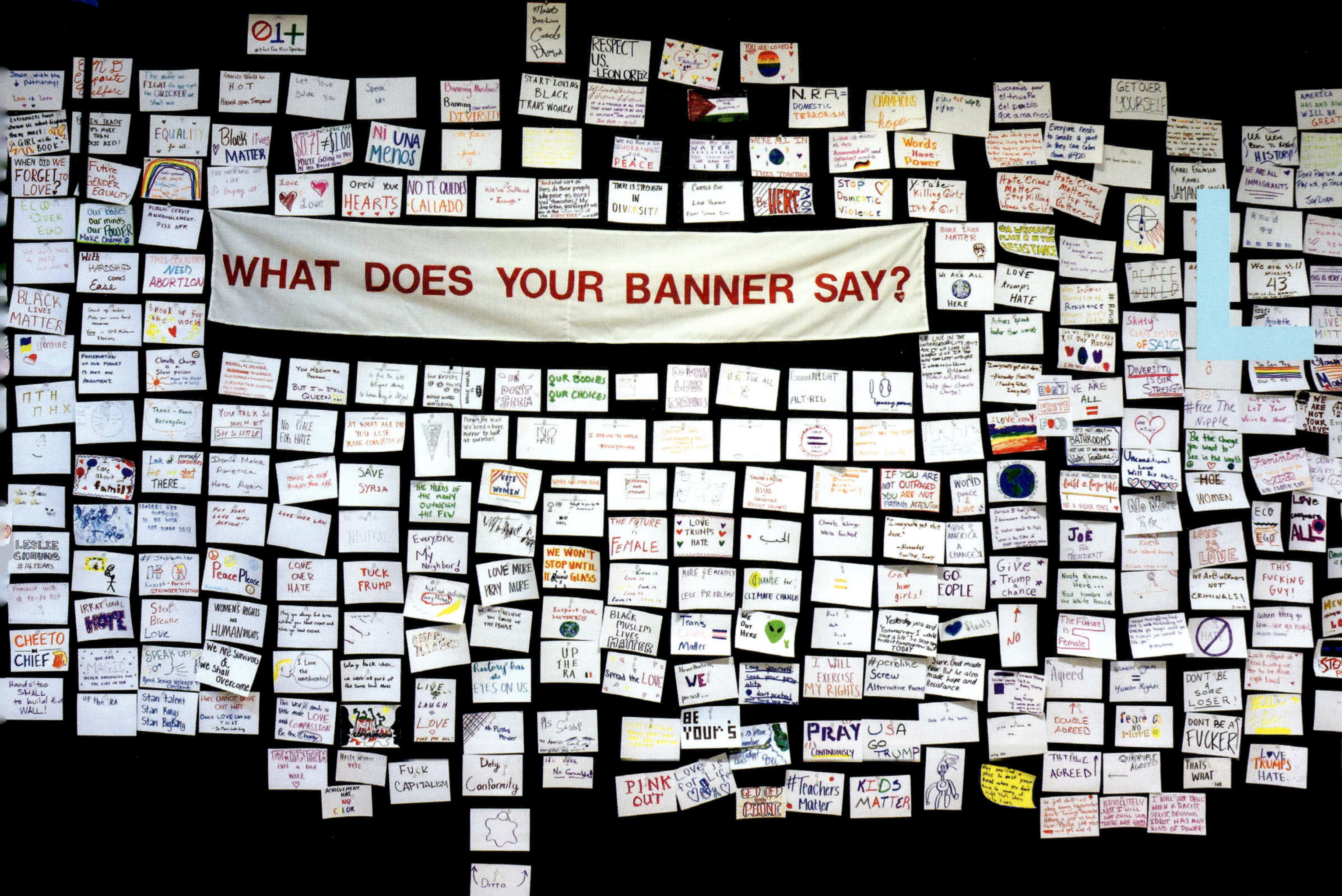

OTEST BANNER NDING LIBRARY

2016–present

I was devastated by the 2016 elections, as many were. I needed a platform to be angry. Immediately after the elections, I started to make protest banners in my apartment. I then started to invite friends over to make banners with me because I needed to feel a sense of community. Then I quickly started to lead workshops for the public.

Banners were, and continue to be, a way for me to resist what is happening in the United States and in the world. Making the banners has been a way for me to put my voice out there and not stay silent. I cannot be silent. At the time I started, I was a non-citizen and a new mother and could not always go to protests. In the workshops I organized for the public, I realized that many people came because they needed to find a way to participate, resist, and speak up. They could not always go to protests because they too were mothers, non-citizens, undocumented – those who would be at great risk if arrested. My protest banner making workshops have become a place where people come together in solidarity through making.

The ***Protest Banner Lending Library*** is a space for people to gain skills to learn to make their own banners, a communal sewing space where we support each other's voices, and a place where people can contribute or check out handmade banners for use.

The words and these banners have a growing history. They are made by someone, used in a protest, returned to the library, and then taken by someone else to a different protest. The banners carry the histories of the hands that made and held them, and the places they have traveled.

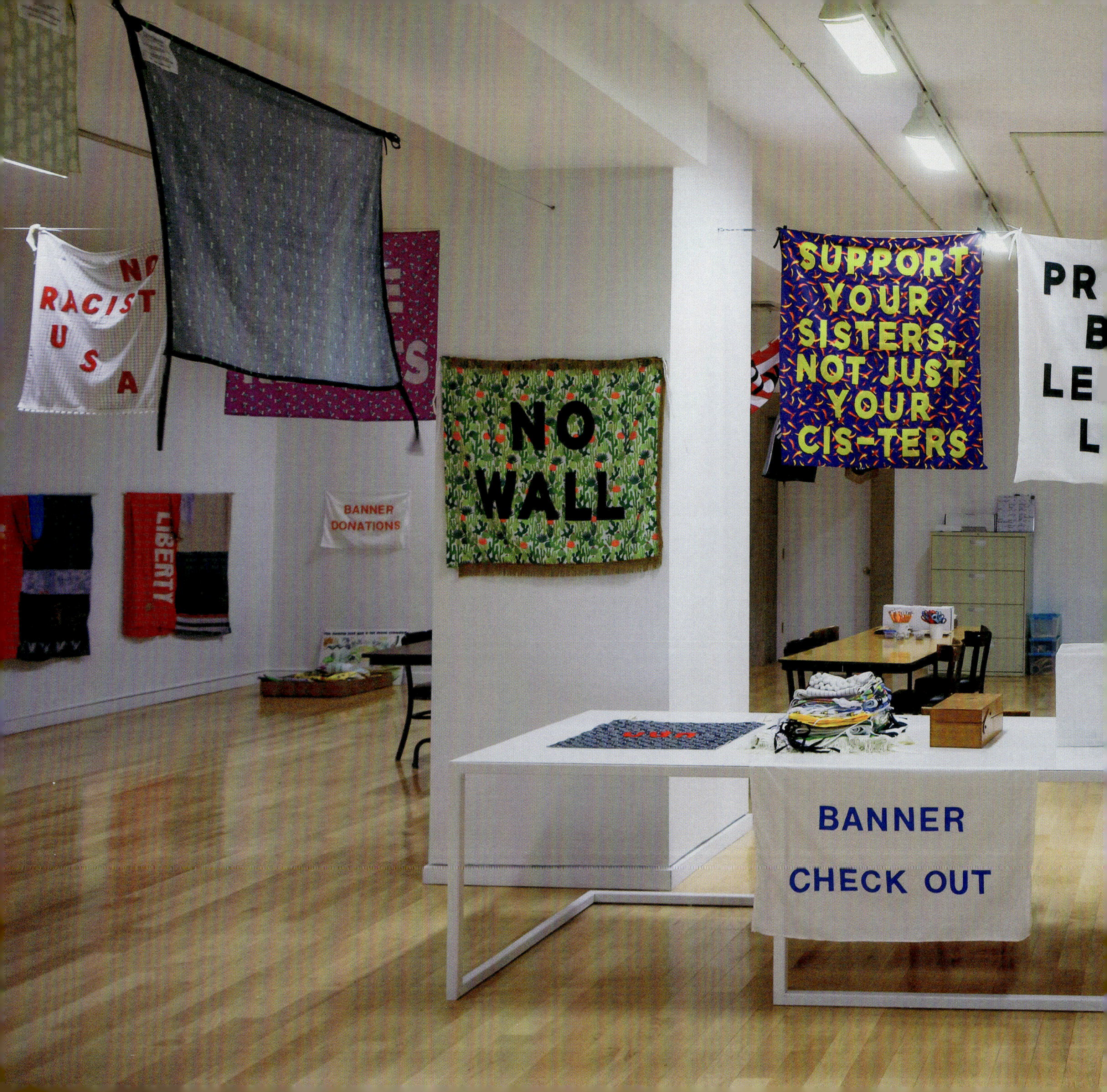
NO RACIST U S A
NO WALL
SUPPORT YOUR SISTERS, NOT JUST YOUR CIS-TERS
LIBERTY
BANNER DONATIONS
BANNER CHECK OUT

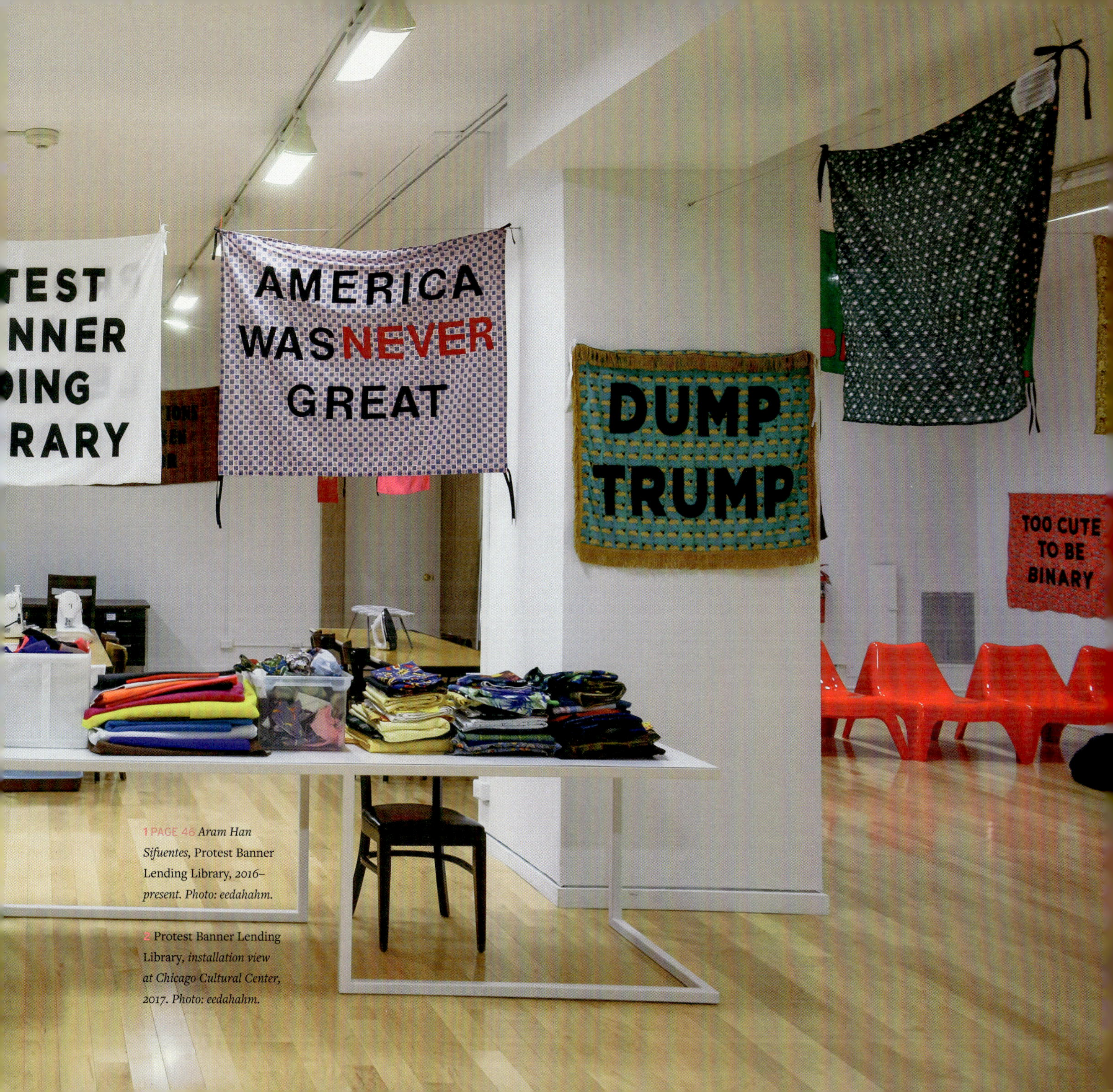

1 PAGE 46 *Aram Han Sifuentes,* Protest Banner Lending Library, *2016–present. Photo: eedahahm.*

2 Protest Banner Lending Library, *installation view at Chicago Cultural Center, 2017. Photo: eedahahm.*

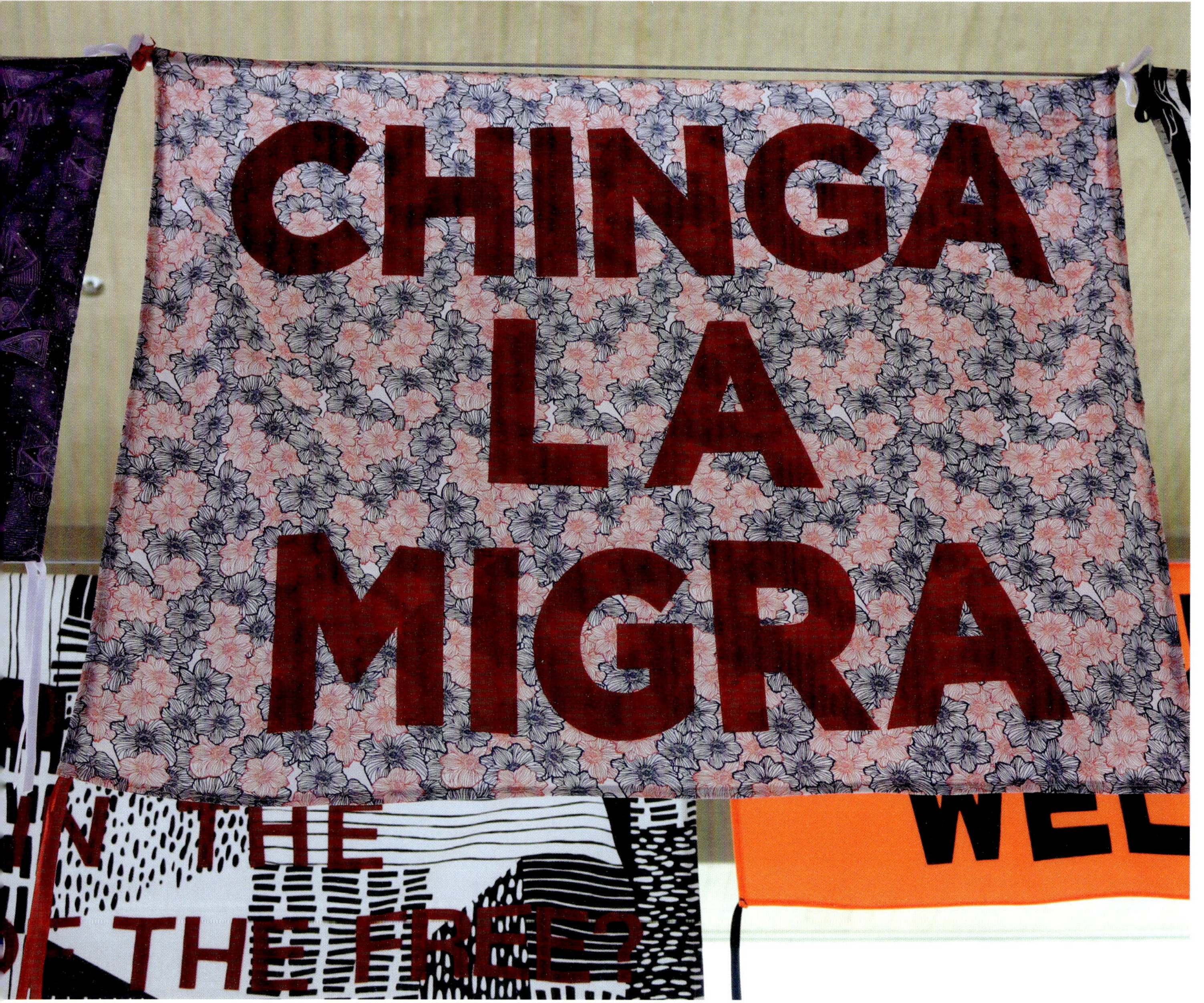

3 Protest Banner Lending Library, *installation views at Herbert F. Johnson Museum of Art, Ithaca, New York, 2019. Photo: Aram Han Sifuentes.*

4 Protest Banner Lending Library, *installation view at Chicago Cultural Center, 2017. Photo: eedahahm.*

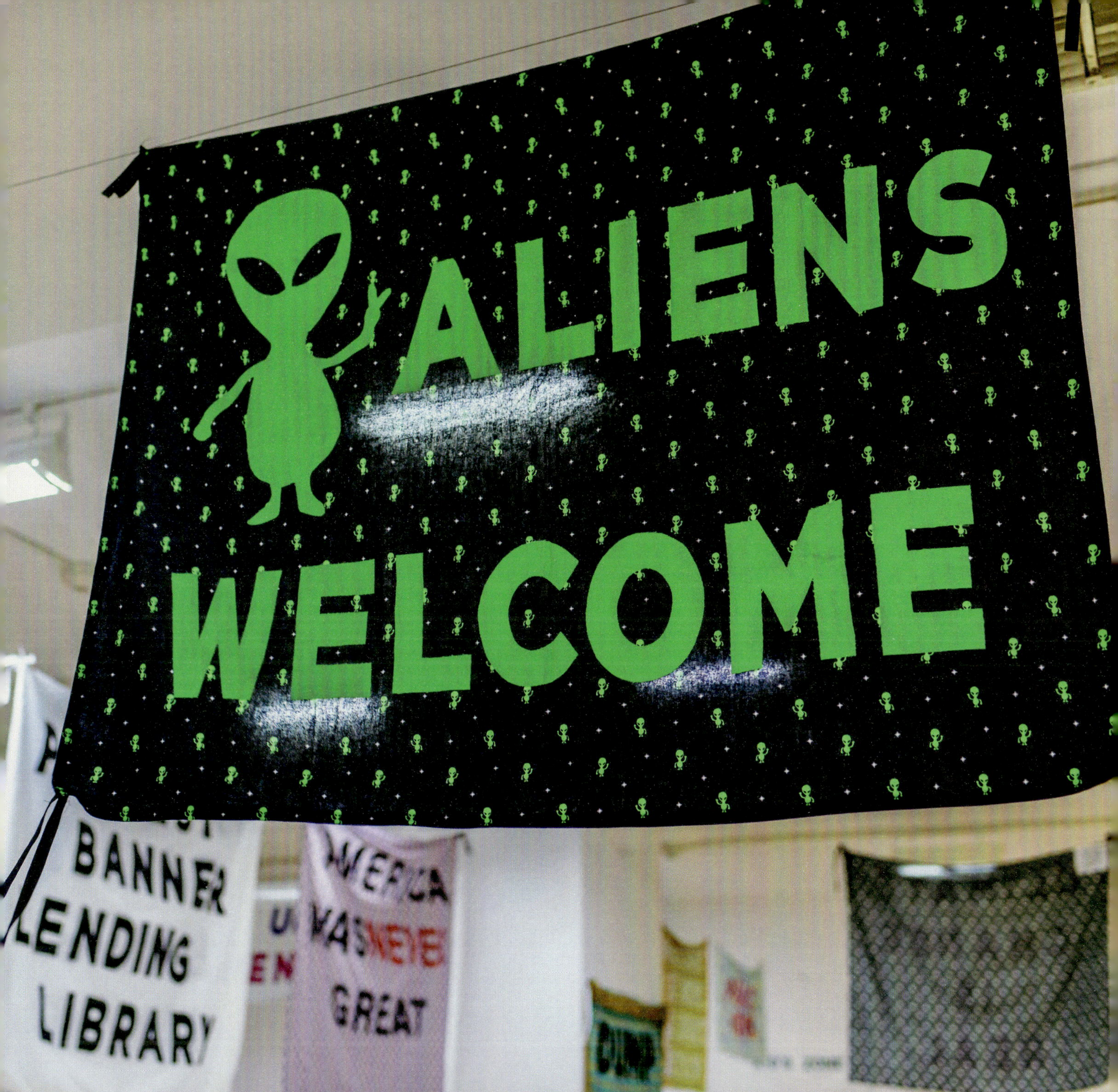
ALIENS
WELCOME
BANNER
LENDING
LIBRARY
GREAT

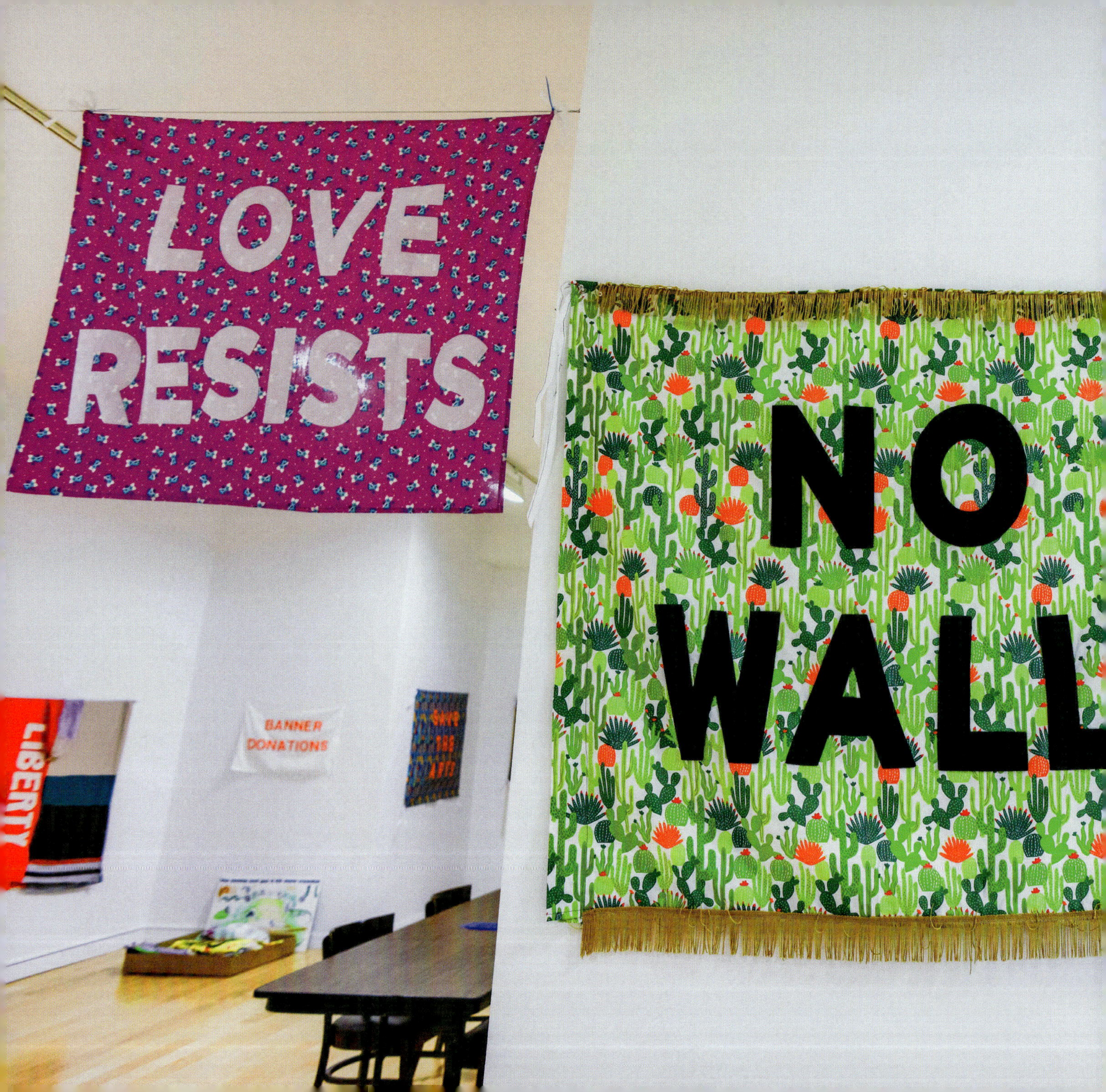

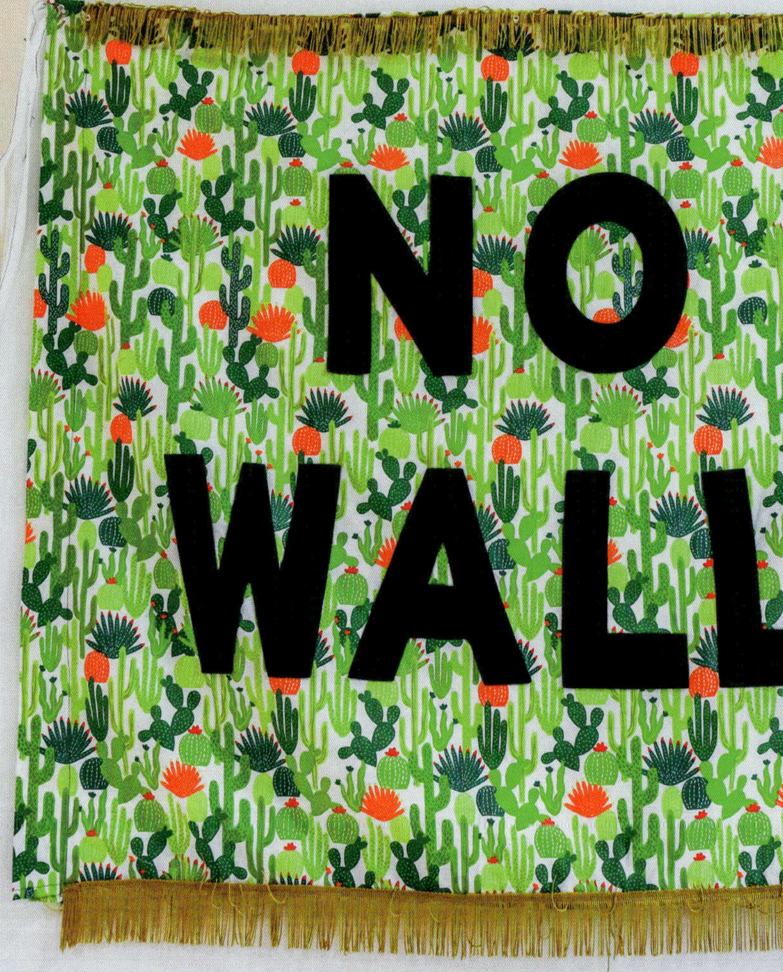
LOVE
RESISTS
LIBERTY
BANNER
DONATIONS
NO
WALL

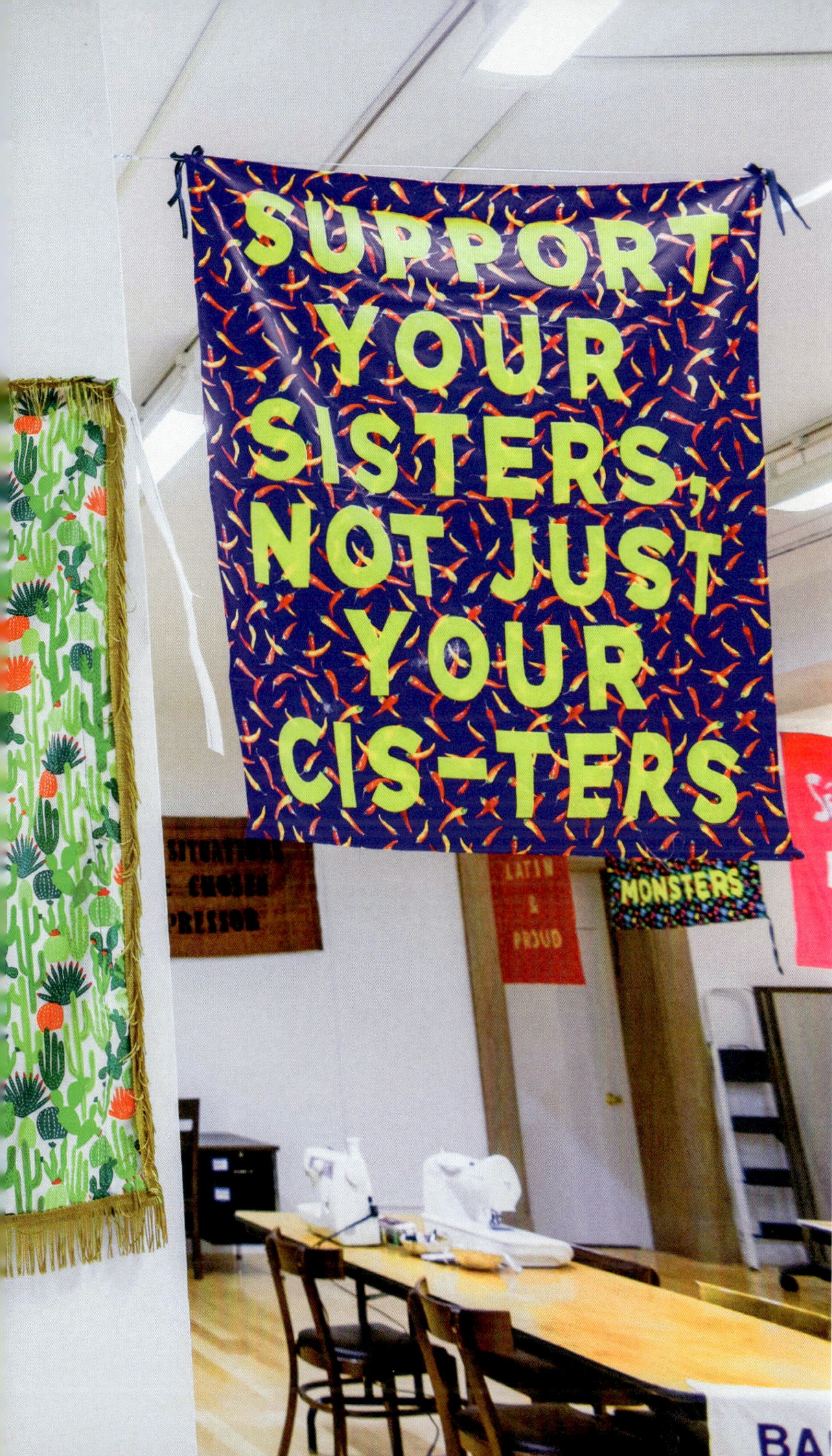

Protest Banner Lending Libraries

Aram Han Sifuentes' studio, Chicago, Illinois

University Galleries of Illinois State University, Normal, Illinois

Tufts University Library, Boston, Massachusetts

Ithaca College Library, Ithaca, New York

Herbert F. Johnson Museum of Art, Ithaca, New York

Yeyo Arts Collective, St. Louis, Missouri (from banners created for a temporary site at Pulitzer Arts Foundation, St. Louis)

Canadian Filmmakers Distribution Centre, Toronto, Canada

Leather Archives and Museum, Chicago, Illinois

Temporary sites
banners gifted to organizations after the exhibition

Tarble Arts Center, Eastern Illinois University, Charleston, Illinois

Asian Arts Initiative, Philadelphia, Pennsylvania

Cardinal Space, Baltimore, Maryland

Upcoming

Skirball Cultural Center, Los Angeles, California

5 Protest Banner Lending Library, *installation view at Chicago Cultural Center, 2017. Photo: eedahahm.*

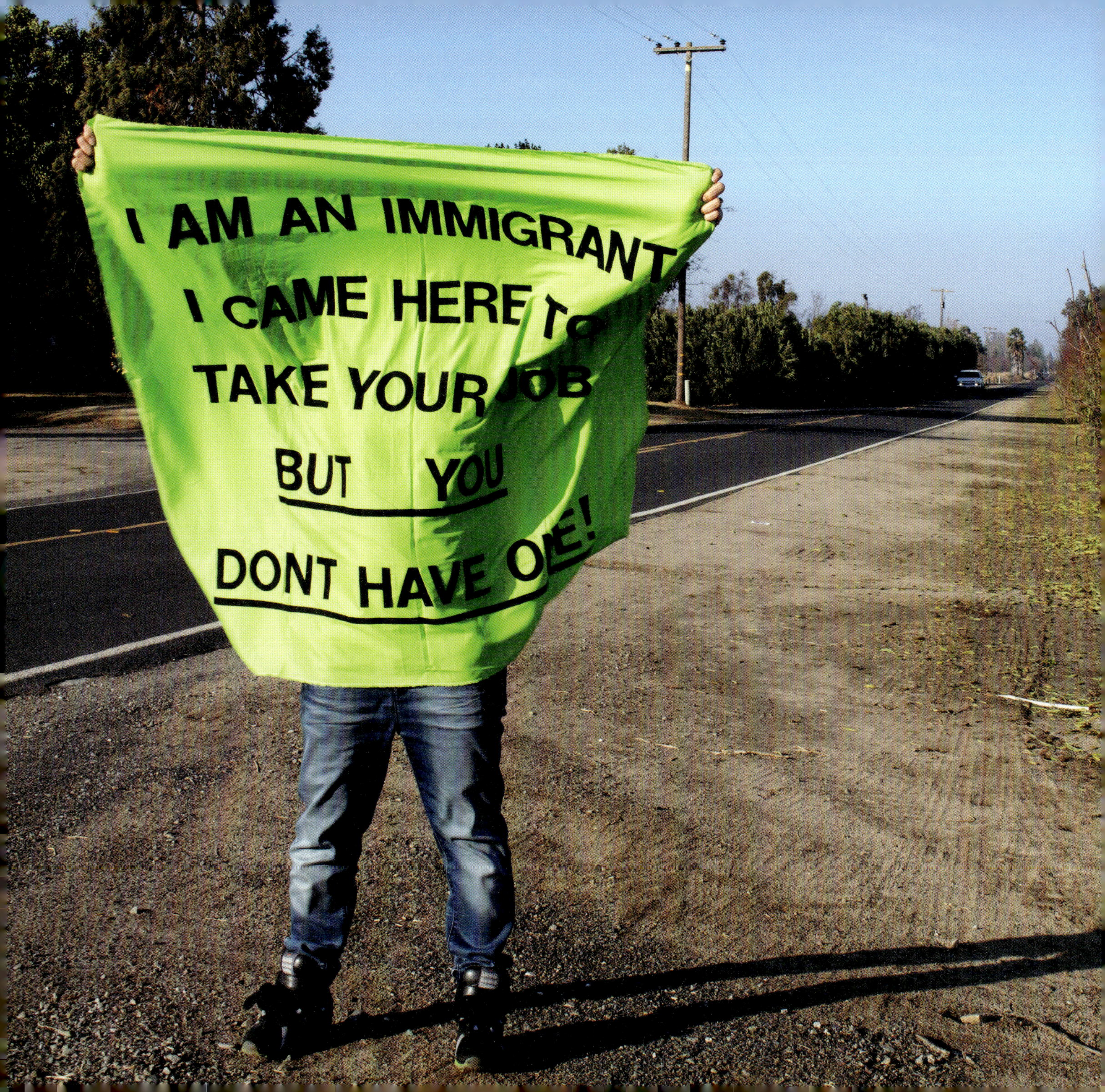
I AM AN IMMIGRANT
I CAME HERE TO
TAKE YOUR JOB
BUT YOU
DONT HAVE ONE!

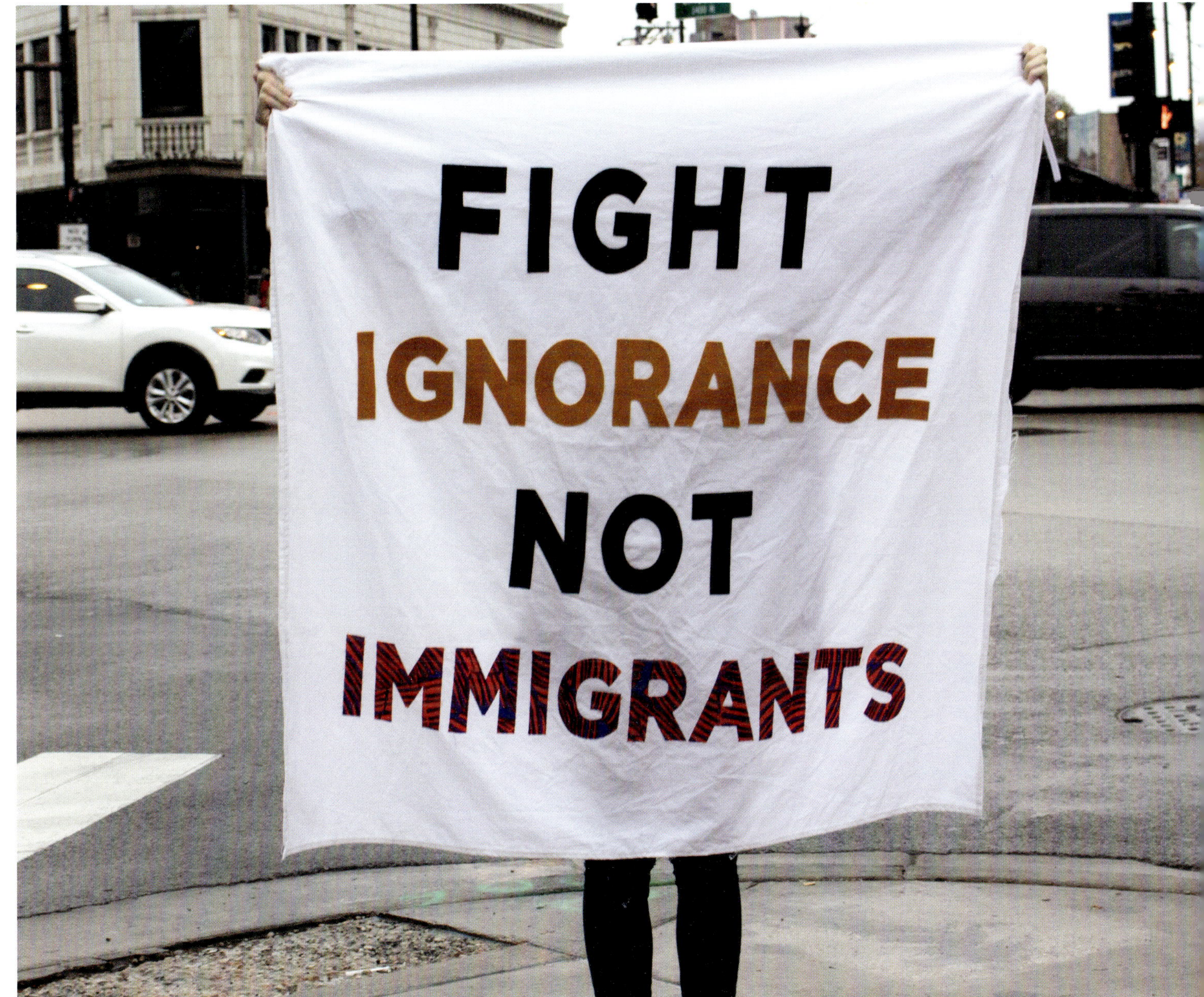

6 *Photo: Aram Han Sifuentes.*

7 *Photo: Ishita Dharap.*

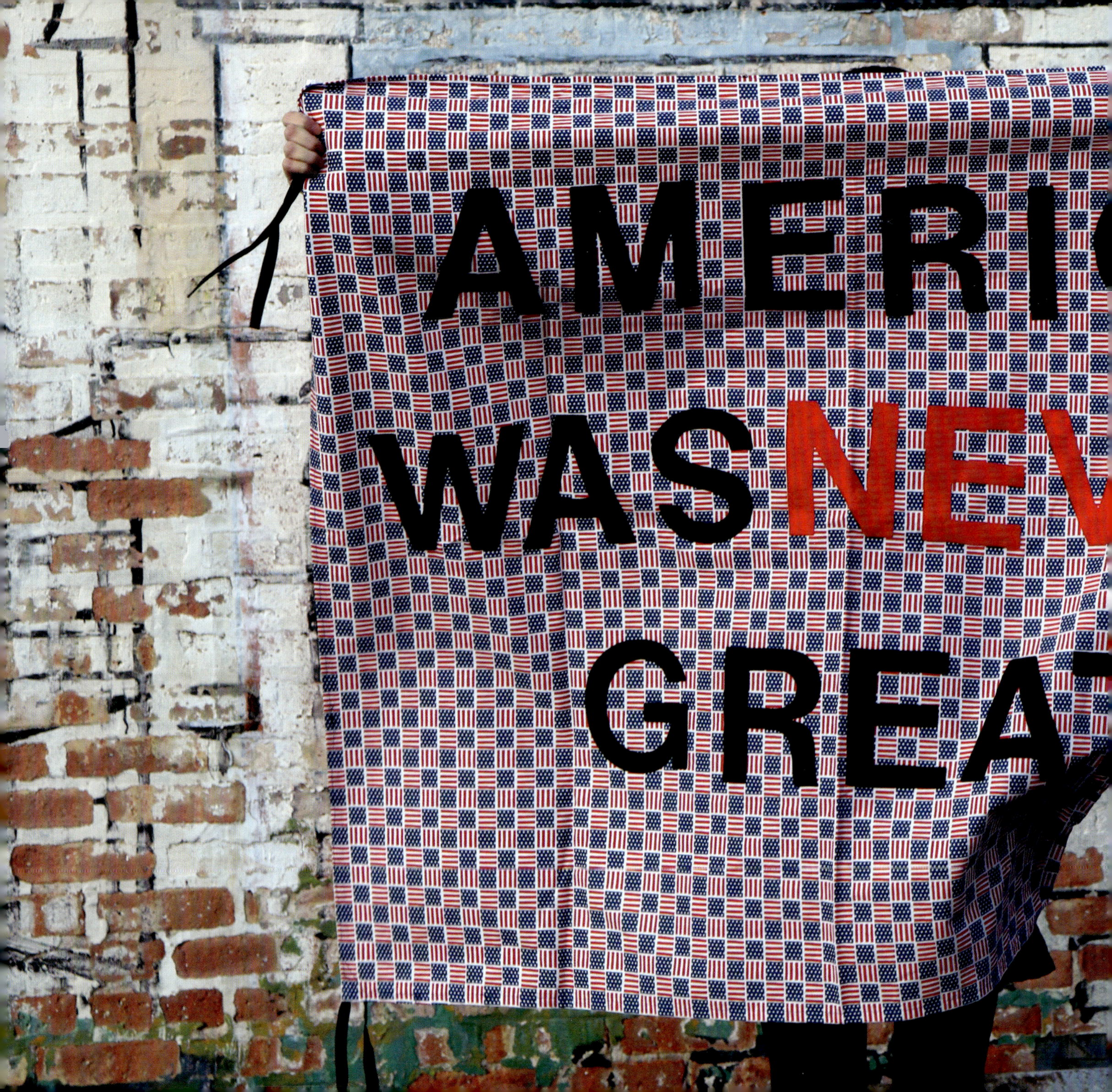
AMERI
WASNE
GREA

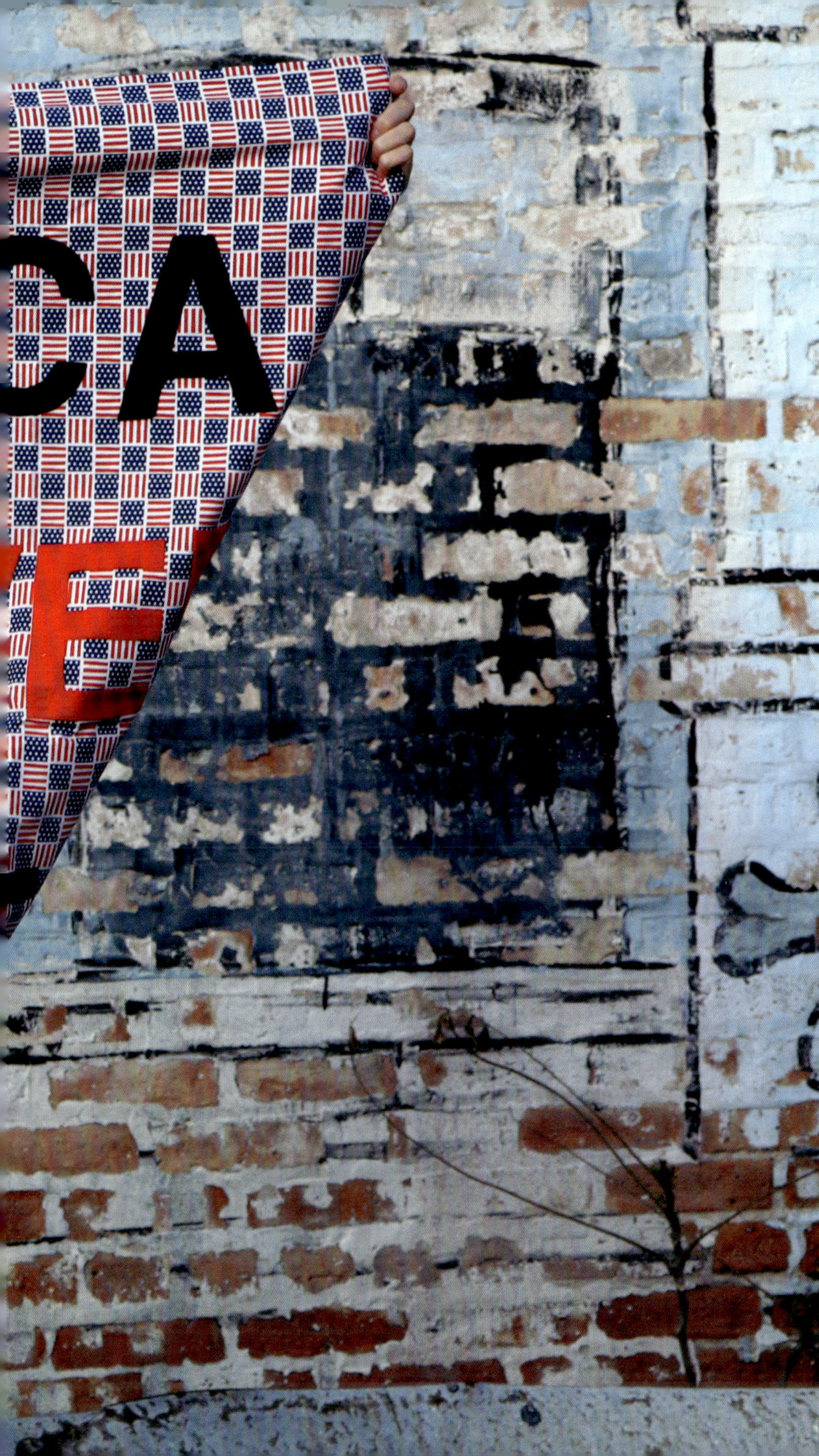

8 *Photo: Ishita Dharap.*

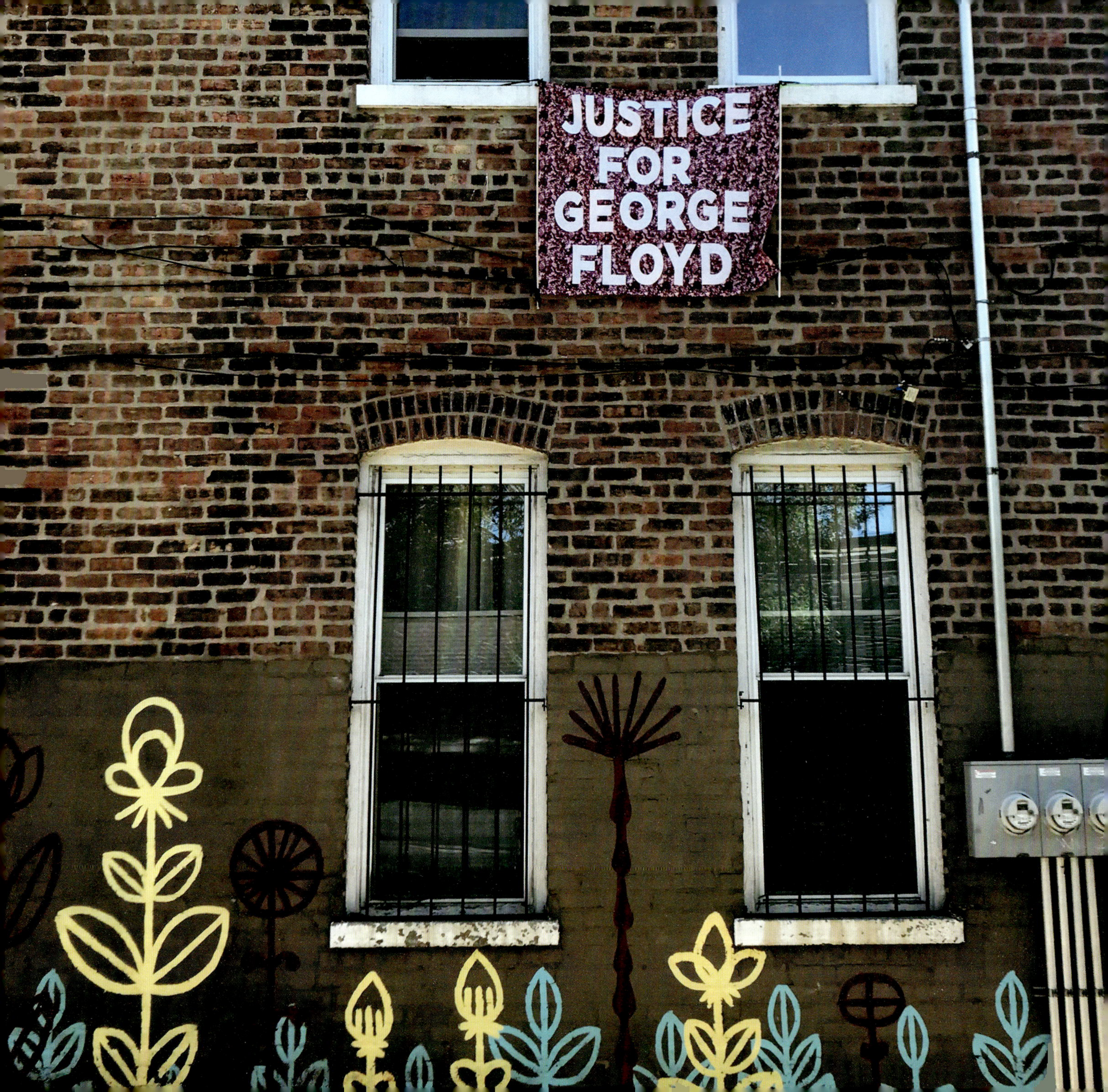
JUSTICE
FOR
GEORGE
FLOYD

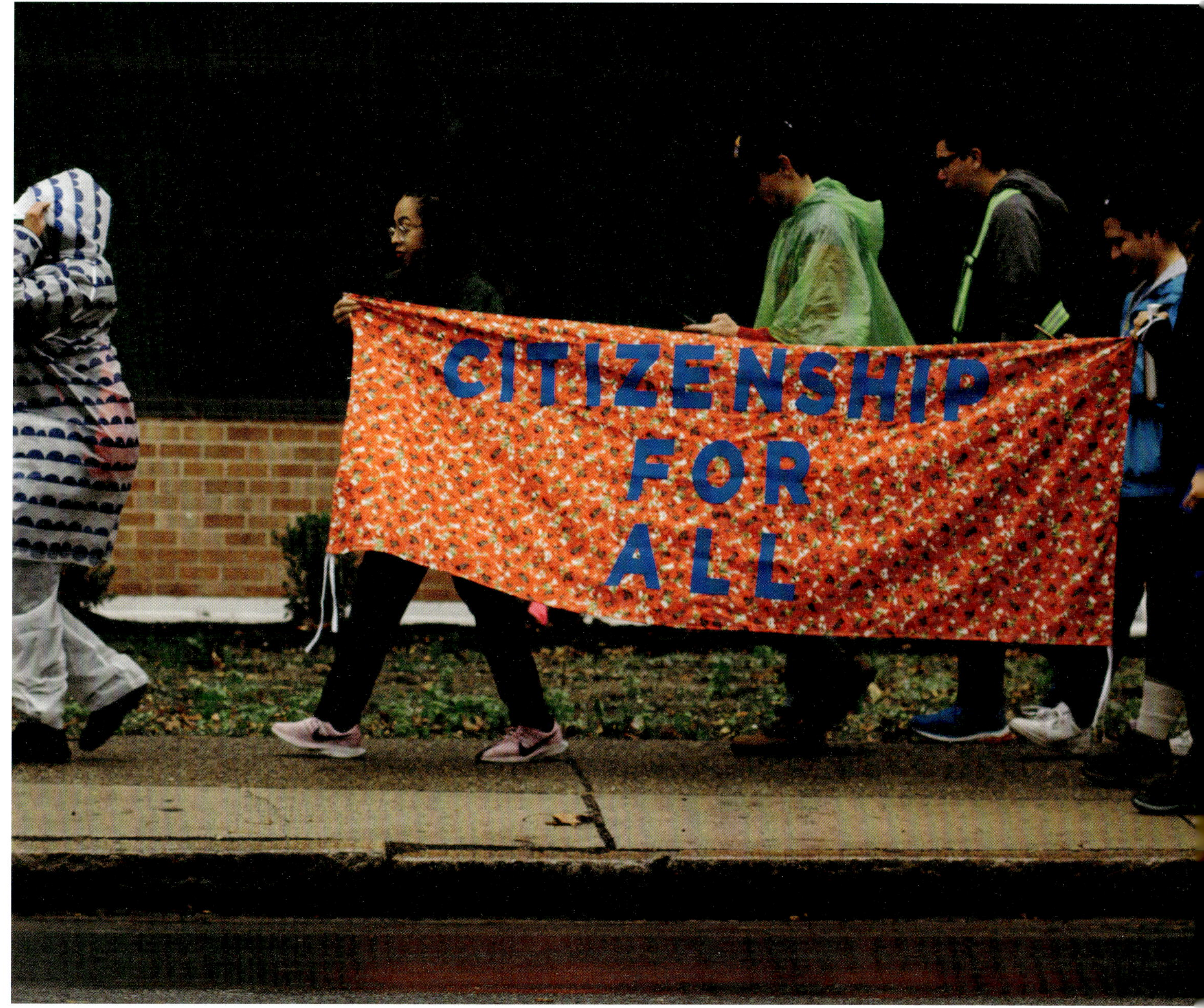

9 *Photo: Lydia Ross.*

10 Home is Here! *March to Defend DACA AND TPS, October–November 2019 in New York, Philadelphia, Baltimore, and Washington, D.C. Organized by a coalition of immigrant rights organizations including Hana Center and NAKASEC. Photo: OffThaRecord x Steer.*

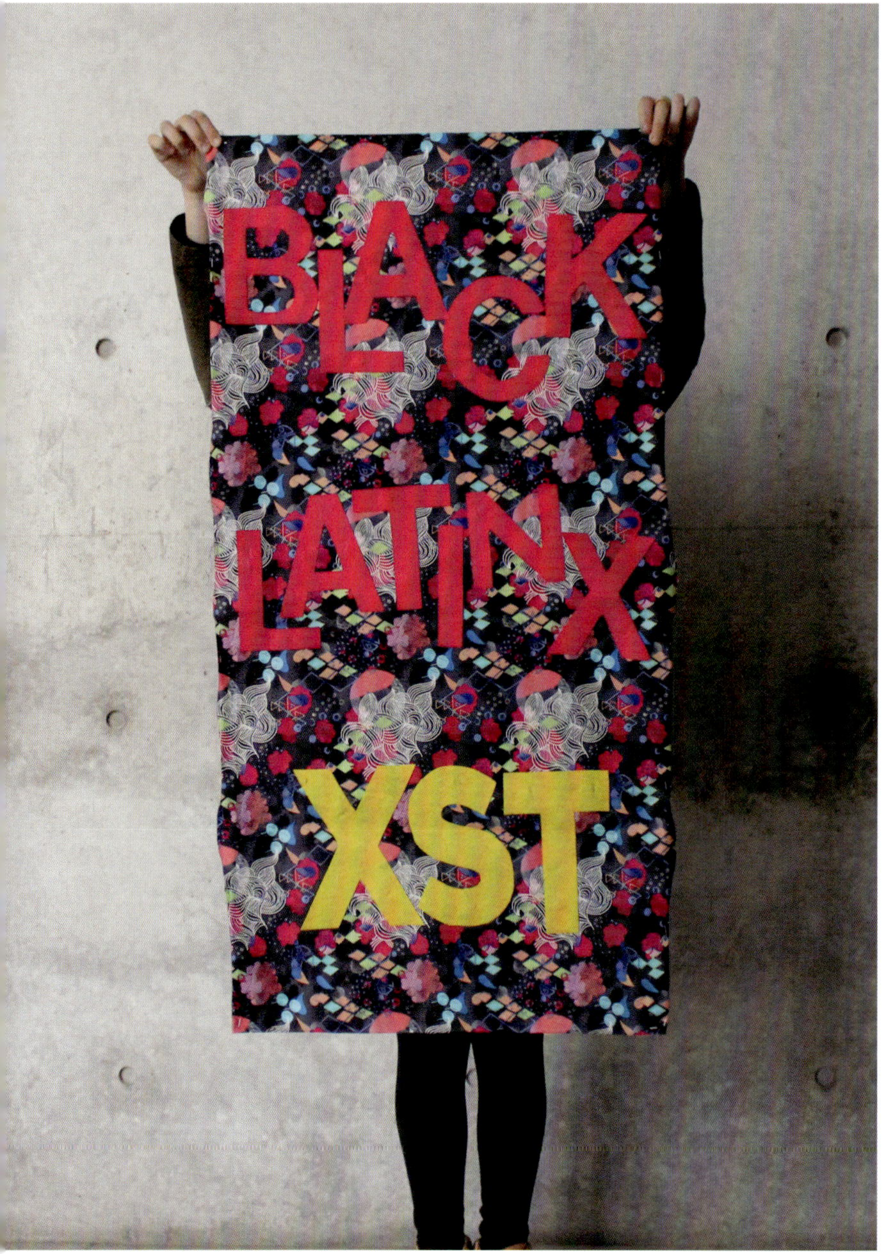

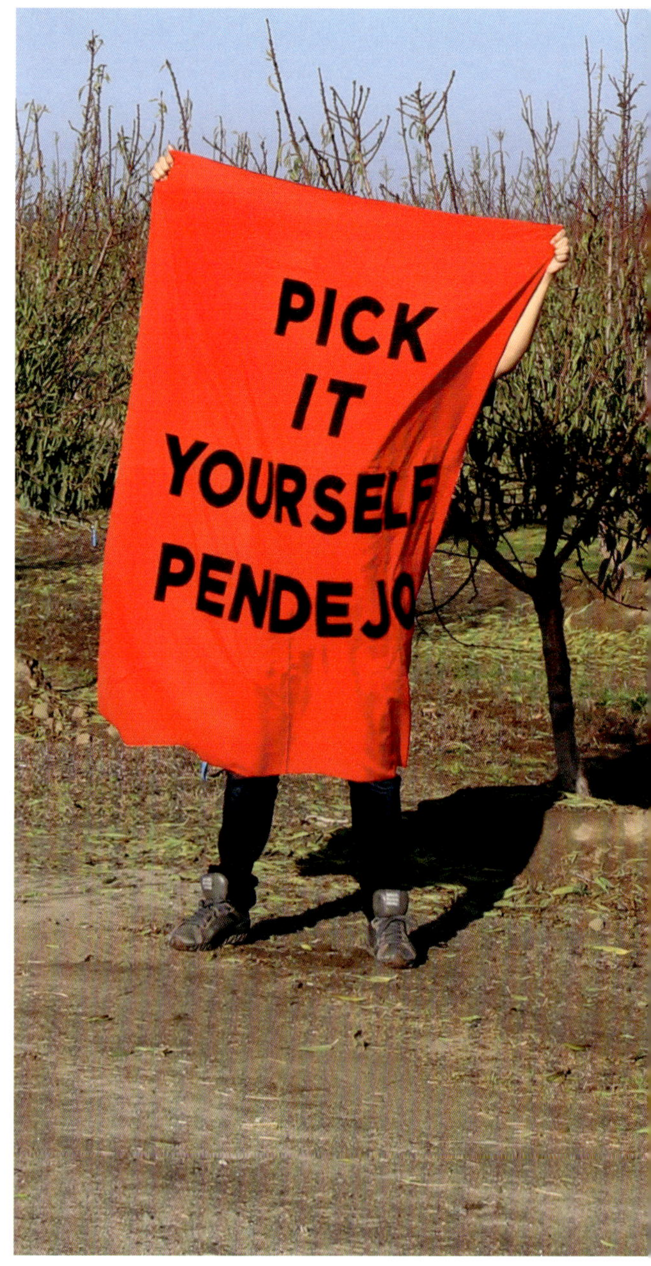

11 *Photo: Pulitzer Arts Foundation, St. Louis. Courtesy of Pulitzer Arts Foundation.*

12 *Photo: Aram Han Sifuentes.*

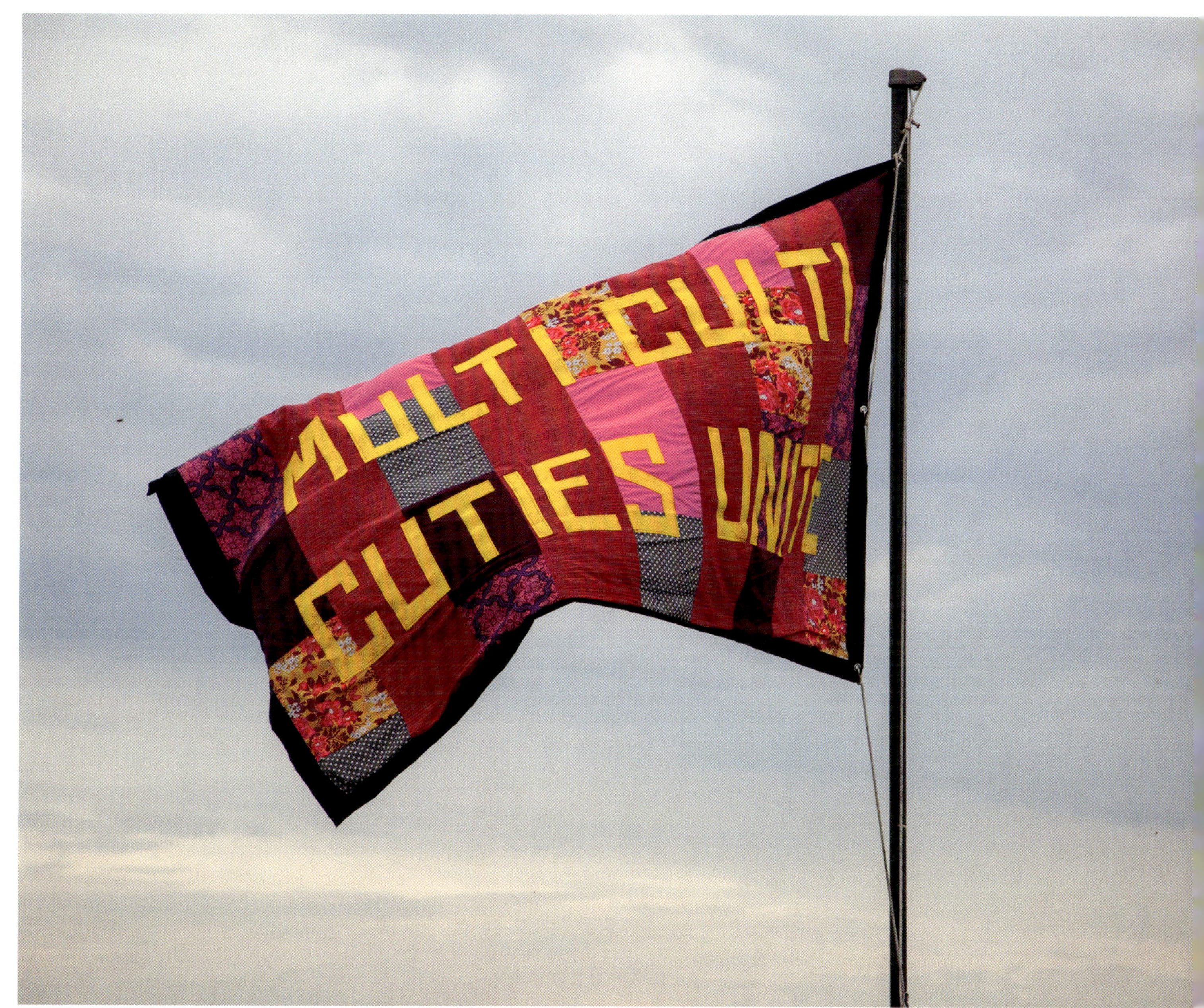

13 Wave Your Freak Flag, *installation of four flags by Aram Han Sifuentes, Verónica Casado Hernández, Ishita Dharap, and Tabitha Anne Kunkes at Lillstreet Art Center, Chicago. Photo: Nora Renick Rinehart.*

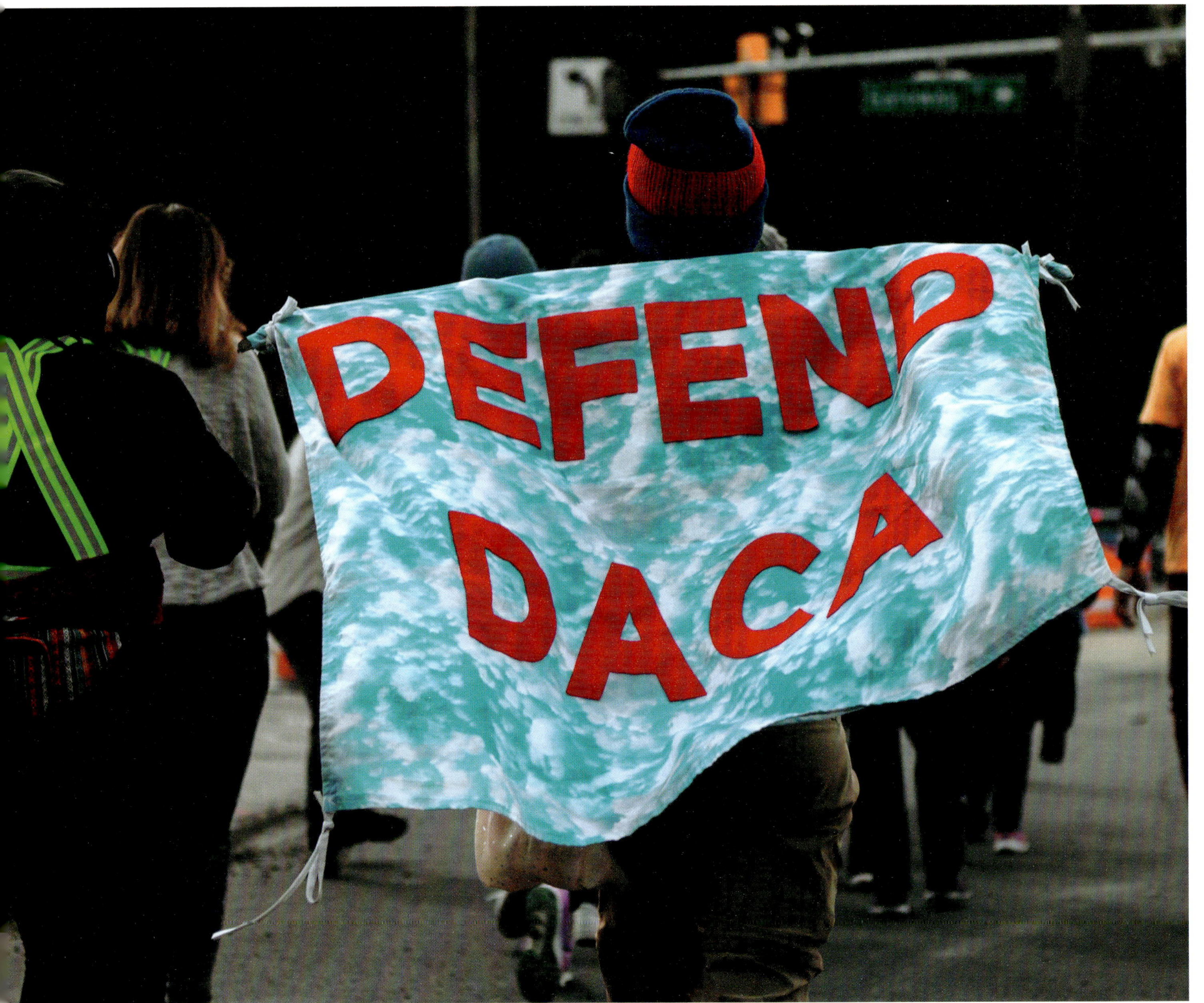

14 *Home is Here! March to Defend DACA AND TPS, October–November 2019 in New York, Philadelphia, Baltimore, and Washington, D.C. Organized by a coalition of immigrant rights organizations including Hana Center and NAKASEC. Photo: OffThaRecord x Steer.*

15 *Photo: Kelly Kristin Jones.*

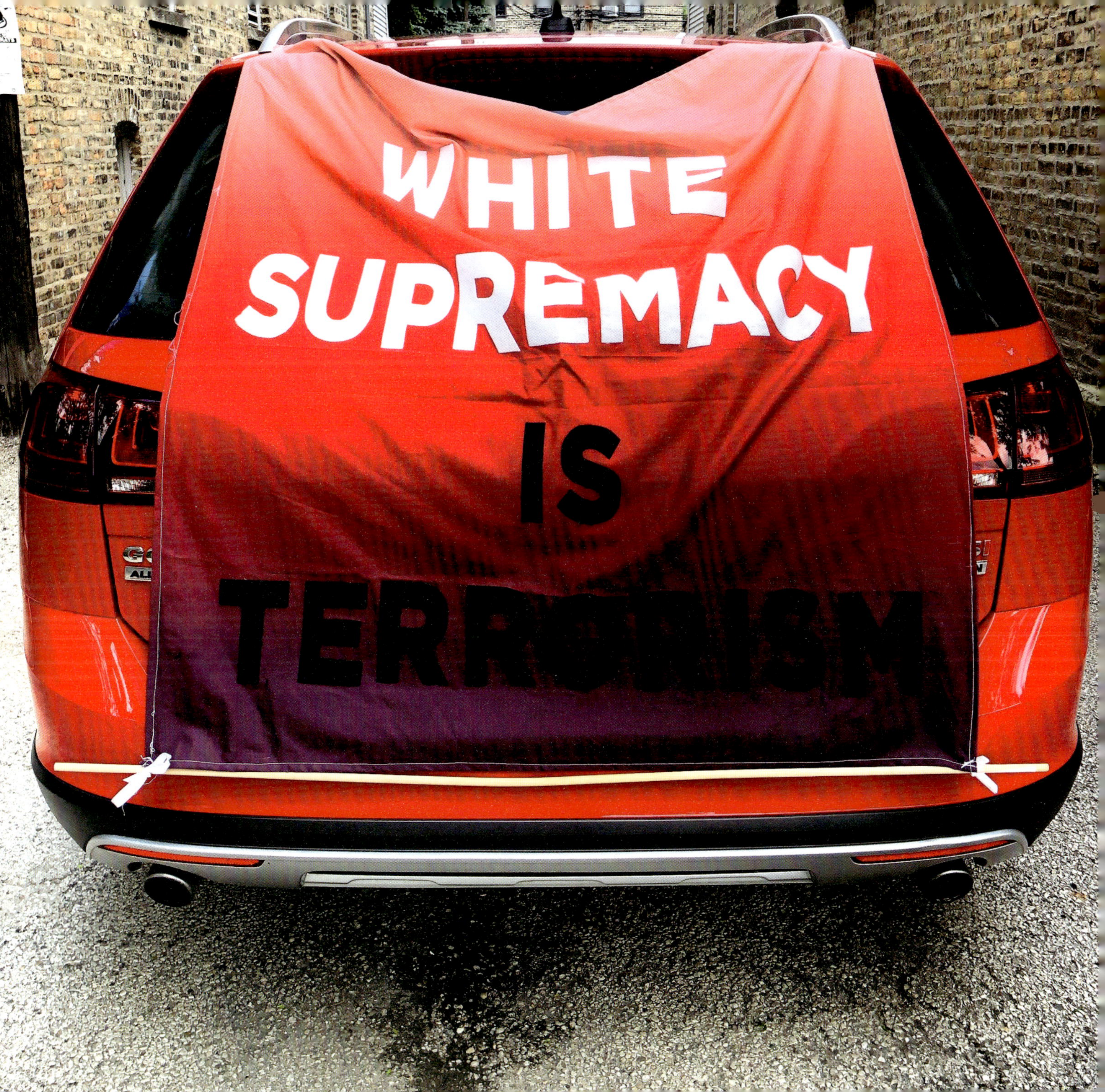
WHITE
SUPREMACY
IS
TERRORISM

Why Fabric Protest Banners?

1. Fabric banners are generally easy to carry around with you. You can fold fabric and carry it around in your bag.

2. The second advantage of fabric is that they last longer than posters and can be reused many times. In this way, they address time. It may be a bit pessimistic, but we are going to be fighting for these causes for a long time.

How to Make a Protest Banner

There are a few different ways to make protest banners.

Option 1
Grab some fabric and permanent markers (optional: textile markers) and draw your banner.

Option 2
Grab some acrylic paint, paint brushes, and fabric, and paint your banner.

Option 3
Create a fabric banner with felt letters. This is how most of the banners in the *Protest Banner Lending Library* are made. You will need to use an iron, scissors, and pins. The instructions are below.

Step 1: Think of a slogan.
There are different ways you can approach your slogan. You know what you stand for and against.

You can turn this into a slogan. Sometimes it is as simple as the word itself, such as **LOVE** or **PEACE**, or putting **NO** in front of what you stand against, such as **NO HATE** or **NO GUNS**.

We are in a time when even an affirmation statement about who you are can be a bold slogan.

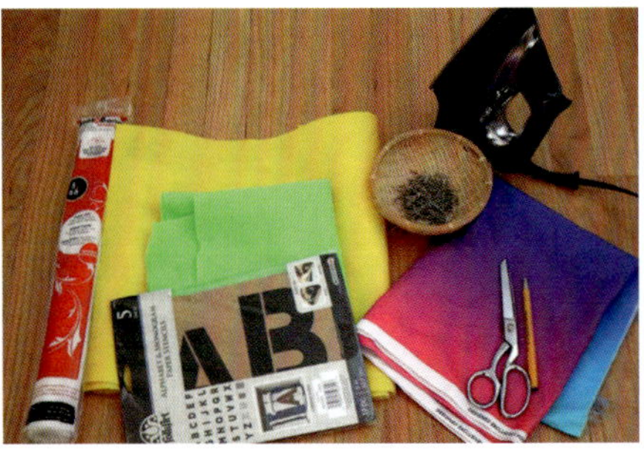

Step 2: Grab materials.

— 1 yard of background fabric
cotton preferable

— ½ yard of felt for the letters
felt preferable because it does not fray

— Scissors

— Pencil

— Stencils

— Pins *T-pins work best*

— HeatnBond Ultra Hold Iron-On Adhesive
about one yard per banner

—Iron

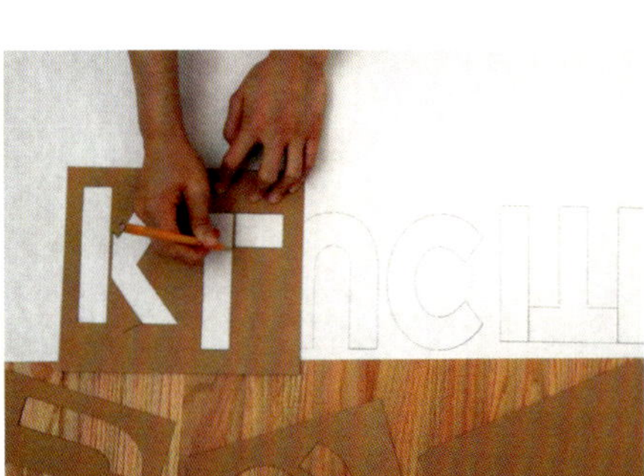

Step 3: Trace the stencils onto the paper side of the HeatnBond. For images, you can also use stencils or draw directly onto the HeatnBond. Make sure the letters and images are flipped horizontally.

Step 1 examples:
Brown and Proud
Black is Beautiful
Multi Culti Cutie
They/Them/Theirs
Young, Latin & Proud
song by Helado Negro
Proud Immigrant

Another way to find a slogan is to complete this sentence:
The Future is ________.

For instance:
The Future is Female and Brown
The Future is Accessible
The Future is Non-Binary
The Future is Queer AF
The Future is Me

16–26 *First published in* The Funambulist Magazine, *N°26, Kids of the World, UNITE!, November–December 2019. Photos: Aram Han Sifuentes and Sarah Whyte.*

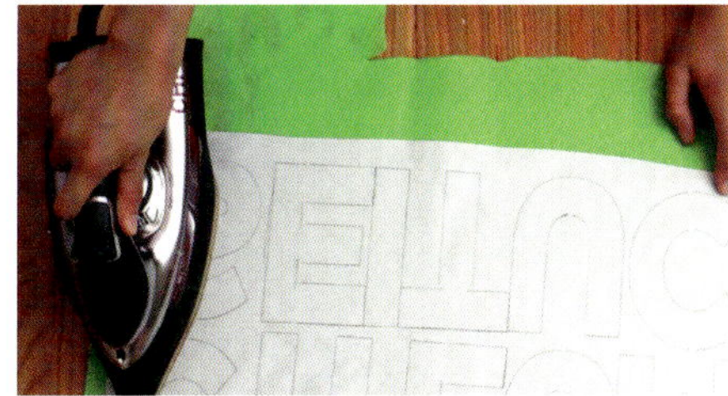

Step 4: Iron the rough side down onto the felt. Iron on medium heat (wool setting). *Watch out though, it's hot!*

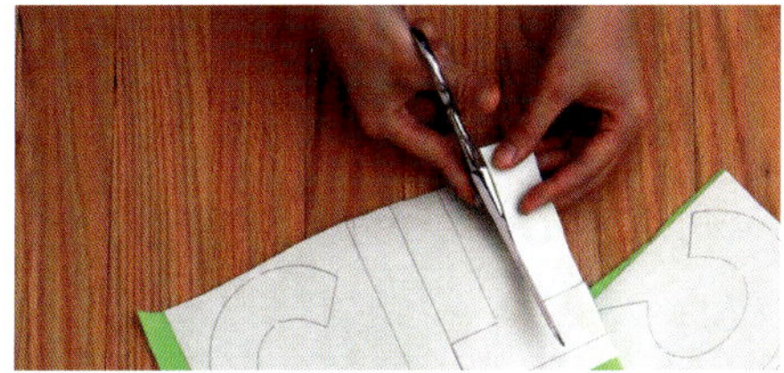

Step 5: Cut out the letters and images.

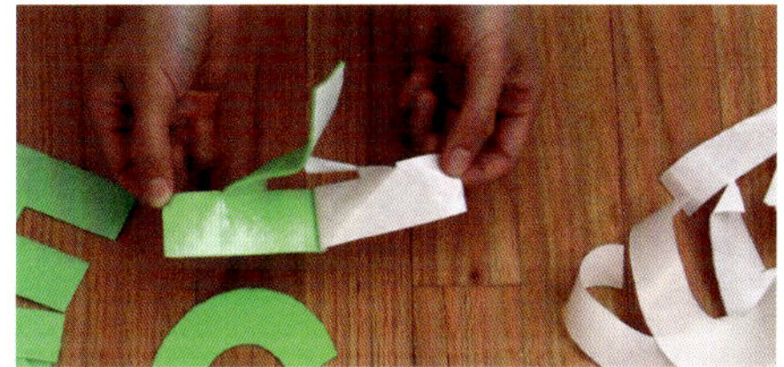

Step 6: Peel off the paper.

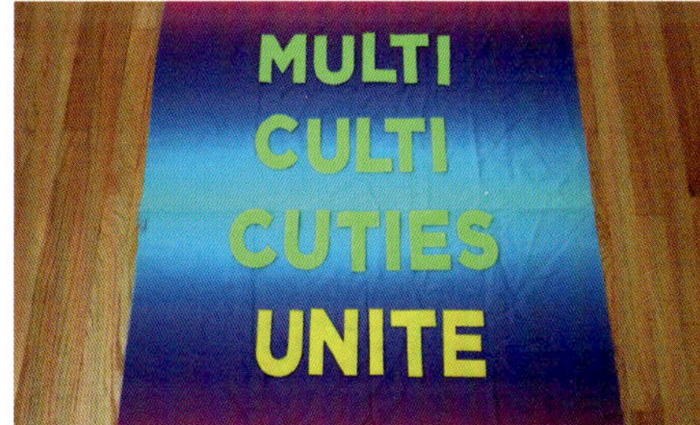

Step 7: Put the shiny peeled side down onto the background fabric. Place as you would like the final design to be.

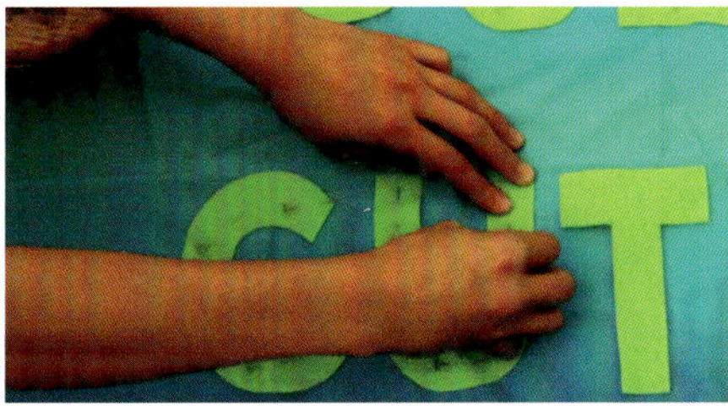

Step 8: Pin down the letters to the background fabric. Pin down every leg of the letter so it does not move around. The best way to pin is to pinch both fabrics, stab the fabrics with the pin, then flatten it out.

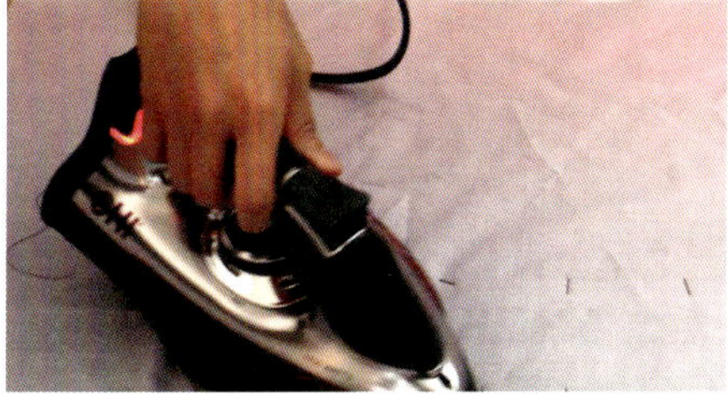

Step 9: Flip the fabric over and iron on medium heat from the back.

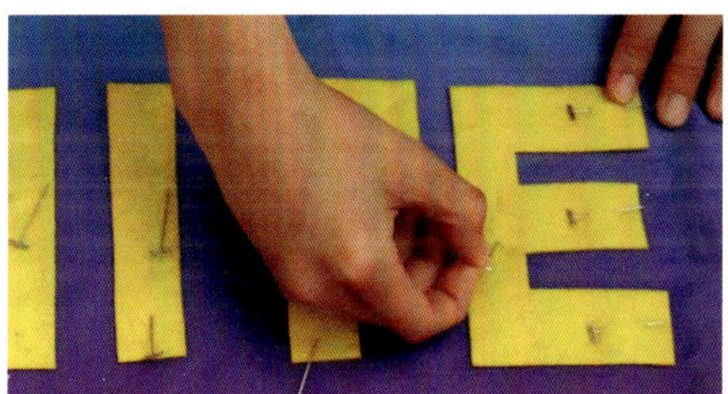

Step 10: Flip the fabric over and remove the pins. The letters should be stuck to the fabric. If not, flip over again and iron again until all letters are firmly adhered.

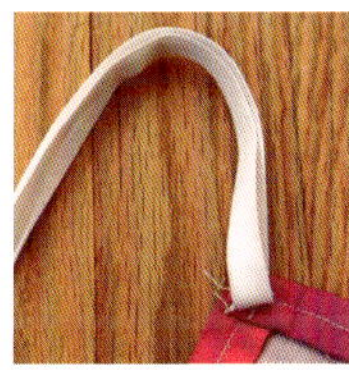

Step 11: Optional. You can sew the edges of the banner and add straps to the corners. We use bias tape for the straps.

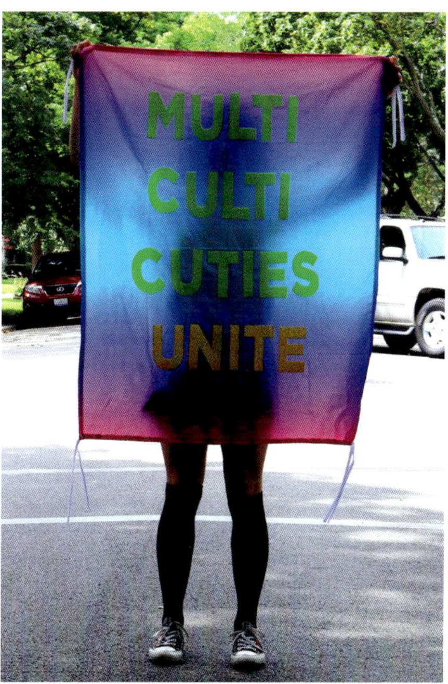

Step 12: Use.
Consider where you would like to see this banner in the world. Consider who you want to see this banner, and what type of impact this can create?

You can put the banner up in your room, display it in your window, take it to your school, use it in a protest or march, donate it to a local organization and/or activist.

You can also always donate your banners to the *Protest Banner Lending Library* so the public can check out and use your banner.

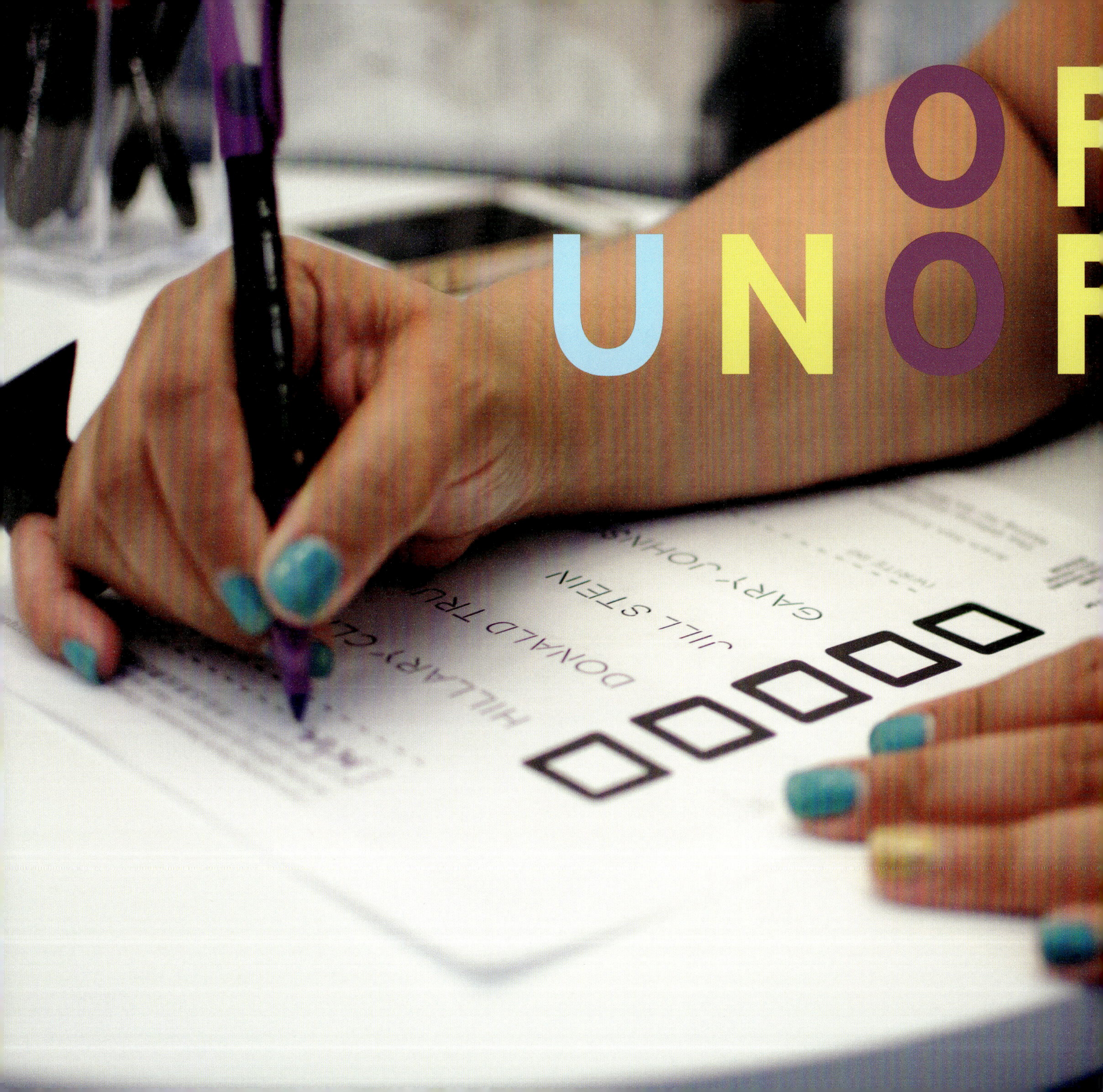
OF
UNOF
JILL STEIN

FICIAL
FICIAL
VOTING
STATION

Voting for All Who Legally Can't

2016 and 2020

According to the U.S. Election Project, in 2016, 28.6% of Americans, equating to more than 92 million people, were disenfranchised and ineligible to vote in the presidential election. The disenfranchised groups include youth under 18, non-citizens, incarcerated and formerly incarcerated people (depending on state laws), residents of U.S. territories, those without government issued IDs (depending on state laws), and those declared "mentally incapacitated" (depending on state laws). This monumental number does not even factor in voter suppression.

In 2016, I created the first iteration of this project by collaborating with more than 15 artists, activists, and organizations to create more than 25 imaginative voting stations in cities throughout the United States and Mexico. Each of these voting stations took different forms, including sculptural public installations, performative guerrilla actions, or pedagogical tools to encourage students to create their own voting stations open to all. In a season where the disenfranchised were deemed to be silent and invisible, these events were not only a site for casting symbolic votes but also for loud celebration and protest.

For the 2020 iteration, I created 50 *Voting Kits for the Disenfranchised*. These kits were available to anyone who requested them for creating their own ***Official Unofficial Voting Station*** for the presidential election. All 50 kits were requested and distributed to voting station activators all over the world.

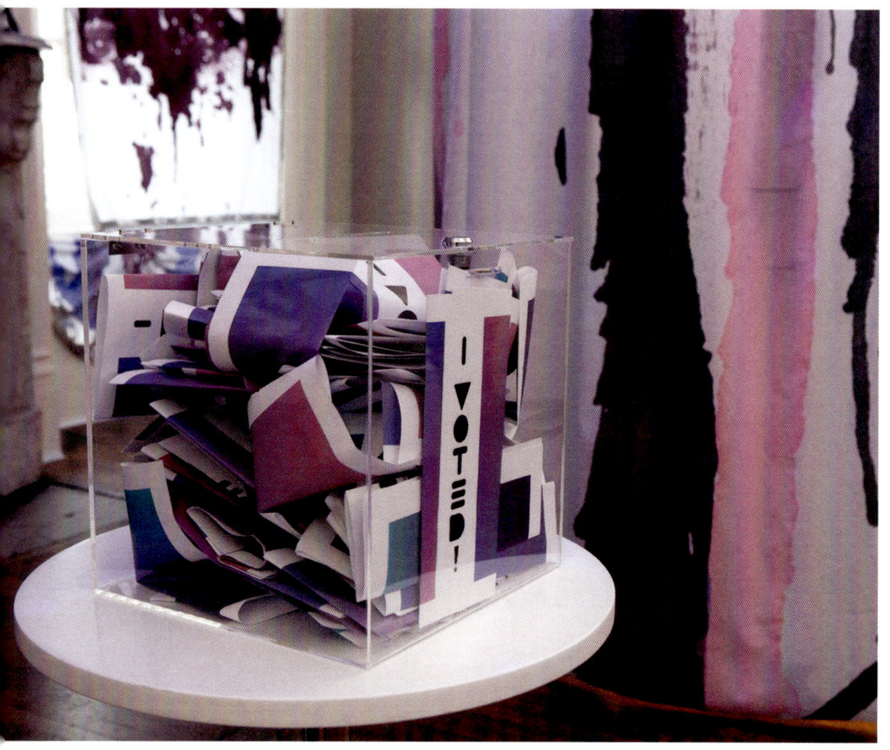

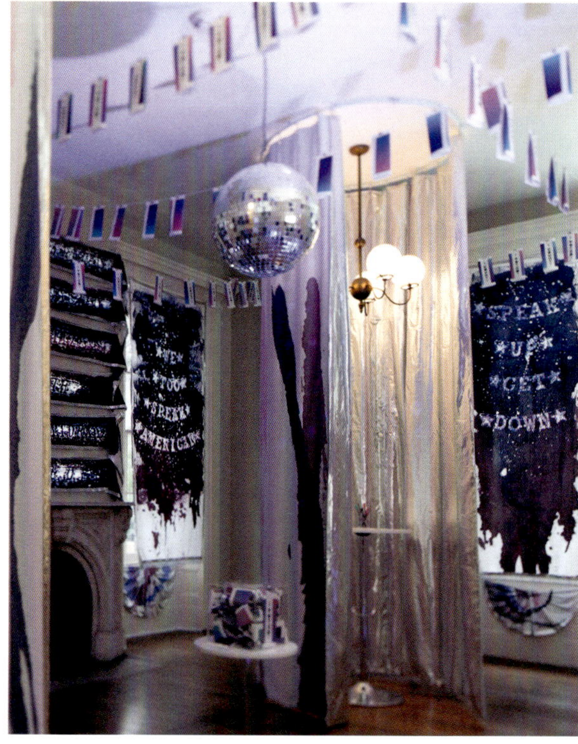

1 PAGE 66 Vox Pop: The Disco Party, *2016, by Aram Han Sifuentes in collaboration with Lise Haller Baggesen and 24-hour playlist of protest songs by DJ Sadie Woods. Jane Addams Hull-House Museum, Chicago. Photo: Tonika Johnson.*

2 + 3 Vox Pop: The Disco Party, *2016, by Aram Han Sifuentes in collaboration with Lise Haller Baggesen and 24-hour playlist of protest songs by DJ Sadie Woods. Jane Addams Hull-House Museum, Chicago. Photos: Sara Pooley.*

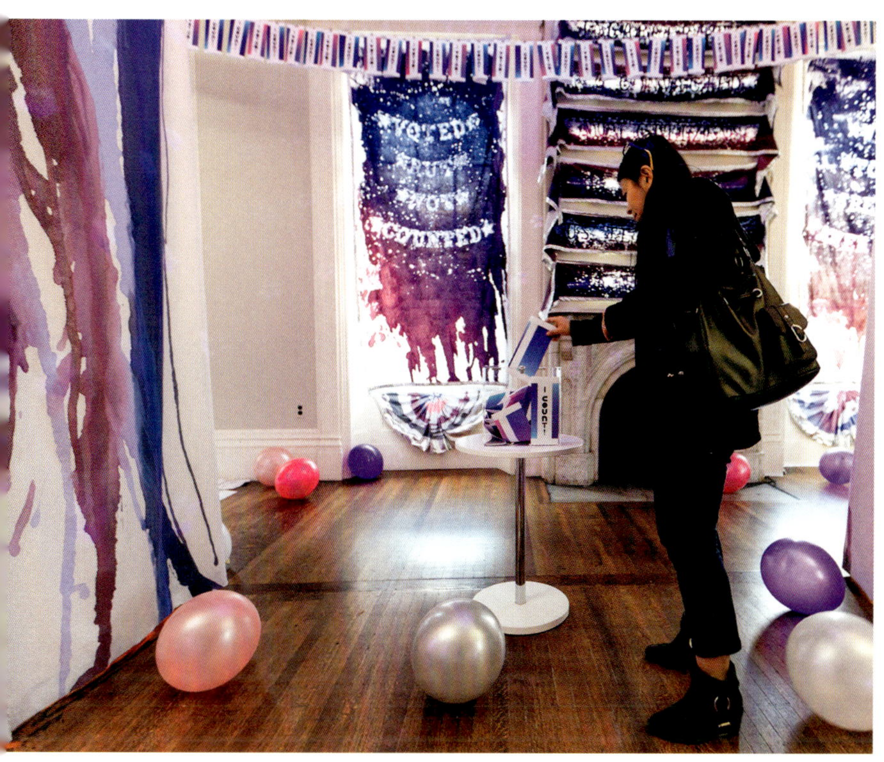

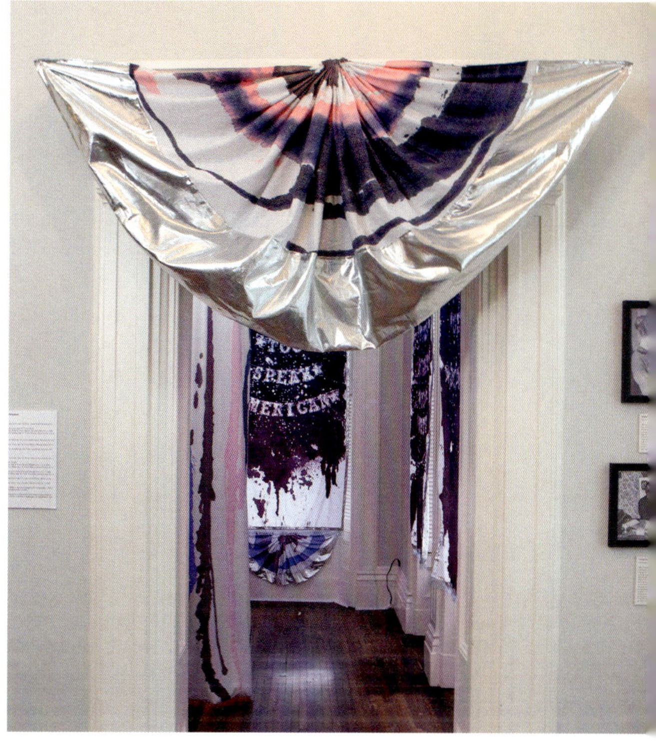

4 Vox Pop: The Disco Party, 2016, *by Aram Han Sifuentes in collaboration with Lise Haller Baggesen and 24-hour playlist of protest songs by DJ Sadie Woods. Jane Addams Hull-House Museum, Chicago. Photo: eedahahm.*

5 Vox Pop: The Disco Party, 2016, *by Aram Han Sifuentes in collaboration with Lise Haller Baggesen and 24-hour playlist of protest songs by DJ Sadie Woods. Jane Addams Hull-House Museum, Chicago. Photo: Sara Pooley.*

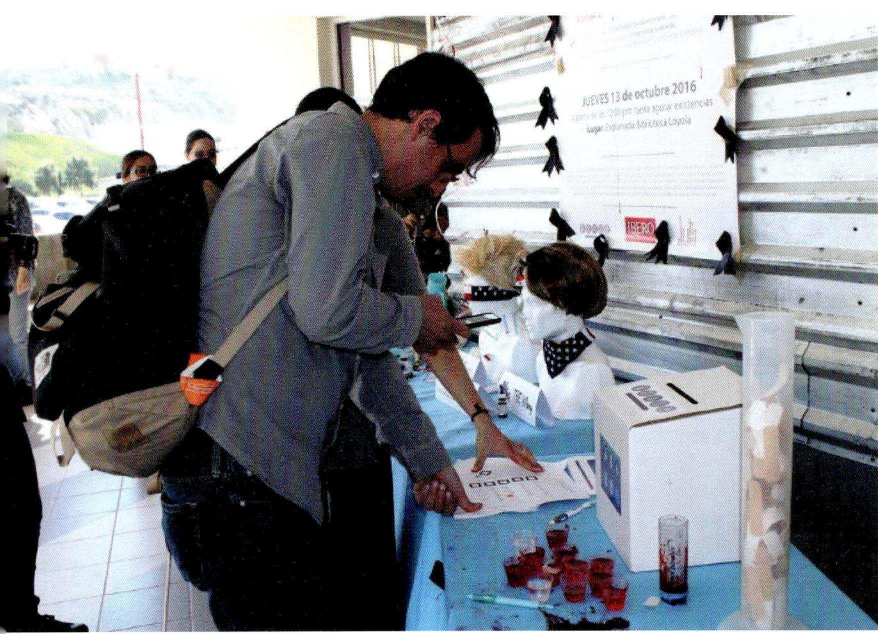

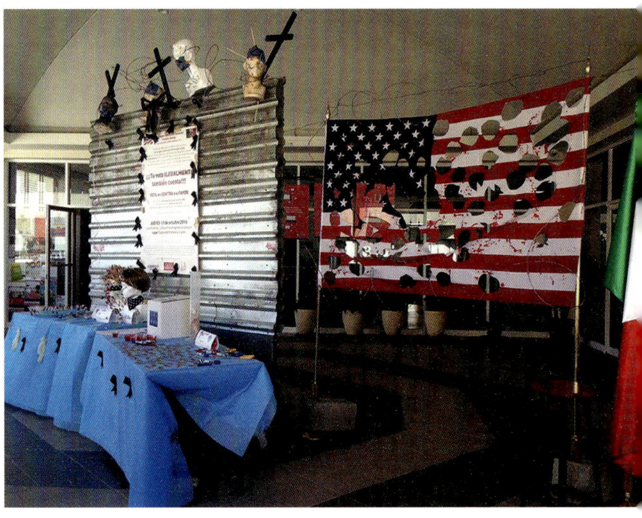

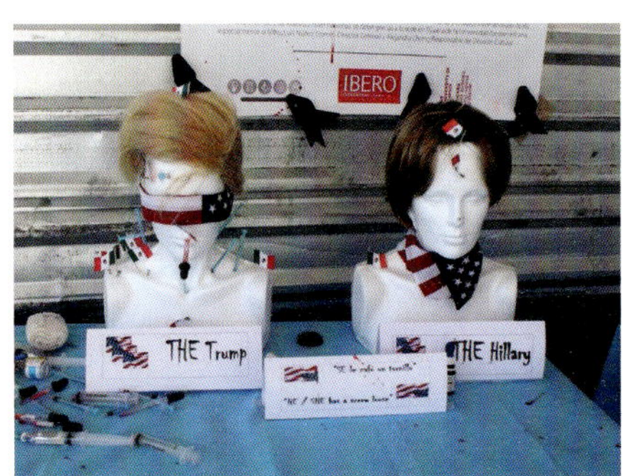

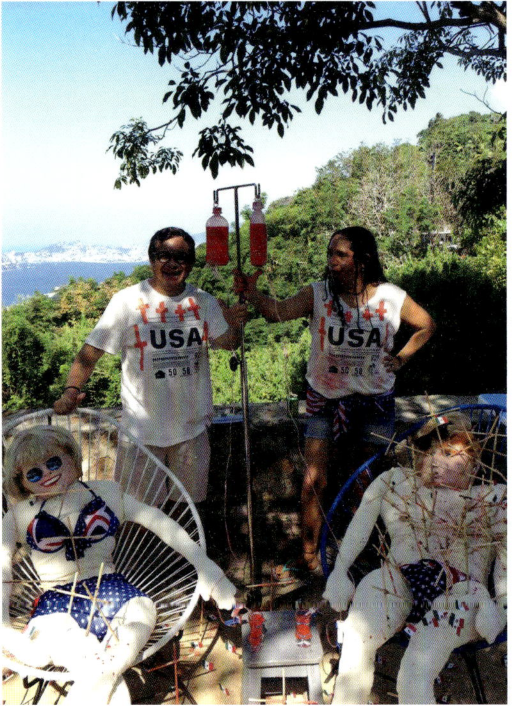

OFFICIAL UNOFFICIAL VOTING STATION

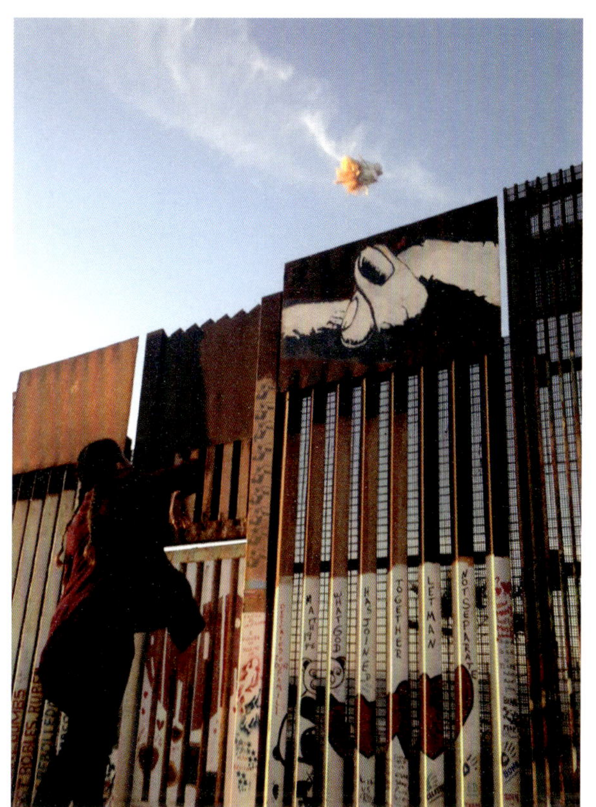

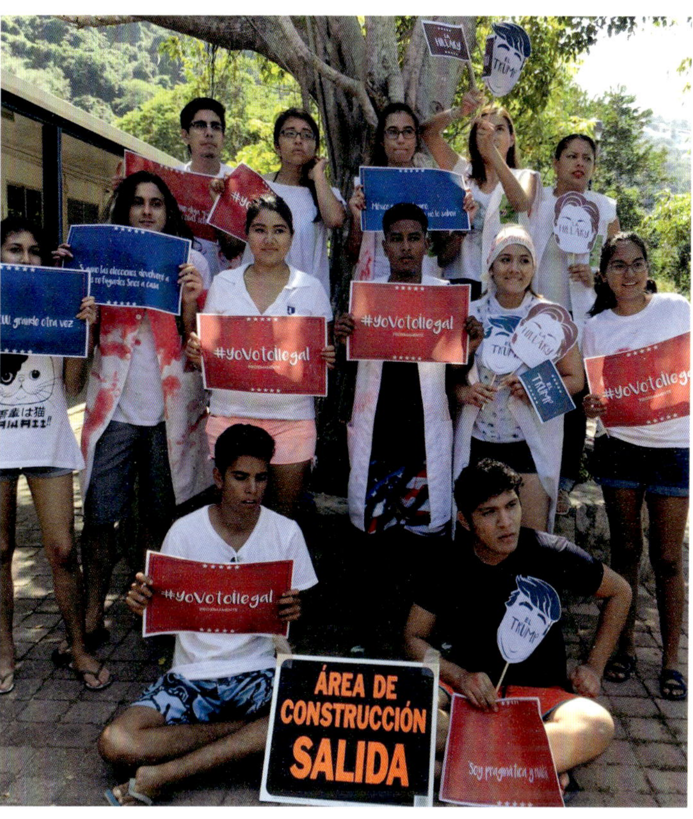

6-11 Voto Ilegal *by Cecilia Aguilar Castillo and Erick Fernández Saldaña, Mexico City, Acapulco, and Tijuana. Photos: Cecilia Aguilar Castillo and Erick Fernández Saldaña.*

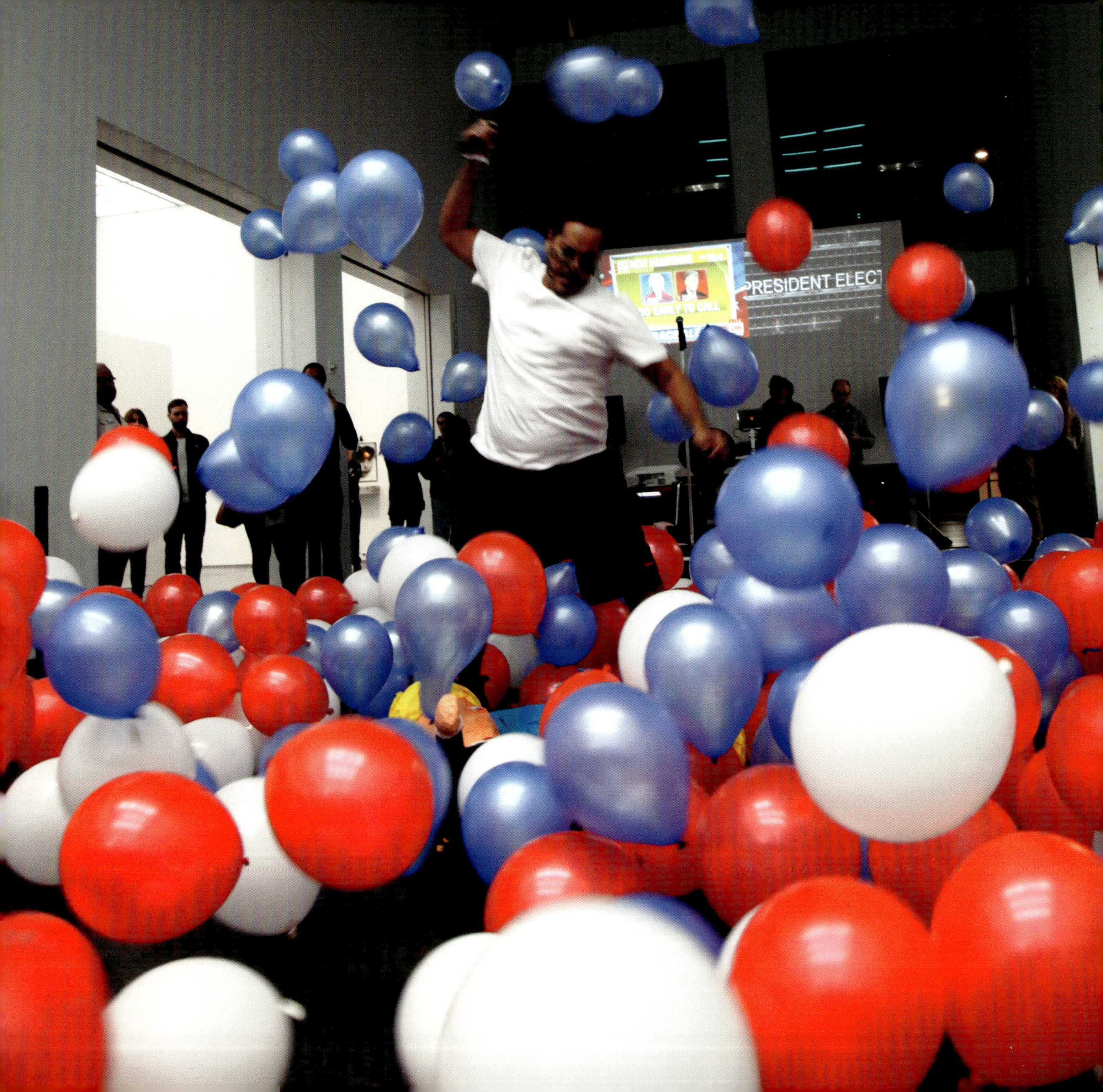
EARLY TO CALL
PRESIDENT ELECT

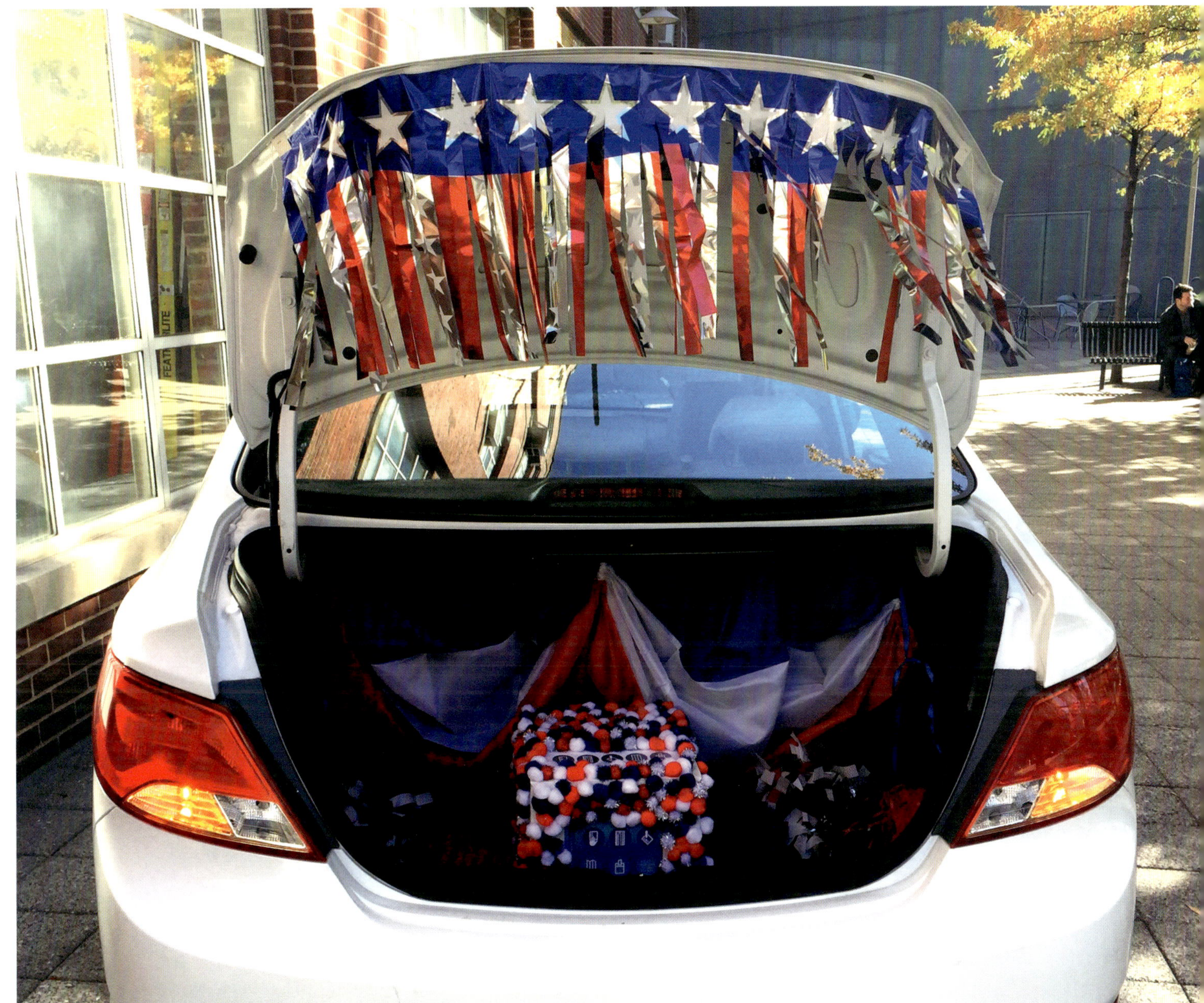

12 Official Unofficial Voting Station Election Viewing Party (*Performances, music, and balloon drop*) *by Aram Han Sifuentes, Roberto Sifuentes, and DJ Sadie Woods, Museum of Contemporary Art, Chicago. Photo: Kanthy Peng.*

13 Mobile Trunk Voting Station *by Verónica Casado Hernández in collaboration with Hannah Hiaasen, Baltimore and Washington, D.C.*

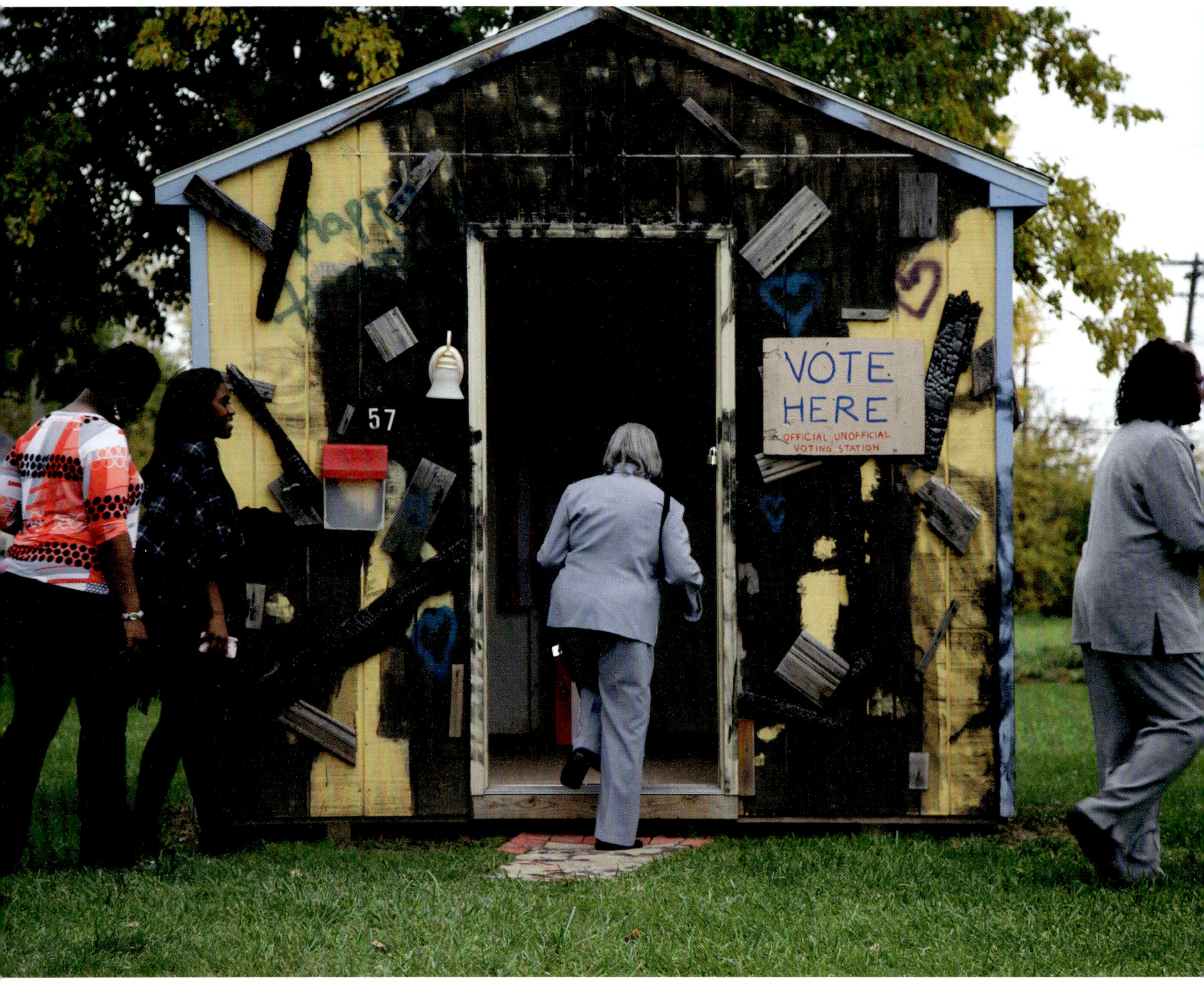

OFFICIAL UNOFFICIAL VOTING STATION

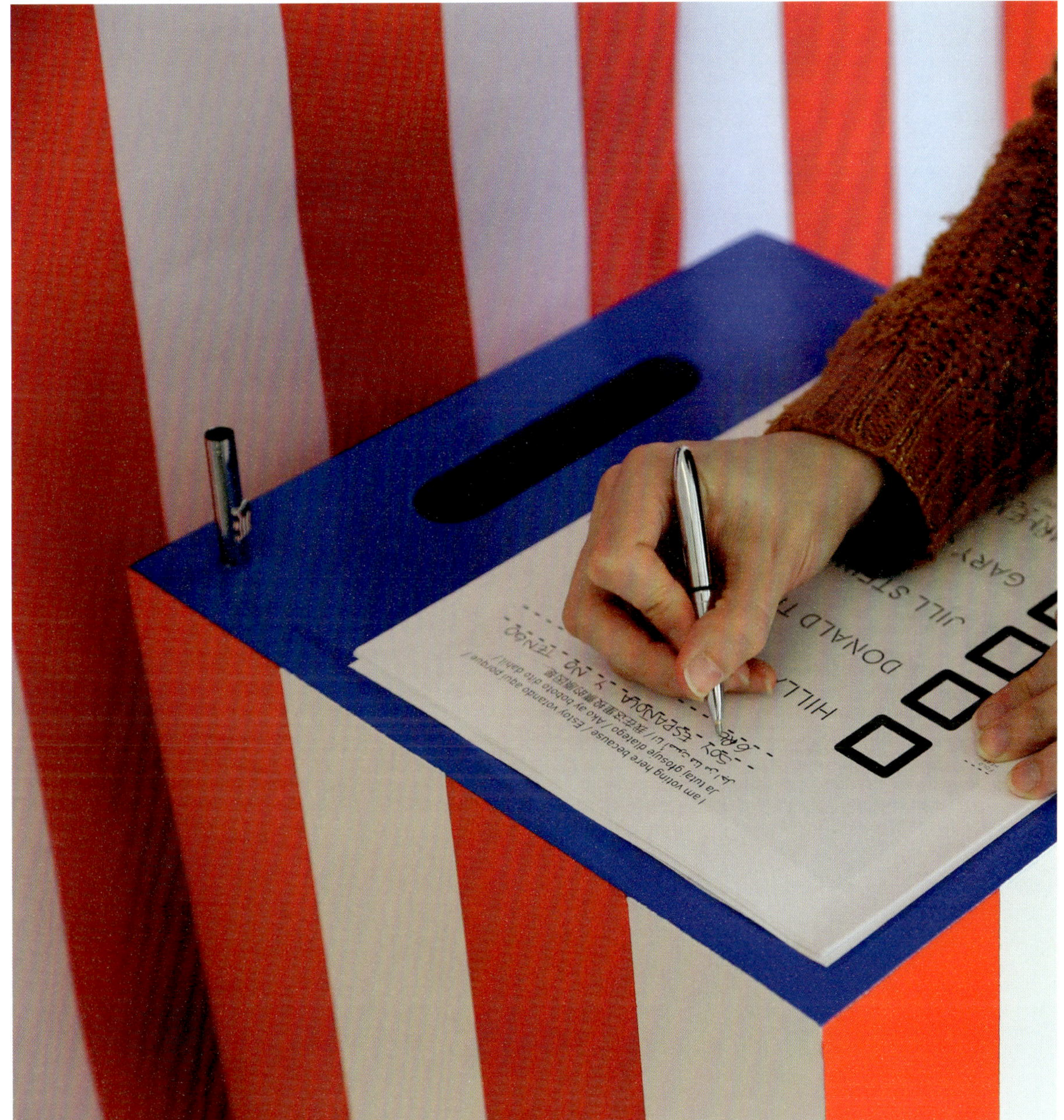

14 Vote Here *by Brandon Bullard at Heidelberg Project, Detroit. Photo: Brandon Bullard.*

15 Official Unofficial Voting Station *by Brandon Bullard at Museum of Contemporary Art, Detroit. Photo: Brandon Bullard.*

2016 Official Unofficial Voting Stations

Project commissioned by Jane Addams Hull-House Museum, Chicago

Aram Han Sifuentes in collaboration with Lise Haller Baggesen, ***Vox Pop: The Disco Station*** at Jane Addams Hull-House Museum, Chicago.

Cecilia Aguilar Castillo and Erick Fernández Saldaña, ***Voto Ilegal*** in Mexico City, Tijuana, and Acapulco.

Brandon Bullard at the Mobile Homestead's exhibition ***Art as Social Force: It's Your Part*** at the Museum of Contemporary Art, Detroit and The Heidelberg Project, Detroit.

Maritea Daehlin at La Cosecha Librería in San Cristobal de las Casas, Mexico.

Mara Baldwin, Anna Gardner, and Michele Hau at Handwerker Gallery, Ithaca College, Ithaca, New York.

Marianne Sadowski, ***Voto o Muerte*** at Plaza de la Raza, Los Angeles.

Verónica Casado Hernández in collaboration with Hannah Hiaasen, ***Mobile Trunk Voting Station*** in Washington, D.C. and Baltimore.

Roberto Sifuentes' ***Border Crossers*** course (student group activations), in the Performance Department, School of the Art Institute of Chicago, Chicago.

Yvette Mayorga and Aram Han Sifuentes, ***Imagining a Border with Piñata Walls*** at Jane Addams Hull-House Museum, Chicago.

Roberto Sifuentes, Aram Han Sifuentes, and DJ Sadie Woods, ***Election Night Official Unofficial Voting Party*** at the Museum of Contemporary Art, Chicago.

Lilah Rose Thompson in Philadelphia.

Latino Advocacy in various cities, Washington.

Haitian American Museum of Chicago, Chicago.

Bennie Lee in Illinois.

Various voting activations by Aram Han Sifuentes, Jennifer Scott (then-director, Jane Addams Hull-House Museum), and Ross Jordan (Curatorial Manager, Jane Addams Hull-House Museum) in Chicago, Los Angeles, London, and beyond.

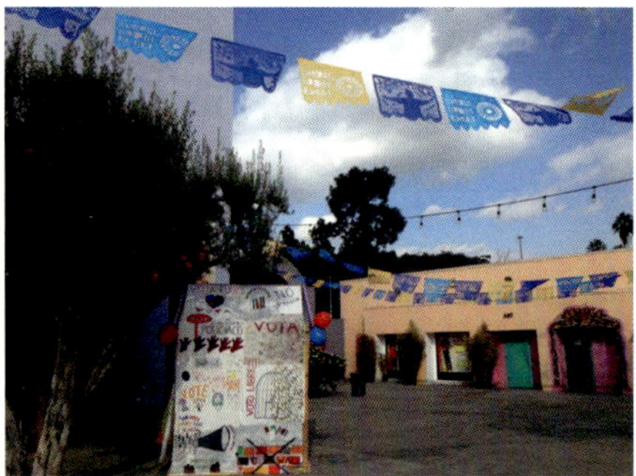

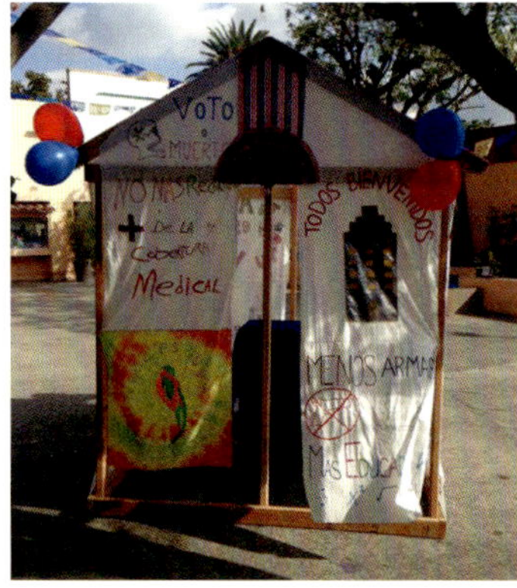

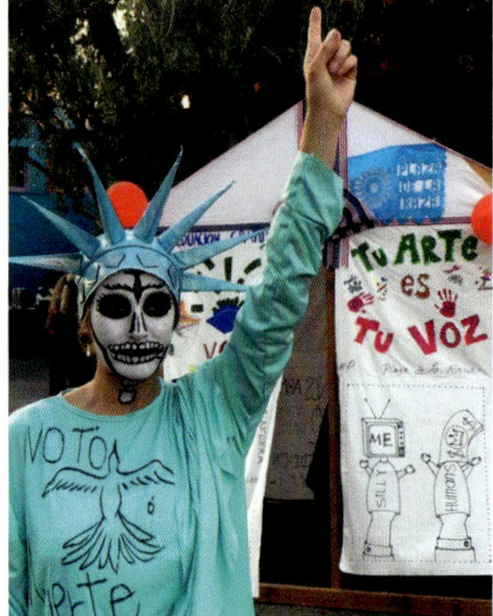

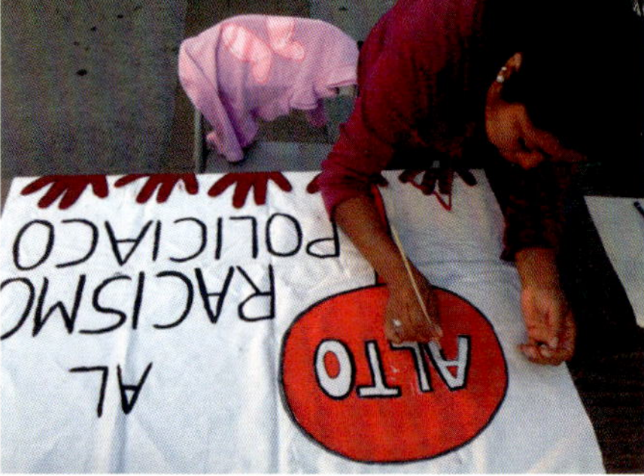

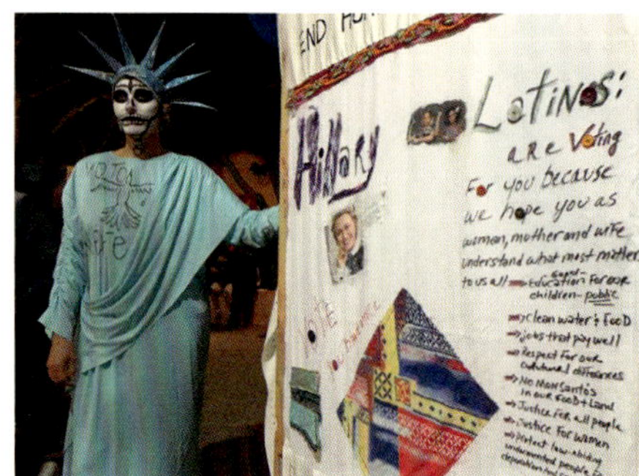

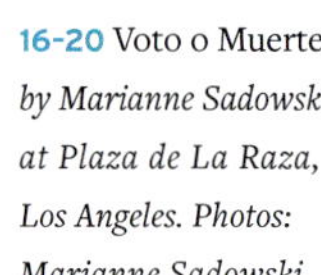

16–20 Voto o Muerte *by Marianne Sadowski at Plaza de La Raza, Los Angeles. Photos: Marianne Sadowski.*

2016 OFFICIAL UNOFFICIAL VOTING RESULTS

I AM VOTING HERE BECAUSE...

(Selected responses. Results are typed exactly as submitted.)

I am a legal alien I cannot vote anywhere.

Me siento que todo deben tener un voz.

I need hope.

I care about the future of this country.

Voting matter! Thank You!

People need to feel the fun and power in making their voice heard and spoken for.

I hate that some who should be able to cannot.

I want justice.

I legally can't. I've never been able to vote anywhere.

In solidarity for undocumented people, this is a blank vote. THEY NEED A VOICE!

I can't vote until next election.

I want my voice to be heard.

Me acabo de hacer ciudadana hace una semana y estoy emocionada.

Gunki ben Amerikan Vatandasi degilim ve oy kullan ami yorum.

I'm scared for the future of America.

I'm not old enough. I'm only 11.

I can cast a symbolic vote in an act of responsibility & I hope for those who are denied the right-here in the US & throughout the world.

I am voting here b/c I legally cannot. Dream Act!

I'm afraid my absentee ballot will get lost (or "lost").

This initiative rocks and is moving boundaries (all the way to the Netherlands).

I'm not sure I'm going to get my absentee ballot in time!!

I'm not old enough (17).

I may be young, but I am knowledgeable and aware of the political situation.

Quiero un pais para todos.

No puedo votar legalmente. F-1 visa sucks!

Enfranchisement kicks in two years' time!!!

Much is at stake!

I am registered to vote in another state & my papers were not returned to me on time.

I stand in solidarity with all those who don't have a say in this election. And Trump is a racist bigot representing the worst of humanity.

I cannot register in Illinois.

Que los sueños de los niños se hagan realidad!

Pasa que yo pueda seguir estudiar y seguridad con mi mama.

Porque creo en la justicia social.

Por la seguridad para que yo pueda tener un seguridad con mis hijos.

I have to constantly lie on my visa renewal form that I don't have the intent to immigrate to the U.S.

They didn't let me at the official voting station.

Nowhere else let me vote.

Because I can. I'm a felon!

America needs to do better.

Basic preservation of the republic in the face of rising American fascism.

I am not a United States citizen yet! This makes me feel like I am!

My faith in democracy is dwindling.

I believe in democracy.

I can't actually vote because I'm Canadian.

Does it matter anymore?

I want my vote to count.

Quiero hacer una diferencia en el mundo.

I love mother earth!

I want the USA to be a better citizen of the world.

I want to have a voice, even if I'm 11.

I'm voting because it's time we are recognized as a part of this country!

They asked nicely.

The power of legislation can determine our future.

I want America to be Mexico Again.

I don't feel represented in the actual election.

Me dan la oportunidad.

No puedo en mi pais ni en los Estados Unidos.

Amerikkkan Democracy is Fucked.

My cousin Oscar is in jail and can't vote yet.

America and its government failed the people of Detroit.

I'm scared.

My ancestors fought 4 this right.

Revolution!!!

Fucked if ya do. Fucked if ya don't.

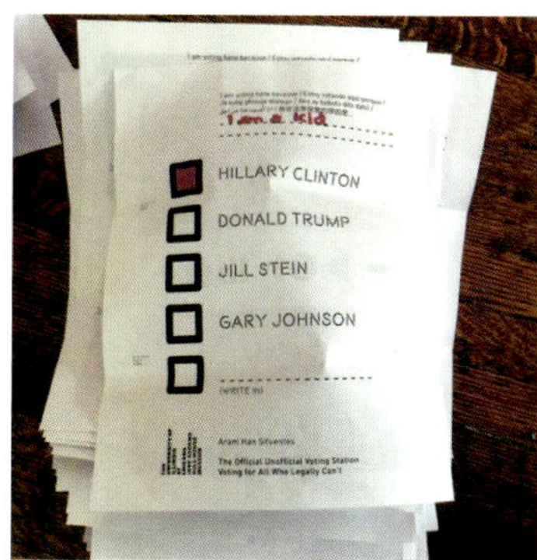

TOTAL VOTES
4317

...

CLINTON
2356

...

TRUMP
278

...

STEIN
302

...

JOHNSON
147

...

WRITE IN
1121
(Bernie Sanders, Barack Obama, and Michelle Obama in the lead)

...

NO VOTE
113

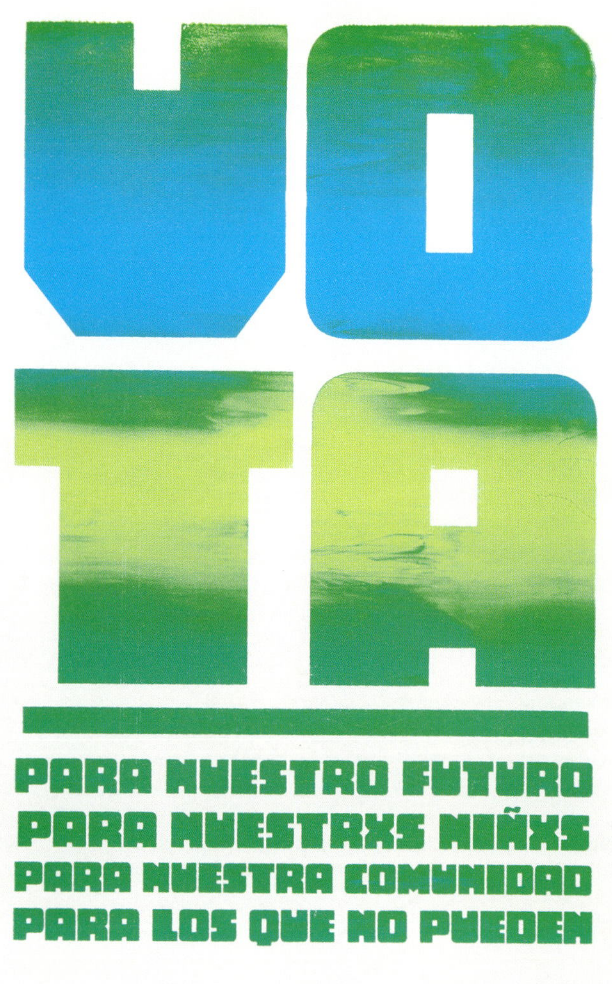

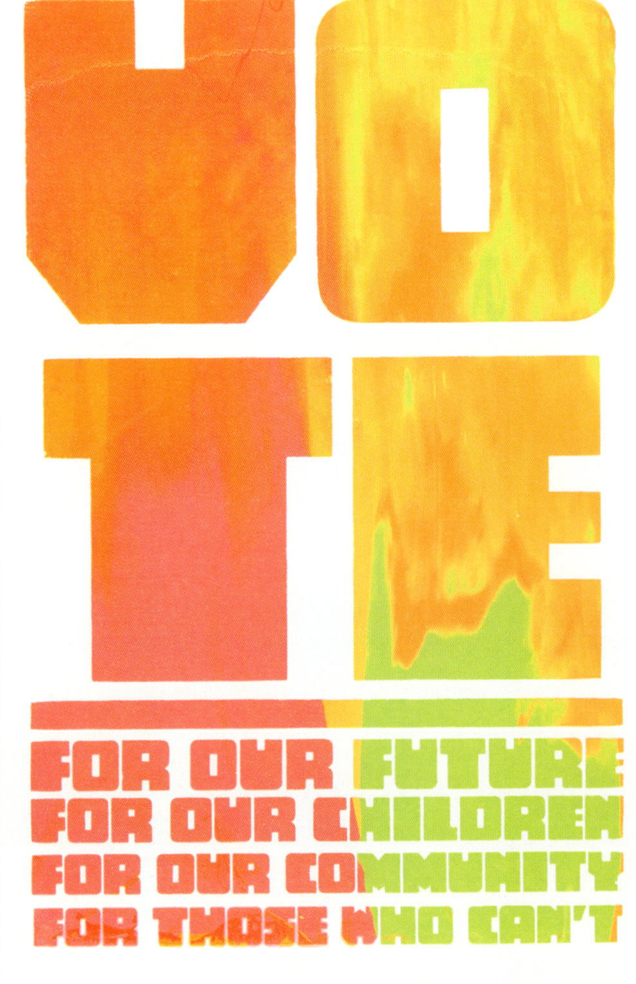

22-26 *Objects included in the* 50 Voting Kits for the Disenfranchised, *a kit for people to activate their own* Official Unofficial Voting Stations, *2020.*

22 *William Estrada,* Vote for Our Future, For Our Children, For Our Community, For Those Who Can't, *screen printed posters available in eight different languages, 18 x 12 inches. Photos: Thaib Wahab.*

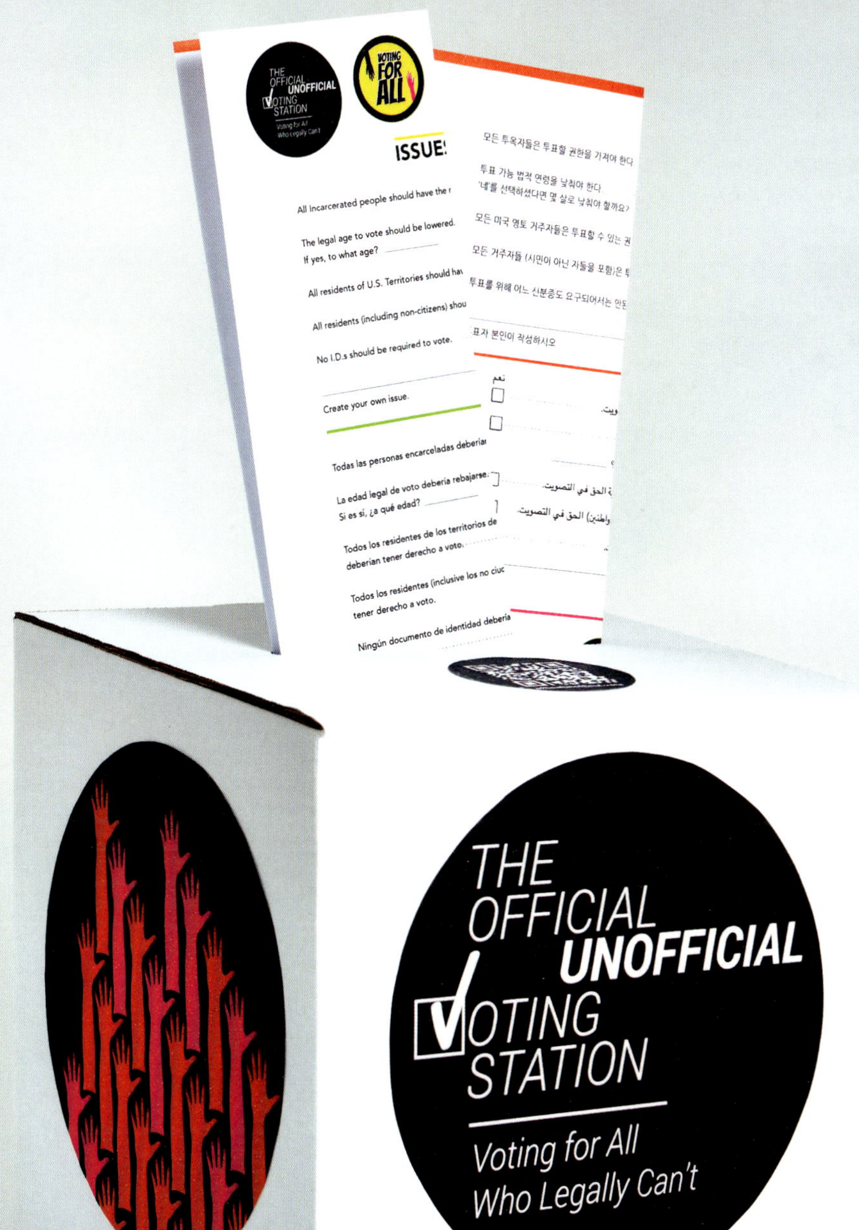

23 Official Unofficial Voting Station *ballot box, 100 candidate ballots, and 100 issues ballots. Photo: Thaib Wahab.*

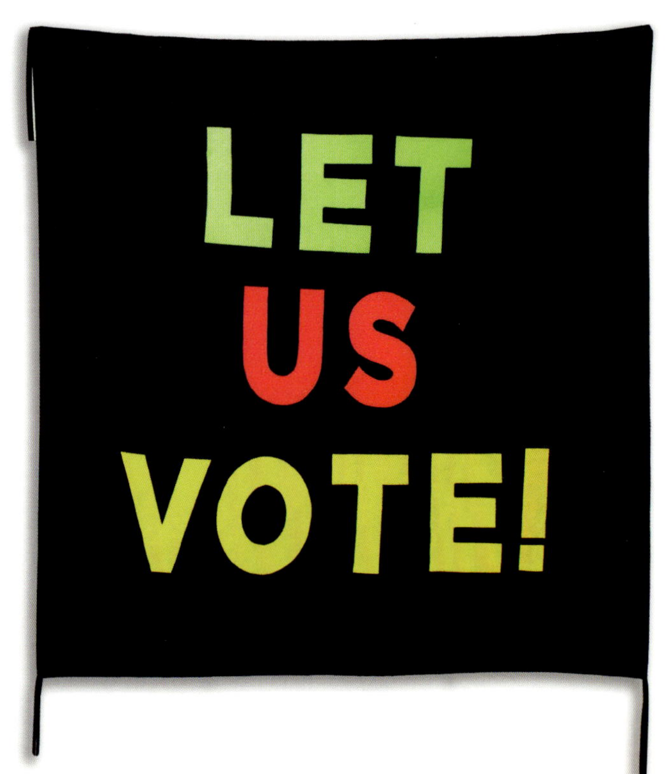

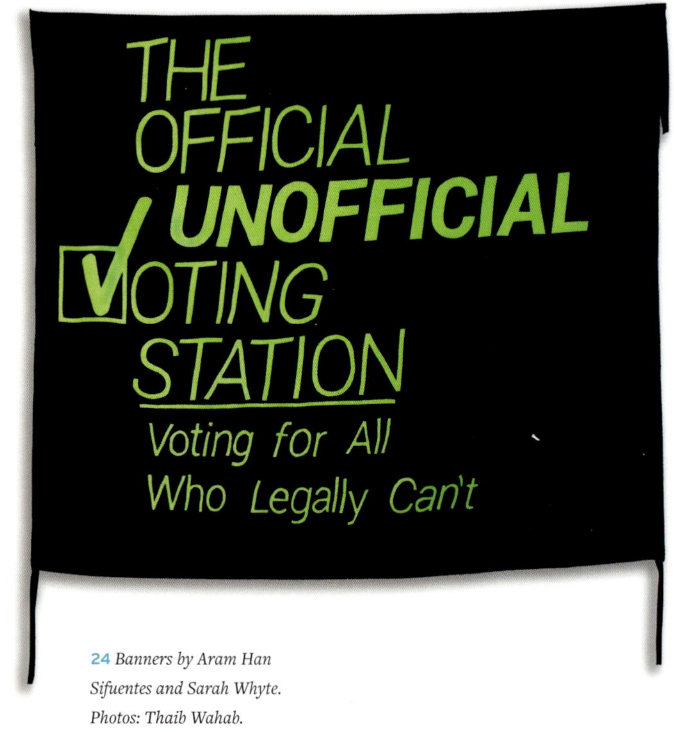

24 *Banners by Aram Han Sifuentes and Sarah Whyte. Photos: Thaib Wahab.*

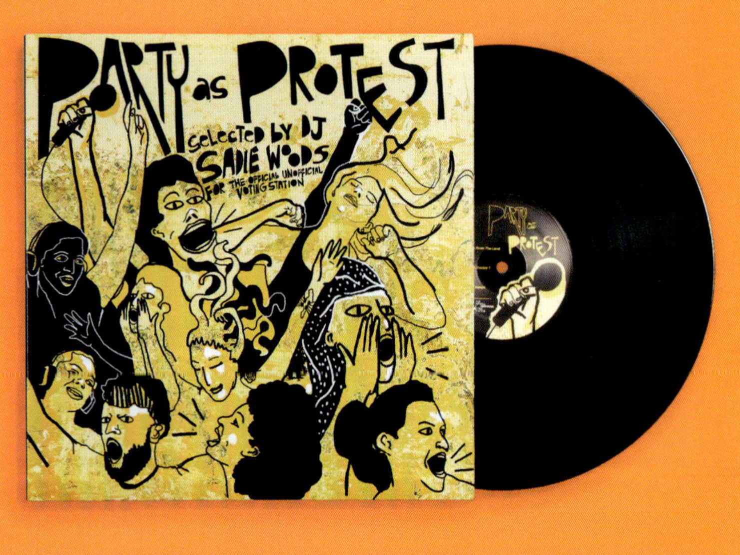

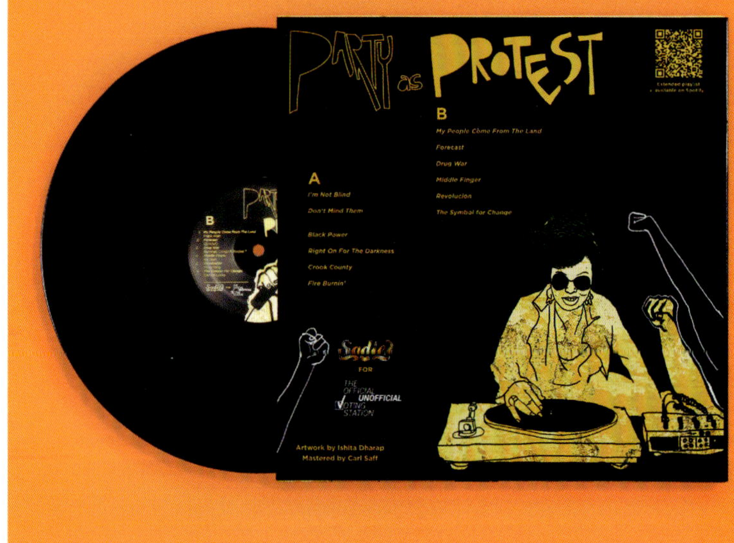

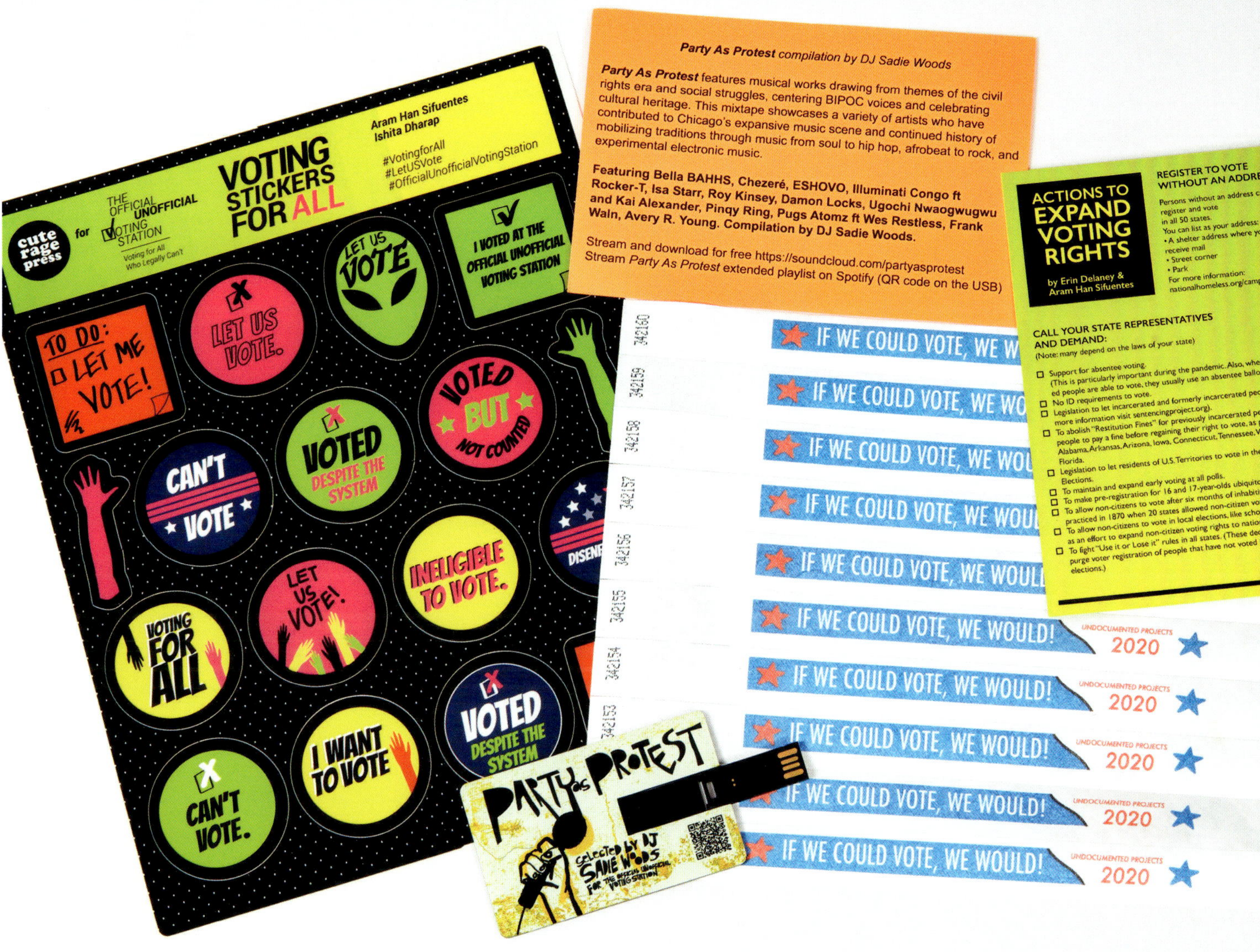

25 Party as Protest *vinyl record featuring Bella BAHHS, Chezeré, ESHOVO, Illuminati Congo ft Rocker-T, Isa Starr, Roy Kinsey, Damon Locks, Ugochi Nwaogwugwu and Kai Alexander, Pinqy Ring, Pugs Atomz ft Wes Restless, Frank Waln, avery r. young. Compilation by DJ Sadie Woods. Photos: Thaib Wahab.*

26 *Voting Stickers FOR ALL by Cute Rage Press (Aram Han Sifuentes and Ishita Dharap). If We Could Vote, We Would! Wristbands by Undocumented Projects. Actions to Expand Voting Rights by Erin Delaney and Aram Han Sifuentes. Photo: Thaib Wahab.*

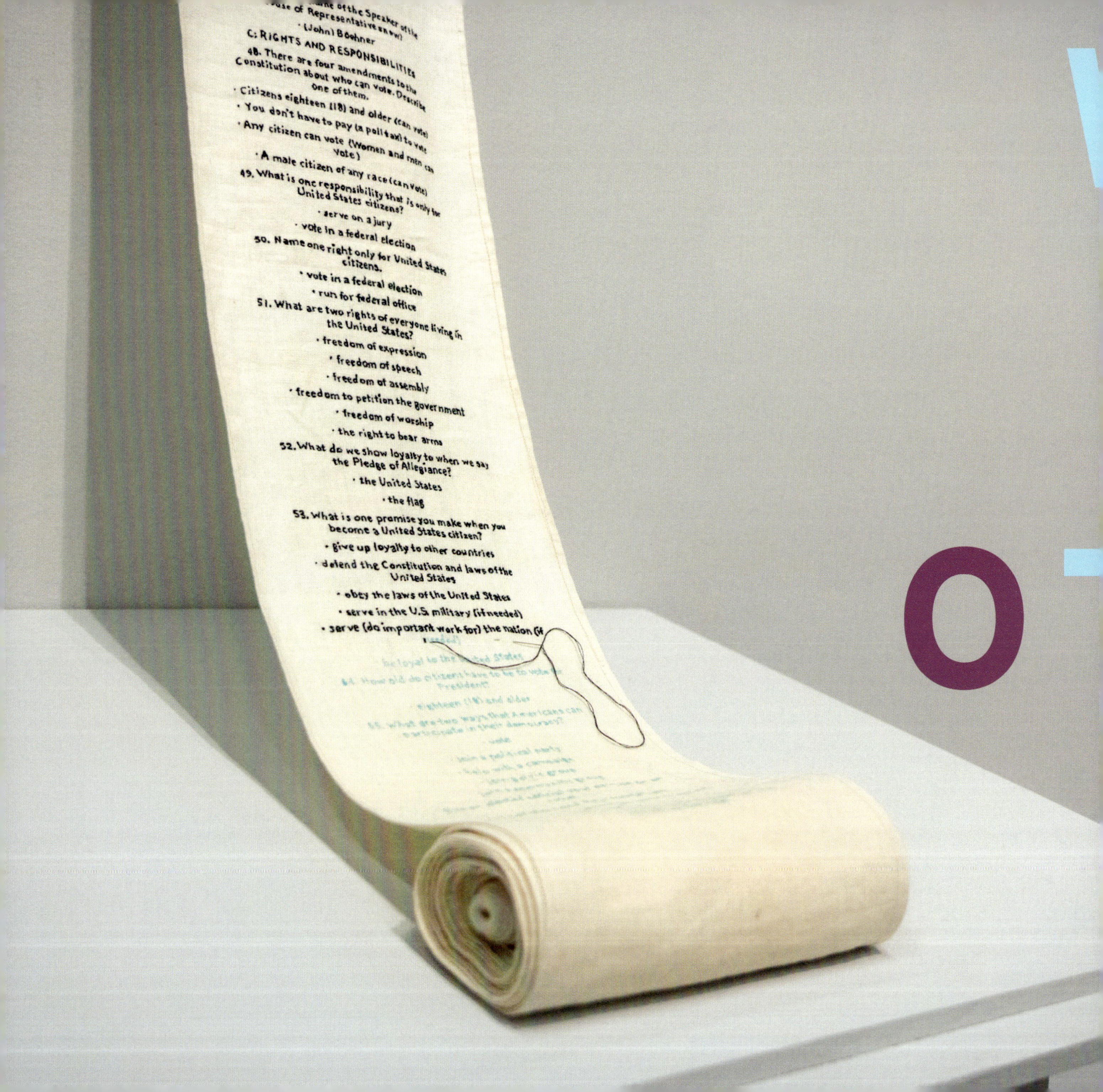

...name of the Speaker of the House of Representatives now?

· (John) Boehner

C: RIGHTS AND RESPONSIBILITIES

48. There are four amendments to the Constitution about who can vote. Describe one of them.

· Citizens eighteen (18) and older (can vote)

· You don't have to pay (a poll tax) to vote

· Any citizen can vote (Women and men can vote)

· A male citizen of any race (can vote)

49. What is one responsibility that is only for United States citizens?

· serve on a jury

· vote in a federal election

50. Name one right only for United States citizens.

· vote in a federal election

· run for federal office

51. What are two rights of everyone living in the United States?

· freedom of expression

· freedom of speech

· freedom of assembly

· freedom to petition the government

· freedom of worship

· the right to bear arms

52. What do we show loyalty to when we say the Pledge of Allegiance?

· the United States

· the flag

53. What is one promise you make when you become a United States citizen?

· give up loyalty to other countries

· defend the Constitution and laws of the United States

· obey the laws of the United States

· serve in the U.S. military (if needed)

· serve (do important work for) the nation (if needed)

WE ARE NEVER NEVER OTHER

Exhibition Views

University Galleries of Illinois State University
Normal, Illinois
August 15–October 13, 2019
Curated by Kendra Paitz

We Are Never Never Other brought together three of Aram Han Sifuentes' projects for the first time: ***Protest Banner Lending Library*** (2016-present), ***U.S. Citizenship Test Sampler*** (2012-present), and ***A Mend*** (2011-present). Rooted in her experiences as an immigrant from South Korea, the artist developed her community-based textile projects to confront social justice issues including racial inequity, economic disparities, and political disenfranchisement. She writes, "Much of my communal work revolves around sharing skills as a point of connection. We share sewing techniques to create multiethnic and intergenerational sewing circles, which become a place for empowerment, subversion, and protest." The exhibition premiered Han Sifuentes' ***A Mend: A Collection of Stories from Local Seamstresses and Tailors (Chicago)*** (2019-present). Workshops and materials were provided throughout the duration of the exhibition for visitors to create their own protest banners.

Han Sifuentes gave an artist talk and led a community banner-making workshop that was attended by more than 90 people of all ages, including a three-generation family. Additionally, staff-led workshops and materials were available daily for visitors to create their own banners. Individuals, classes, and groups (including Student Leadership Council, Design Streak, and students involved with organizing Queertober and the Climate Strike) took part. Han Sifuentes and several participants generously donated banners to University Galleries' permanent collection. They continue to be used for protests, classes, and exhibitions.

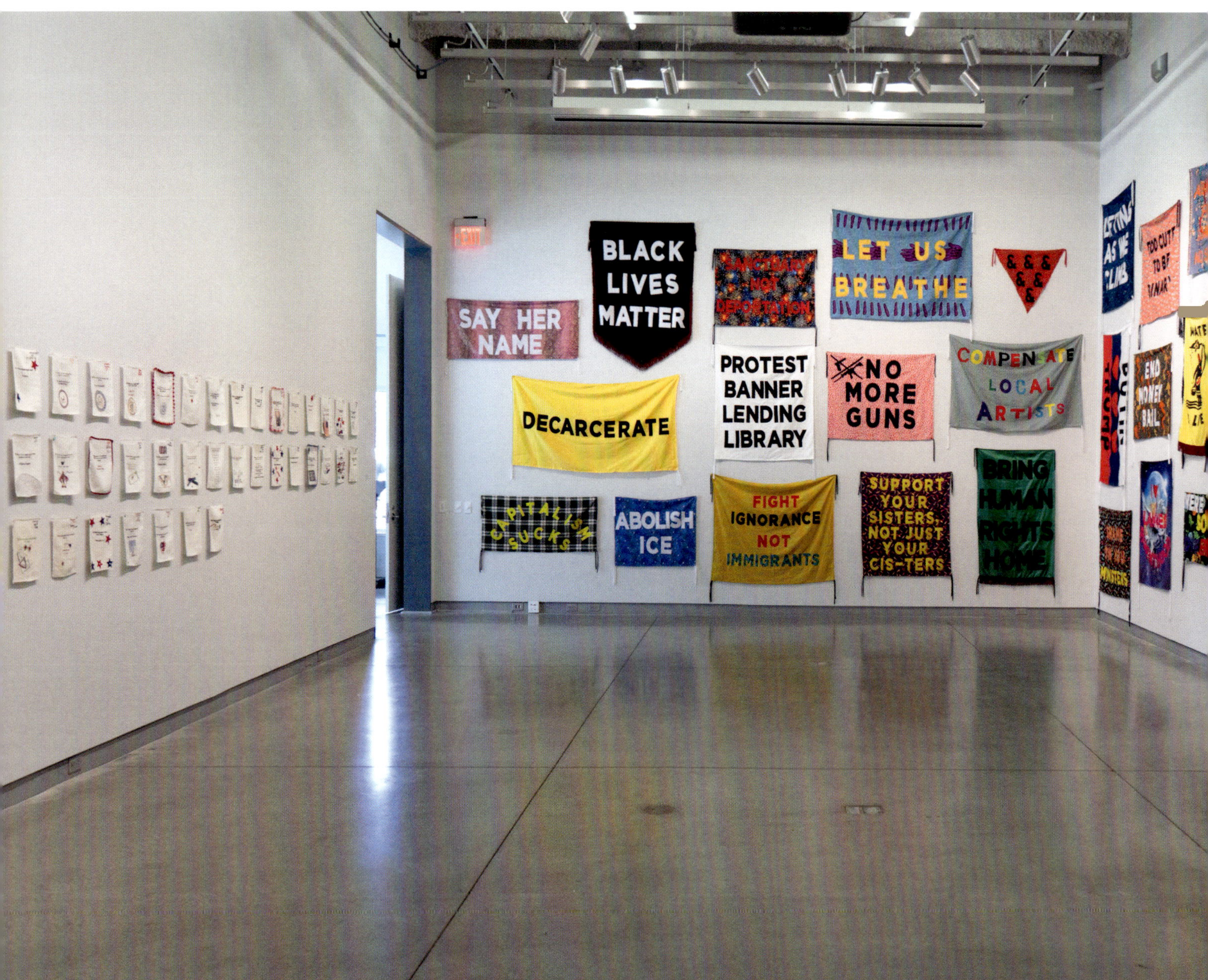

1 PAGE 82 *Aram Han Sifuentes,* U.S. Citizenship Test Sampler: 100 Questions and Answers *(detail), 2012–present. Cotton thread on linen, 25 feet x 8.5 inches. Installation view at University Galleries of Illinois State University, Normal, 2019. Photo: Jessica Bingham.*

2 *Installation view of* Aram Han Sifuentes: We Are Never Never Other *at University Galleries of Illinois State University, 2019. Photo: Jessica Bingham.*

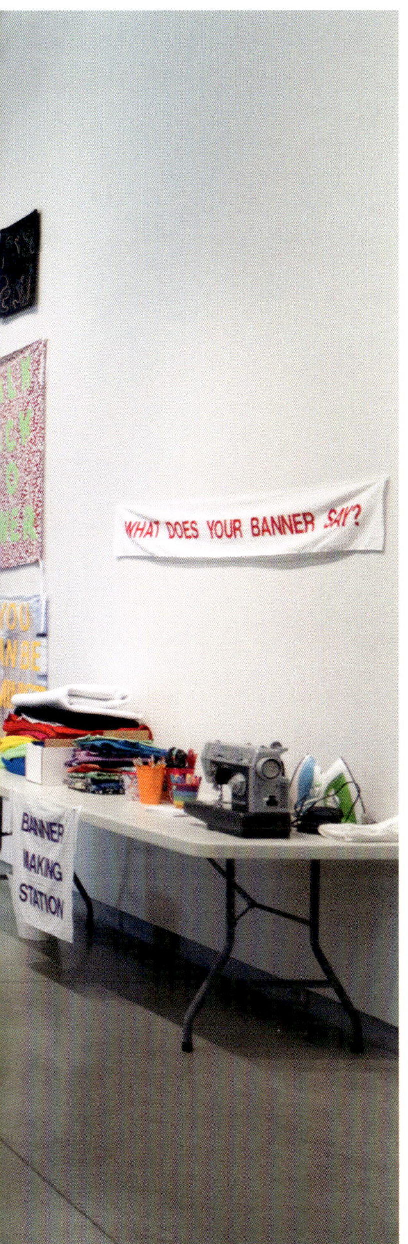

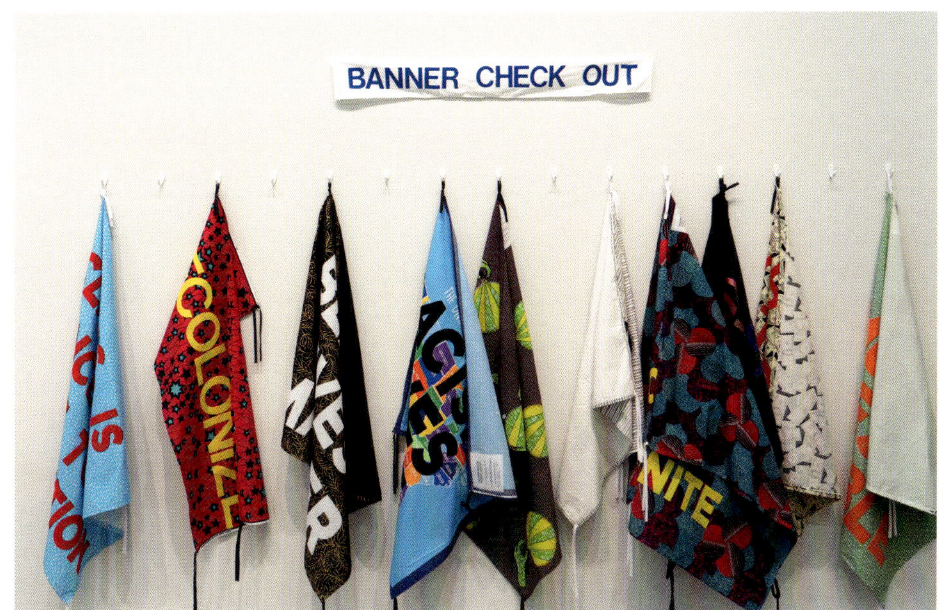

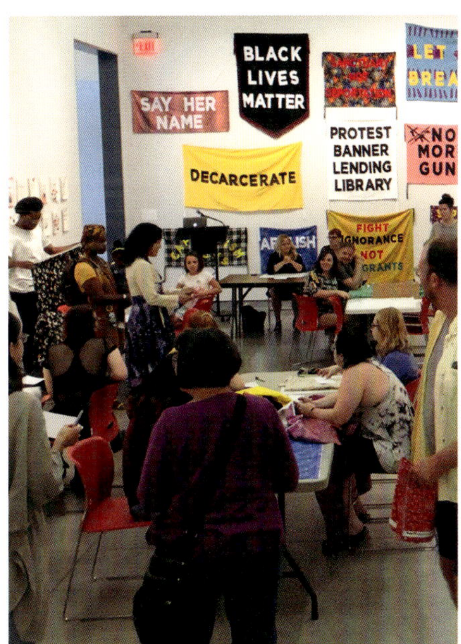

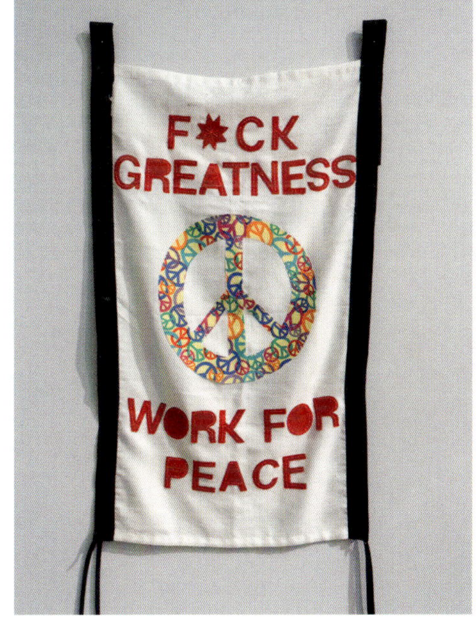

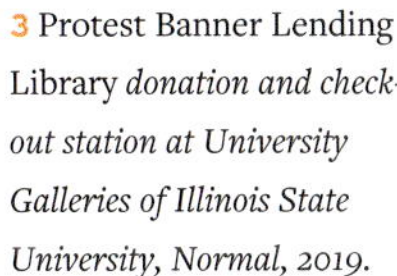

3 Protest Banner Lending Library *donation and check-out station at University Galleries of Illinois State University, Normal, 2019.*

4 *Brainstorming before creating banners at University Galleries of Illinois State University, Normal, 2019.*

5 *Installation view at University Galleries of Illinois State University, 2019.*

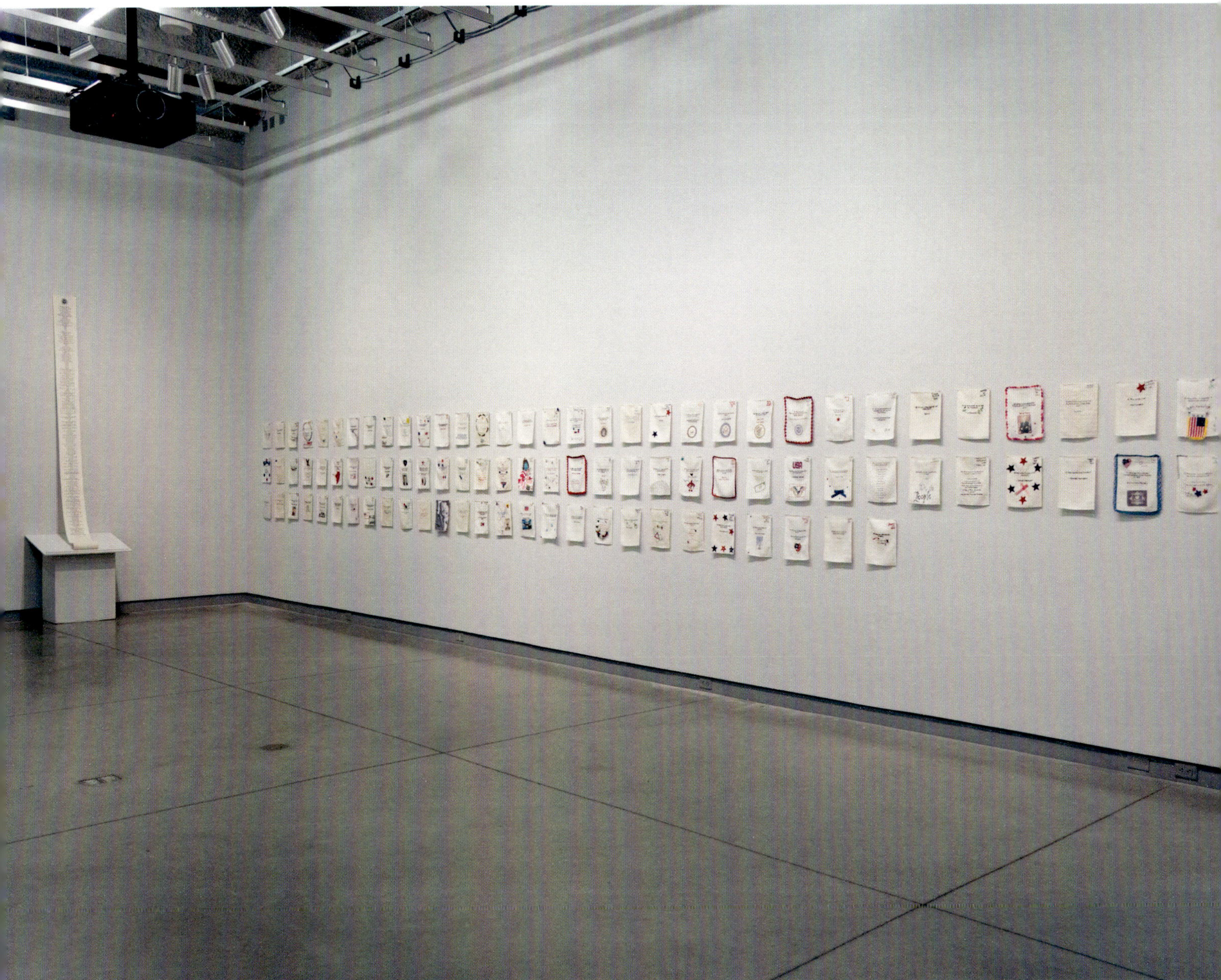

4 *Aram Han Sifuentes,* U.S. Citizenship Test Sampler (Made by non-citizens who live and work in the U.S.), *2013–present. Cotton thread, sequins, beads, photo transfers, patches, felt, and yarn on linen. 8.5 x 11 inches each. Installation view at University Galleries of Illinois State University, Normal, 2019. Photo: Jessica Bingham.*

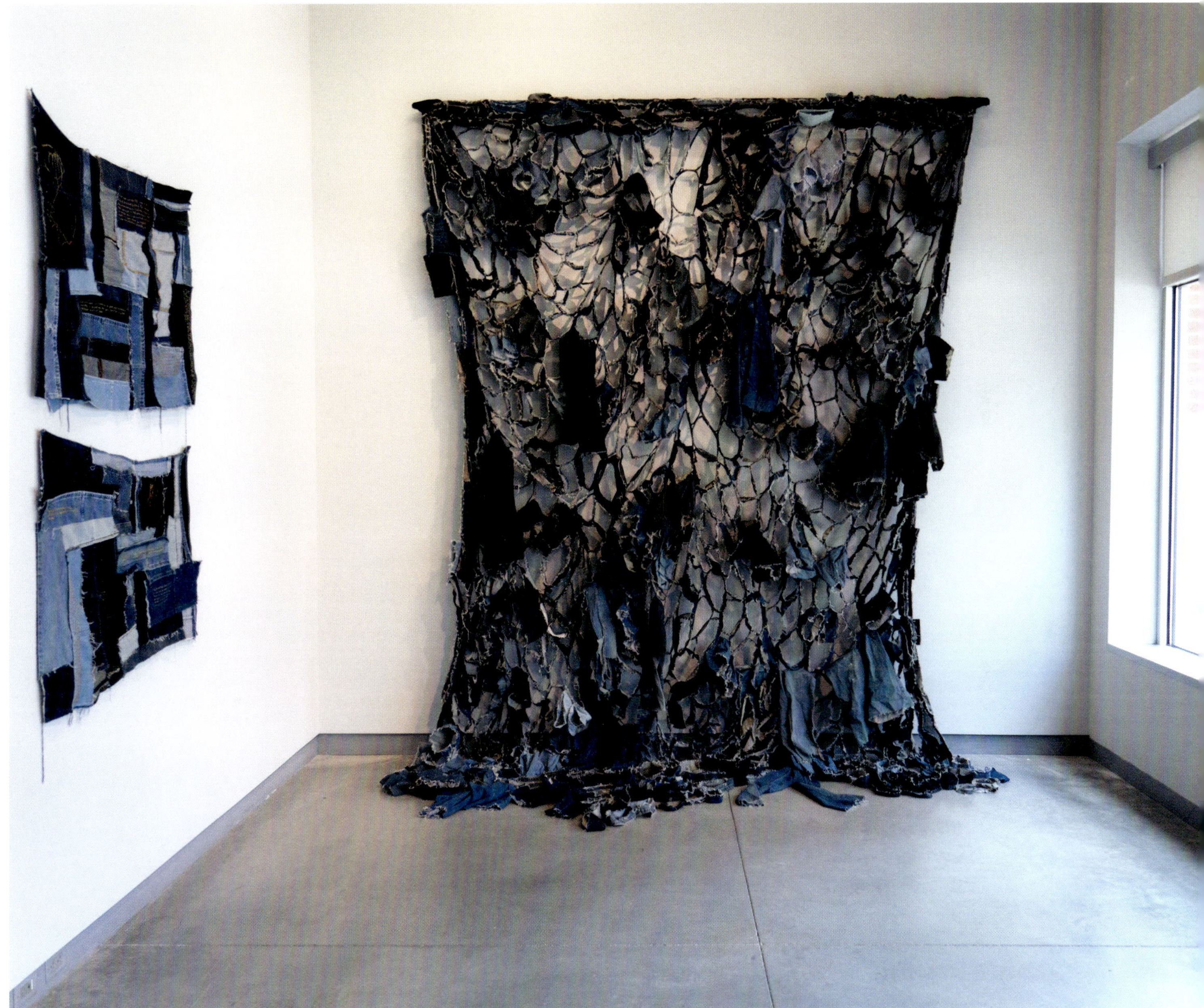

5 *Aram Han Sifuentes,* A Mend: A Collection of Stories from Local Seamstresses and Tailors (Chicago), *2019 and* A Mend: A Collection of Scraps from Local Seamstresses and Tailors (Chicago), *2011–13. Installation view at University Galleries of Illinois State University, Normal, 2019. Photo: Jessica Bingham.*

6 PAGE 88 *Aram Han Sifuentes,* U.S. Citizenship Test Sampler: 100 Questions and Answers *(detail), 2012–present. Cotton thread on linen, 25 feet x 8.5 inches. Installation view at University Galleries of Illinois State University, Normal, 2019. Photo: Jessica Bingham.*

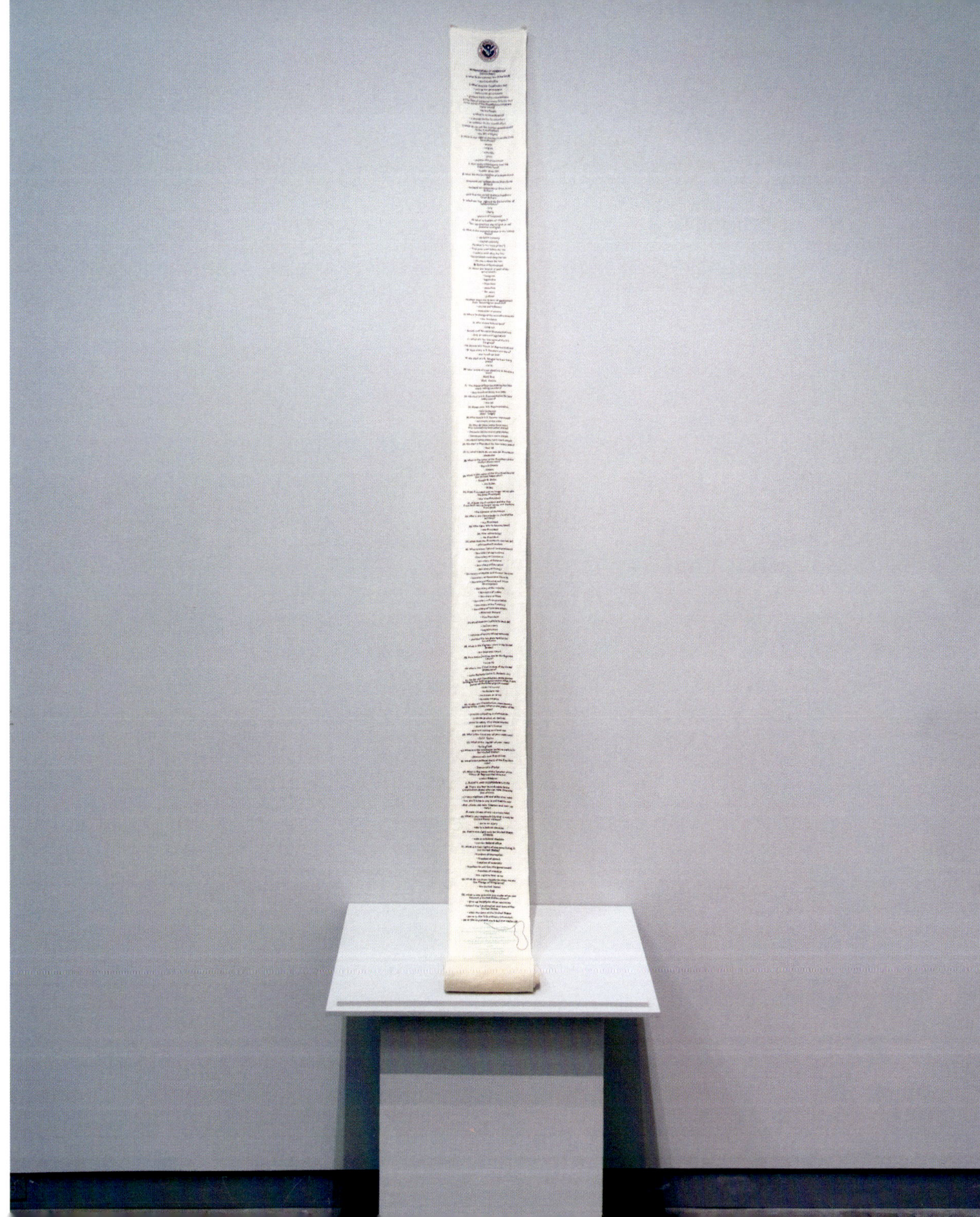

ARAM HAN SIFUENTES

EDUCATION

2013: M.F.A. Studio Art/Fiber & Material Studies, School of the Art Institute of Chicago, Chicago

2011: Post-Baccalaureate Certificate in Fine Art, Maryland Institute College of Art, Baltimore, Maryland

2008: B.A. Practice of Art and Latin American Studies, University of California, Berkeley
Regents and Chancellor's Scholar

AWARDS

2020: Grantee, Andrew & Barbara Choi Family Foundation Grant, AHL Foundation, New York City

2020: Grantee, Map Fund, New York City

2020: Artist Fellowship Finalist, Illinois Arts Council Agency

2020: Individual Artist Grant, City of Chicago's Department of Cultural Affairs and Special Events

2019: Visual Artist Grant, Bloom Fund

2019: Propeller Grant, Gallery 400 and Threewalls, Chicago

2019: MAKER Grant, Chicago Artists Coalition, Chicago

2019: Emerging Voices Award Finalist, American Craft Council, Minneapolis, Minnesota

2018: Part-Time Faculty of the Year, School of the Art Institute of Chicago

2017: Sustainable Arts Foundation Awardee, Sustainable Arts Foundation, San Francisco, California

2017: Beazley Design of the Year Finalist, Design Museum, London

2016: 3Arts Awardee, 3Arts, Chicago

2015: Creative Project Grant, City of Chicago's Department of Cultural Affairs and Special Events

2015: Grant, Puffin Foundation LTD, Teaneck, New Jersey

2015: Craft Research Fund Travel Grant, Center for Craft, Creativity and Design, Asheville, North Carolina

FELLOWSHIPS

2019: Individual Fellowship Program, Collaborator of Roberto Sifuentes, Asian Cultural Council, New York City

2016: Smithsonian Artist Research Fellowship, Smithsonian Institution, Washington, D.C.

RESIDENCIES

2021: Getting to Know You Artist in Residence, Museum of Contemporary Art, Cleveland, Ohio

2019: Artist in Residence, A. Farm, Ho Chi Minh City, Vietnam

2018: Artist in Residence, Pulitzer Arts Foundation, St. Louis, Missouri

2018: Gyopo in Residence, The Back Room at Kim's Corner, Chicago

2018: Artist in Residence, Hyde Park Art Center exchange with Frise Künstlerhaus Hamburg, Hamburg, Germany

2018: HCL Sponsored Artist Program, High Concept Labs, Chicago

2017: Facebook Artist in Residence, Facebook, Chicago

2017: Take Action, Alphawood Gallery, Chicago

2017: DCASE Public Studio, Chicago Cultural Center, Chicago

2015–16: Bolt Residency Mentor, Chicago Artists Coalition, Chicago

2015: Artist in Residence, Trenza Negra, Chiapas, Mexico

2014–15: Bolt Resident, Chicago Artists Coalition, Chicago

2014: Residency and Grant, Est-Nord-Est résidence d'artistes, Saint-Jean-Port-Joli, Québec

SOLO EXHIBITIONS

2020–2022: *Talking Back to Power: Projects by Aram Han Sifuentes*, curated by Laura Mart, Skirball Cultural Center and Museum, Los Angeles

2020: *Official Unofficial Voting Station*, Site Gallery at the School of the Art Institute of Chicago, Chicago

2020: *Protest Banner Lending Library*, curated by Amanda Shore, Art in the Open, Prince Edward Island, Canada

2019: *Protest Banner Lending Library*, curated by Tim Abel, Tarble Arts Center, Eastern Illinois University, Charleston, Illinois

2019: *We Are Never Never Other*, curated by Kendra Paitz, University Galleries of Illinois State University, Normal, Illinois (catalog)

2019: *Protest Banner Lending Library*, curated by Mara Baldwin, Handwerker Gallery at Ithaca College, Ithaca, New York

2018: *To Ward Off Authorities and To Protect My Neighbors*, Hyde Park Art Center, Chicago

2018: *Protest Banner Lending Library*, Cardinal, Baltimore, Maryland

2018: *We Are Never Never Other*, Pulitzer Arts Foundation, St. Louis, Missouri

2018: *We Are Not the Other. We Are the Center*, Frise Künstlerhaus, Hamburg, Germany

2018: *Take Receipts and Put it on Blast*, The Luminary, St. Louis, Missouri

2018: *Those Who Talk Back: U.S. Citizenship Test Samplers and Protest Banner Lending Library*, Asian Arts Initiative, Philadelphia, Pennsylvania

2017: *Protest Banner Lending Library*, Chicago Cultural Center, Chicago

2017: *Wave Your Freak Flag by the Protest Banner Lending Library*, Lillstreet Art Center, Chicago

2016: *The Official Unofficial Voting Station: Voting for All Who Legally Can't*, Jane Addams Hull-House Museum, Chicago

2016: *Younghye Han: My Mother's First Exhibition*, Chicago Artists Coalition, Chicago

2015: *A Mend*, curated by Danielle Krcmar, Babson College, Wellesley, Massachusetts

2015: *Kim Jong Un Americans*, Chicago Artists Coalition, Chicago

GROUP EXHIBITIONS

2020–21: *Citizenship*, curated by Zoe Larkins, Museum of Contemporary Art Denver, Colorado (catalog)

2020: *State of Mind*, curated by Ylinka Barotto, Moody Center for the Arts, Houston, Texas

2020: *Official Unofficial Voting Station and Never Again is Now*, Southern Exposure, San Francisco, California

GROUP EXHIBITIONS continued

2020: *Coexistence: Discourse on Traditional and Contemporary Art*, Sookmyung Women's University Museum, Seoul, South Korea (catalog)

2020: *To the Polls*, Mural Arts Philadelphia, Philadelphia, Pennsylvania

2020: *Here to Stay: Braving Barriers Through Performance*, curated by Danielle Paswaters, Union Art Gallery, Milwaukee, Wisconsin

2020: *City of Chicago's Artist Billboards Project*, led by artist Amanda Williams, Department of Cultural Affairs and Special Events, Chicago

2020: *City of Chicago's Make Yourself Count Census Campaign*, Department of Cultural Affairs and Special Events, Chicago

2020: *The Future We Roll, The More We Gain*, curated by Janeil Engelstad, Make Art With Purpose, Dallas, Texas (catalog)

2019: *How the Light Gets In*, curated by Andrea Inselmann, Herbert F. Johnson Museum of Art, Cornell University, Ithaca, New York

2019: *Tense Present*, curated by Sarah Darro, BOK, Philadelphia, Pennsylvania (catalog)

2019: *Take Refuge*, curated by Alejandro Acierto, Coop, Nashville, Tennessee

2019: *Ready*, curated by Related Tactics, Berkeley Art Center, Berkeley, California

2019: *Parallels and Peripheries: Migration and Mobility*, curated by Larry Ossei-Mensah, VisArts, Rockville, Maryland

2019: *Race and Revolution: Still Separate — Still Unequal*, curated by Katie Fuller and Larry Ossei-Mensah, the August Wilson African American Cultural Center, Pittsburgh, Pennsylvania

2019: *Asian American Storytelling Through Art*, HANA CENTER, Chicago

2019: *Everyday, Everyday, Everyday, Everyday Freedoms*, organized by Curatorial Practice MFA at MICA Class of 2020, Maryland Institute College of Art, Baltimore, Maryland

2019: *Race and Revolution: Still Separate — Still Unequal*, co-curated by Katie Fuller and Larry Ossei-Mensah, Woskob Family Gallery, Penn State University, State College, Pennsylvania

2018: *Case Study*, Houston Center for Contemporary Craft, Houston, Texas

2018: *Culinary Roots/Migratory Routes*, curated by Nancy Comorau and Anna Davies, Richard M. Moss Art Museum, Ohio Wesleyan University, Delaware, Ohio

2018: *This Country*, curated by Kahlil Irving, Ezra and Cecile Zilkha Gallery at Wesleyan University, Middletown, Connecticut

2018: *Life as We Know It*, curated by Penny Duff and Michael Slaboch, Eckert Art Gallery at Millersville University, Millersville, Pennsylvania

2018: *Forward Union Fair*, Red Bull Arts, New York City

2018: *Cry of Victory and Short Walks to Freedom*, curated by Modou Dieng projects + gallery, St. Louis, Missouri (catalog)

2018: *Through Her Eye*, organized by Ysabel Pinyol and Mashonda Tifrere, Mana Contemporary, Chicago (catalog)

2018: *Elegant Disruption*, curated by Joseph Ravens, Zhou B Art Center and Defibrillator Gallery, Chicago

2018: *Living Architecture*, curated by Tricia van Eck, 6018 North, Chicago

2018: *Banner! 100 Years of Protest*, New Brewery Arts, Cirencester, Gloucestershire, United Kingdom

2018: *What We Make*, curated by Erin Fletcher and Ashley Biser, Ross Art Museum, Ohio Wesleyan University, Delaware, Ohio

2018: *Making Change: The Art and Craft of Activism*, curated by Betsy Greer, Museum of Design Atlanta, Atlanta, Georgia

2018: *Slouching Toward Sunshine*, curated by Kimberly McKinnis, Rutter Family Art Foundation, Norfolk, Virginia

2017: *2017 Beazley Design of the Year*, Design Museum, London (catalog)

2017: *The Art Next Door: Chicago's Exemplars*, curated by Tami Miller, Krasl Art Center, St. Joseph, Michigan

2017: *Over and Over*, curated by Debra Kayes, Glass Curtain Gallery at Columbia College, Chicago

2017: *Human Human*, curated by Jessica Cochran, Ralph Arnold Gallery, Chicago

2017: *VIP: Very Important Platforms*, EXPO Chicago, 6018North and 3Arts, Chicago

2017: *A Matter of Conscience*, curated by Mia Lopez, DePaul Art Museum, Chicago

2017: *Race and Revolution: Still Separate — Still Unequal*, co-curated by Katie Fuller & Larry Ossei-Mensah, Smack Mellon, Brooklyn, New York

2017: *Art Work: An Exploration of Labor*, curated by Jennie Lamensdorf, Love Apple Art Space, Ghent, New York

2017: *Making Plans*, organized by Kyle Bellucci Johanson and Matthew Lax, Human Resources, Los Angeles (catalog)

2017: *Fierce Tiding*, Gene Siskel Film Center, Chicago

2016: *Splendor of Threads*, Chung Young Yang Embroidery Museum at Sookmyung Women's University, Seoul, South Korea (catalog)

2016: *Everything has been material for scissors to shape*, curated by Namita Gupta Wiggers, Wing Luke Museum of the Asian American Experience, Seattle, Washington

2015: *Make Do*, curated by Mara Baldwin, Handwerker Gallery, Ithaca College, Ithaca, New York

2015: *Elmhurst Art Museum Biennial: Chicago Statements*, curated by Staci Boris, Elmhurst Art Museum, Elmhurst, Illinois

2015: *RaceCraft*, co-curated by Marie Lo and Sarita Echavez See, Center for Art and Thought, Los Angeles

2014: *Material Possessions*, Lubeznik Center for the Arts, Michigan City, Indiana

2013: *Tracing Affinities*, Sullivan Galleries, School of the Art Institute of Chicago, Chicago

PERFORMANCES

2018: #exsanguination excerpt, in collaboration with Roberto Sifuentes and Jon Cates, OKLAHOMO, Chicago

2018: #exsanguination, in collaboration with Roberto Sifuentes and Jon Cates, Art of the Networked Practice Symposium, Chicago

2017: #exsanguination, in collaboration with Roberto Sifuentes and Jon Cates, Defibrillator Performance Art Gallery, Chicago

2016: Official Unofficial Voting Station: Election Night Party for the Disenfranchised with Roberto Sifuentes and Sadie Woods, Museum of Contemporary Art, Chicago

2015: Kim Jong Un Haircuts, Chicago Artists Coalition, Chicago

2015: Kim Jong Un Haircuts, Terrain Biennial, Chicago

COLLECTIONS

Herbert F. Johnson Museum of Art, Ithaca, New York

DePaul Art Museum, Chicago

Design Museum, London

Facebook, Chicago

University Galleries of Illinois State University, Normal, Illinois

Textile Resource Center, Fiber and Material Studies Department, School of the Art Institute of Chicago, Chicago

Wing Luke Museum of the Asian Pacific American Experience, Seattle

Denver Art Museum, Denver

The Renwick Gallery of Smithsonian American Art Museum, Washington, D.C.

WORKSHOPS

Take Receipts and Put it on Blast
(Aram Han Sifuentes and Ishita Dharap)

2019
Vends + Vibes, Arts + Public Life, Chicago

Creating Justice Symposium at Oakton Community College, Des Plaines, Illinois

2018
The Luminary, St. Louis, Missouri

Protest Banner Lending Library

2020
Skirball Cultural Center, Los Angeles (virtual)

Art in the Open, Prince Edward Island, Canada (virtual)

2019
Houston Center for Contemporary Craft, Houston, Texas

Herbert F. Johnson Museum of Art, Cornell University, Ithaca, New York

Vis Arts, Rockville, Maryland

Leather Archives and Museum, Chicago

Ithaca College, Ithaca, New York

Re-Joyce at Canadian Filmmakers Distribution Centre, Toronto

University Galleries of Illinois State University, Normal, Illinois

Tarble Arts Center, Eastern Illinois University, Charleston, Illinois

University of Florida, Gainesville

2018
Forward Union Fair, Red Bull Arts New York, New York City

Cardinal, Baltimore, Maryland

Maryland Institute College of Art, Baltimore, Maryland

Pulitzer Arts Foundation, St. Louis, Missouri

Latina Mothers at LifeWise STL, St. Louis, Missouri

Covenant House, St. Louis, Missouri

Metro Academic & Classical High School, St. Louis, Missouri

Grand Center Arts Academy, St. Louis, Missouri

Lewis Place Camp, St. Louis, Missouri

Sewcial Impact Project, St. Louis, Missouri

Latinos en Axion STL, St. Louis, Missouri

Senior Living at Renaissance Place, St. Louis, Missouri

Design Museum, London

Sojourner Scholars, Smart Museum of Art, University of Chicago, Chicago

Asian Arts Initiative, Philadelphia, Pennsylvania

School of the Museum of Fine Arts at Tufts University, Boston, Massachusetts

2017
Alphawood Gallery, Chicago

Protest Banner Making Workshop with Cauleen Smith, Whitney Museum of American Art, New York City

Albany Park Theater Project, Chicago

Pick Museum of Anthropology, Northern Illinois University, DeKalb, Illinois

Art Institute of Chicago, Chicago

Chicago Cultural Center, Chicago

Truth. Climate. Now. Symposium, School of the Art Institute of Chicago, Chicago

Jane Addams Hull-House Museum in partnership with Gallery 400, Chicago

Comfort Station, Chicago

Teaching Artist Summit for Chicago Artists Coalition at Hyde Park Art Center, Chicago

2016
Jane Addams Hull-House Museum, Chicago, Comfort Station, Chicago

US Citizenship Test Sampler

2018
Museum of Fine Arts, Boston, Massachusetts

2017
The Wing Luke Museum of the Asian Pacific American Experience, Seattle, Washington

Smart Museum of Art, University of Chicago, Chicago

Jane Addams Hull-House Museum, Chicago

2016
Elmhurst Art Museum, Elmhurst, Illinois

Jane Addams Hull-House Museum, Chicago

Pulaski International School of Chicago, Chicago

Rodolfo Lozano Bilingual and International Center Elementary School, Chicago

Benito Juarez Community Academy, Chicago

2015
Chicago Humanities Festival, Chicago

Smithsonian's Archives of American Art, Donald W. Reynolds Center for American Art and Portraiture, Washington, D.C.

Rodolfo Lozano Bilingual and International Center Elementary School, Chicago

Center for Craft, Creativity, and Design, Asheville, North Carolina

Embroidery in Translation: Traditional Korean Embroidery

2015
Centro de Textiles del Mundo Maya, Chiapas, Mexico

CURATED EXHIBITIONS

2015
Work Werq, co-curated with Jacqueline Chao, for the Association for Asian American Studies FlATStudios, Chicago

2014
On Craft, curation of oral histories on American craft, Archives of American Art, Smithsonian Institution, Washington, D.C.

2013
MFA Show 2013, Curatorial Fellows at the School of the Art Institute of Chicago, Sullivan Galleries, Chicago

INVITED PUBLICATIONS

Han Sifuentes, Aram. "Protest Making: How Crafting Collectively Can Empower Disenfranchised People." *Crafts Council*, October 20, 2020.

Han Sifuentes, Aram. "Official Unofficial Voting Station: Voting for All Who Legally Can't." *Art Journal Open*, October 1, 2020.

Han Sifuentes, Aram. "My Immigrant Parents Won't Close Their Shop (And They Really Should)." *Quarantine Times*, April 18, 2020.

Han Sifuentes, Aram. "Be Bold. There is No Other Option." *The Funambulist Magazine*, Kids of the World: Unite!: 26. November 2019.

Han Sifuentes, Aram. "For Those Who Talk Back." *Dilettante Army*. Spring/Summer 2019 Issue.

Han Sifuentes, Aram. "A Mother's Work: A Mother/Daughter/Seamstress/Fiber Artist's Merging Practice and Politics," in *Maternal in Creative Work: Intergenerational Discussions on Motherhood and Art*, ed. Elena Marcevska and Velerie Walkerdine (Abingdon-on-Thames, England: Routledge, 2019).

Han Sifuentes, Aram, Lisa Vinebaum, and Namita Gupta Wiggers. "Unsettling Coloniality: A Critical and Radical Fiber/Textile Bibliography." *Critical Craft Forum*, 2018.

Han Sifuentes, Aram. "Steps Towards Decolonizing Craft." *Textile Society of America*, April 23, 2017.

Han Sifuentes, Aram. "Leonard Suryajaya: Don't Hold on to Your Bones." *Asian Diasporic Visual Cultures and the Americas*. Volume 3, Issue 1–2. March 14, 2017.

Han Sifuentes, Aram. "Questioning Americanness: Artists Yasuo Kuniyoshi and Aram Han Sifuentes." *Smithsonian Institution's Archives of American Art Blog*, July 24, 2015.

Han Sifuentes, Aram. "Emerging Voices: Aram Han." *Surface Design Journal: Korea East & West*, July 31, 2014.

KEYNOTE LECTURES

2020

"Creating A Seed for Action," Loyola University, Chicago

"Role of Activism in Mobilizing Society for Social Justice in the Era of Trump." ICGD 9 Annual Symposium, Eastern Illinois University, Charleston, Illinois

2018

"We Are Never Never Other. We Are the Center.," For Freedoms at University of New Mexico Art Museum, Albuquerque, New Mexico

2017

"Towards Decolonizing Craft," Surface Design Association Conference, Portland, Oregon

"Protest Banner Lending Library: Making as Resistance," Chicago Objects Study Initiative, Art Institute of Chicago, Chicago

LECTURES

2020

"Let Us Vote! Election Day Break," Artist talk by Aram Han Sifuentes, Listening party by DJ Sadie Woods, Live performances by Frewuhn, Damon Locks, and Isa Starr, Contemporary Arts Museum Houston, Texas (virtual)

"Here to Stay: Election Day Livestream," United We Dream, Houston, Texas (virtual)

"Side by Side: Beili Lui and Aram Han Sifuentes," Crow Museum of Asian Art, Dallas, Texas (virtual)

"Let Us Vote: An Artist Intervention," Conversation with Lisa Iglesias, Mount Holyoke College, South Hadley, Massachusetts (virtual)

"Generation of Change," Panel with Cecil B. Moore and Mia Velez, moderated by Nina "Lyrispect" Ball, Mural Arts Philadelphia, Philadelphia, Pennsylvania (virtual)

"Artist Talk: Aram Han Sifuentes & DJ Sadie Woods," Wing Luke Museum of the Asian Pacific American Experience, Seattle, Washington (virtual)

"Performance, Protest and Censorship: A Conversation with Aruna D'Souza," Panel with Aruna D'Souza, Sami Ismat, Jeanette Arellano, and Danielle Paswaters, Union Art Gallery, University of Wisconsin-Milwaukee, Milwaukee, Wisconsin (virtual)

"LGBTQ + Immigration Activism," Panel with Liam Garcia and Sheridan Aguirre, Q + EDU (A project of the Central Texas GSA Coalition, Out Youth, and the Texas GSA Network), Texas (virtual)

"Contemporary Voices: Aram Han Sifuentes," George Washington University Museum and The Textile Museum, Washington, D.C. (virtual)

"Our Futures are Tied," Panel with Weston Teruya and Carol Zou, moderated by Megha Ralapati, Asian Cultural Council and Hyde Park Art Center, Chicago (virtual)

"Creating a Seed for Action," Art and Design Lecture Series, Texas State University, San Marcos, Texas (virtual)

"Propositions #1: Activism, Art and Performance," Panel with Maria Gaspar and Nicole Marroquin, Performance Department, School of the Art Institute of Chicago, Chicago (virtual)

"Art in Action," Kansas City Art Institute, Kansas City, Missouri (virtual)

"Being an Immigrant Artist in the Age of Trump," Panel with Amir Fallah, Aliza Nisenbaum, Guadalupe Maravilla, Maryland Institute College of Art, Baltimore, Maryland

2019

"We Are Never Never Other," University Galleries of Illinois State University, Normal, Illinois

"Artist Talk: Roberto Sifuentes and Aram Han Sifuentes," Sàn Art, Ho Chi Minh City, Vietnam

"We Are Never Never Other. We Are the Center," Handwerker Gallery at Ithaca College, Ithaca, New York

"Arts and Immigration," Arts Alliance Illinois, Chicago

"Conversation between Aram Han Sifuentes and Indu Vashist", Re-Joyce at Canadian Filmmakers Distribution Centre, Toronto

2018

"The Official Unofficial Voting Station: Voting for All Who Legally Can't," as part of The Library of Performing Rights Open, Live Art Development Agency, London

"Protest Banner Lending Library," The Risk Society Symposium, Design Museum, London

2016

"Intersection of Politics and Craft," Sookmyung Women's University, Seoul, South Korea

"In Translation," Sungshin University, Seoul, South Korea

"RaceCraft: Decolonizing Craft," Racecraft Symposium, University of California, Riverside

2015

"Immigrant, American/UnAmerican, At least a quarter North Korean," Handwerker Gallery, Ithaca College, Ithaca, New York

"Questioning Americanness: Artists Yasuo Kuniyoshi and Aram Han Sifuentes," Smithsonian's Archives of American Art, Donald W. Reynolds Center for American Art and Portraiture, Washington, D.C.

"A Mend: Immigrant Sewing Projects," Sorenson Center for the Arts, Babson College, Wellesley, Massachusetts

ACADEMIC CONFERENCES

2019

"We Are Never Never Other. We Are the Center.," Creating Justice Symposium at Oakton Community College, Des Plaines, Illinois

2018

Panelist in "Radical Arts Therapies Pedagogy and Praxis: A Cross Disciplinary Dialogue" at Critical Pedagogy in the Arts Therapies, School of the Art Institute of Chicago, Chicago

Panel Chair, "Decolonizing Craft: Critical Craft Forum," College Art Association, Los Angeles

2017

"The Official Unofficial Voting Station: Voting for All Who Legally Can't," Open Engagement — JUSTICE, Chicago

2014

Panelist, "A Community of Non-Citizens: Proving Worth of Citizenship Through Stitching Samplers," and Panel: "Crafting Community: Textiles, Collaboration, and Social Space," College Art Association, Chicago

ACADEMIC AND PROFESSIONAL EXPERIENCE

2020–21

Artist-in-Residence, Loyola University, Chicago

2019–present

Adjunct Associate Professor, School of the Art Institute of Chicago, Chicago

2018–19

Adjunct Assistant Professor, School of the Art Institute of Chicago, Chicago

2013–18

Lecturer, School of the Art Institute of Chicago, Chicago

SELECTED PRESS

Stromberg, Matt. "LA's Art Spaces Are Focusing on the Election." *hyperallergic.com*, October 21, 2020.

Almino, Elisa Wouk. "Colorful and Loving Murals in Philadelphia Are Inspiring People to Vote." *hyperallergic.com*, October 19, 2020.

Henerson, Evan. "Artist Gets Out the Vote at 'Official Unofficial' Exhibition." *jewishjournal.com*, October 7, 2020.

Bassett, Dana. "Episode 753: Aram Han Sifuentes." *Bad at Sports* podcast, October 6, 2020.

MacLeod, Nicola. "Protest banners on display as part of Art in the Open." *cbc.ca*, August 29, 2020.

Mart, Laura. "Artist Q&A: Aram Han Sifuentes." *skirball.org*, August 4, 2020.

Cardoza, Kerry. "Vote of Confidence: Aram Han Sifuentes Radically Reenvisions the Voting Process." *art.newcity.com*, May 12, 2020.

Kennedy, Laura. "Needle and Thread Provide Empowerment." NPR affiliate: WGLT, September 18, 2019.

G'Sell, Eileen. "Labor of Love." *Alive Magazine*, Issue 3, 2018. Print.

Radyk, Michael. "Aram Han Sifuentes and the Protest Banner Lending Library." *American Craft Inquiry*, Volume 2, Issue 2, 2018. Print.

Acierto, Alejandro. "Aram Han Sifuentes: Protest Banner Lending Library." *Asian Diasporic Visual Cultures and the Americas*, Volume 4, 2018. Print.

Hahn, Valerie Schremp. "Fiber artist can teach you to make a protest banner that's also a gallery-worthy work of art." *stltoday.com*, July 22, 2018.

Green, Tyler. "No. 343: Carrie Moyer, Aram Han Sifuentes." *Modern Art Notes* podcast, May 31, 2018.

Miranda, Lynnette. "Dissenting Through Craft with Aram Han Sifuentes." *sixtyinchesfromcenter.org*, May 15, 2018.

Yang, Wenjing. "In the Age of Trump, A Chicagoan Created a Lending Library for Protest Banners." *americaninno.com*, January 3, 2018.

Borrelli, Christopher. "Chicago Artist Creates Ingenious Library of Protest Banners." *Chicago Tribune*, October 15, 2017. Print.

Adamson, Glenn. "The Anatomy of the Protest Banner." *Disegno*, #16, December 4, 2017. Print.

Lau, Barbara, Jennifer Scott, and Suzanne Seriff. "Designing for Outrage: Inviting Disruption and Contested Truth into Museum Exhibitions." *National Association for Museum Exhibition*, Spring 2016. Print.

Yang, Linda. "The Woman Behind the Library Where You Can Rent Signs Protesting Trump." *broadly.vice.com*, December 16, 2017.

Peña, Mauricio. "The Best Protest Banners of 2017 That You Can Borrow." *chicagomag.com*, December 4, 2017.

Voon, Claire. "A Lending Library for Handmade Protest Banners." *hyperallergic.com*, November 2, 2017.

Stephens, Regan. "You can borrow a protest banner from Chicago's newest lending library." *lonelyplanet.com*, October 26, 2017.

Morris, Kadish. "The Protest Banner Library Where You Can Rent Signs of Rage." *broadly.vice.com*, September 28, 2017.

Morris, Kadish. "Turning protest banners into striking, effective works of art." *huckmagazine.com*, September 13, 2017.

Norman, Lee Ann. "Breakout Artists 2017." *Newcity*, May 2017. Print.

Reilly, Alison. "A Protest Banner Lending Library." *Chicago Gallery News, April 28, 2017*. Print.

Rhee, Nissa. "Aram Han Sifuentes." *90days90voices.com*, May 6, 2017.

Ducey, Karen. "Studying for U.S. Citizenship One Stitch at a Time." *features.crosscut.com*, April 6, 2017.

Robertson, Kirsty and Lisa Vinebaum. "Crafting Community." *TEXTILE*. Volume 14, Issue 1, 2016. Print.

Paré, André-Louis. "Aram Han Sifuentes: The Politics of an Immigrant." *Espace Art Actuel Magazine*. No 111, Fall 2015: Migration. Print.

ACKNOWLEDGMENTS

Sharing Aram Han Sifuentes' powerful work at our university and in our community in fall 2019 was deeply moving. We can sometimes feel overwhelmed and defeated by an onslaught of horrific news and hateful rhetoric, but we spent two months surrounded by Han Sifuentes' *Protest Banner Lending Library*, *U.S. Citizenship Test Sampler*, and *A Mend*, all of which demonstrate thoughtful and empowering ways to fight back and to celebrate the vital voices of so many. I particularly appreciate how each project is embedded with the artist's clear sense of ethics. It was thrilling to witness people's reactions and the rate at which they participated, whether checking out banners, making their own banners, or seeing themselves reflected in the works. I am grateful to Aram for her impactful workshops, brilliant lecture, generous donation of protest banners to our permanent collection, and for trusting us with bringing these three projects together. It has been such a joy to work together on this exhibition and monograph.

We are thankful to The Andy Warhol Foundation for the Visual Arts, Illinois Arts Council Agency, Harold K. Sage Foundation, and Illinois State University Foundation Fund for their critical support of this exhibition and publication.

Thank you to Grace Kyungwon Hong for writing such a thoughtful and necessary essay. I appreciate Alice J. Lee and her design skills; she understood what this book needed right from the start and has been an excellent designer to brainstorm and work with. Alice, Aram, and I are grateful to Shannon Brinkley and Matthew Brinkley at Shannon Brinkley Studio for sharing the Dryad fabric pictured on the cover. Thank you to Dennis Simmons, Gary Frantz, and the staff at Taylor Print Impressions for their communication throughout the process of printing this publication.

Jean Miller, dean of the Wonsook Kim College of Fine Arts, and Michael Wille, director of the Wonsook Kim School of Art, are supportive of our programs and welcoming to the artists we bring to campus. Janis Swanton and Corey Oltman at Illinois State University's Research and Sponsored Programs are appreciated for their assistance with grant logistics and payments. Sarah Dick at Milner Library provided helpful copyright information. Thank you to Stephanie Kohl Ringle in the Wonsook Kim College of Fine Arts for proofreading promotional materials and this publication.

The dedicated staff at University Galleries is key to realizing our ambitious exhibitions and providing engaging interactions for our visitors. Registrar Lisa Lofgren skillfully handled loans, travel, honoraria, shipping, supplies, and installation; curator Jessica Bingham helpfully installed, photographed, and promoted; and curator of education Tanya Scott developed guides and led workshops and tours. Each of them also enthusiastically assisted people with making their own protest banners. Graduate assistants Zach Buckley, Aaron Caldwell, and Zachary Sprenger; gallery assistants Antonio Crossley, Ari Garcia, Magon Pedroza, and Anna Tulley; and intern Alice Brandenburg provided assistance with installing and deinstalling the exhibition; setting up for lectures, workshops, and exhibition tours; designing promotional materials; researching educational handouts; and greeting visitors. Garcia and Tulley also assisted with research for this publication. We appreciate alumnus Jason Hoffman for his continued installation assistance.

A tremendous thank you is also due to all the visitors, workshop and tour participants, instructors, and banner contributors who made the entire period of this exhibition such a vibrant and meaningful experience. As Han Sifuentes' work reminds us, I hope that we will all continue to talk back to power.

— **Kendra Paitz**, director and chief curator

CREDITS

This book is published with *Aram Han Sifuentes: We Are Never Never Other*, organized by director and chief curator Kendra Paitz, and presented at University Galleries of Illinois State University from August 15 through October 13, 2019.

The exhibition and publication were made possible by grants from The Andy Warhol Foundation for the Visual Arts, Illinois Arts Council Agency, Harold K. Sage Foundation, and Illinois State University Foundation Fund.

COVER: Banner created by Aram Han Sifuentes in 2020 using Dryad fabric by Shannon Brinkley Studio. Fabric used with permission of Shannon Brinkley Studio.

PHOTO CREDITS:

Pages 2–3 A selection of stickers by Cute Rage Press (Aram Han Sifuentes and Ishita Dharap).

Page 4 Protest Banner-making public workshop, Pulitzer Arts Foundation, St. Louis.
Photo: Michael Thomas. Courtesy of Pulitzer Arts Foundation.

Page 96 Home is Here! March to Defend DACA AND TPS, October–November 2019 in New York, Philadelphia, Baltimore, and Washington, D.C. Organized by a coalition of immigrant rights organizations including Hana Center and NAKASEC. Photo: OffThaRecord x Steer.

PUBLISHER: University Galleries of Illinois State University

EDITOR: Kendra Paitz

DESIGNER: Alice J. Lee — alicejlee.com

TYPEFACES: Freight by Joshua Darden and Interstate by Tobias Frere-Jones

PAPER: McCoy Silk 100#

PRINTER: Taylor Print Impressions, Bloomington, Illinois

DISTRIBUTOR: Artbook L.L.C, D.A.P. Distributed Arts Publishers, New York — artbook.com

ISBN: 978-0-945558-44-6

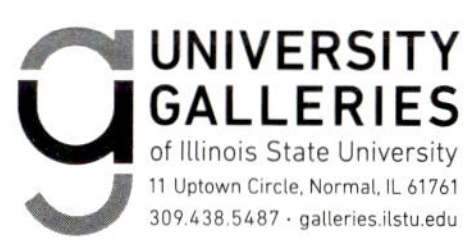

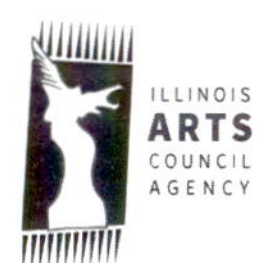

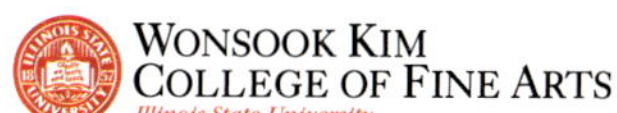

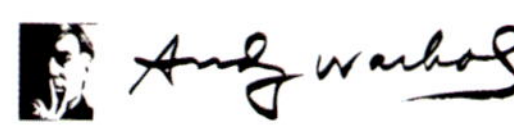

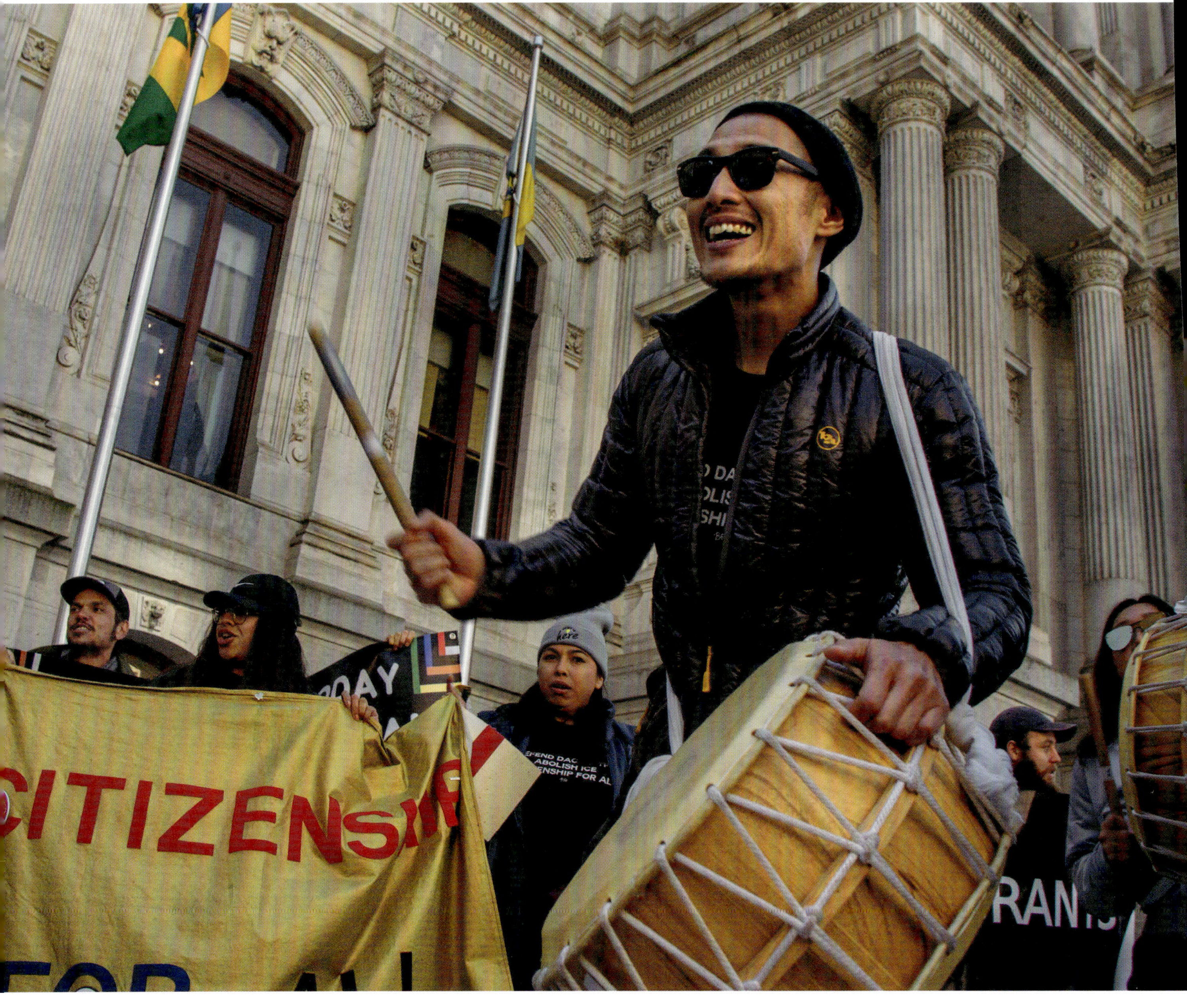
CITIZENS
ABOLISH ICE